RECLAIMING the CULTURE

How You Can Protect Your Family's Future

Focus on the Family

Alan Crippen II, editor

With contributions from
Chuck Colson and Bill Bennett

PUBLISHING
Colorado Springs, Colorado

RECLAIMING THE CULTURE
Copyright © 1996 by Focus on the Family. All rights reserved. International copyright secured.

Library of Congress Cataloging-in-Publication Data
Reclaiming the culture : how you can protect your family's future /
    Alan R. Crippen II, editor.
      p. cm.
    Includes bibliographical references (p. 197).
    ISBN 1-56179-440-6
    1. United States—Moral conditions. 2. United States—Social conditions. 3. Social problems—United States. 4. Church and social problems—United States. 5. Social values—United States. 6. Secularism—United States. I. Crippen, Alan R.
HN90.M6R43   1996
306'.0973—dc20
                        96-10537
                           CIP

Published by Focus on the Family Publishing, Colorado Springs, CO 80995. Distributed in the U.S.A. and Canada by Word Books, Dallas, Texas.

Unless otherwise noted, Scripture quotations are from the HOLY BIBLE, NEW INTERNATIONAL VERSION ®. Copyright © 1973, 1978, 1984 by the International Bible Society. Used by permission of Zondervan Publishing House. All rights reserved.

People's names and certain details of the case studies in this book have been changed to protect the privacy of the individuals involved. However, the facts of what happened and the underlying principles have been conveyed as accurately as possible.

Front cover design: Candi L. Park
Front cover photo: Arthur Tilley/FPG International

Printed in the United States of America

96 97 98 99 00/10 9 8 7 6 5 4 3 2 1

Contents

"Be not afraid!"

—Jesus Christ

*"The most important thing for each of us to do to save
the world . . . is to practice righteousness,
to love God with all our heart and soul and mind and strength
and our neighbor as ourself.
You the individual can make the difference."*

—C.S. Lewis

*"We find ourselves faced with a new reality.
The world, tired of idealogy, is opening itself to truth.
The time has come when the splendor of this truth
(veritatis splendor) has begun anew
to illuminate the darkness of human existence."*

—Pope John Paul II

*"Nothing that is worth doing can be achieved
in our lifetime; therefore we must be saved by hope.
Nothing which is true or beautiful
or good makes complete sense in any immediate context
of history; therefore we must be saved by faith.
Nothing we do, however virtuous,
can be accomplished alone;
therefore we are saved by love.
No virtuous act is quite as virtuous
from the standpoint of our friend or foe
as it is from our standpoint.
Therefore we must be saved
by the final form of love which is forgiveness."*

—Reinhold Niebuhr

Foreword

by Tom Minnery

Every life takes surprising turns that come to us at unexpected times and in unplanned ways. If someone had told the young Peter he would forever leave his career as a fisherman to become an apostle of the Messiah, he probably would have laughed. What appears to be a bend in the road of our lives ends up taking us on an entirely new course. Looking back 20 or 30 years later, we can hardly believe how far we've come. This book represents one of those moments for me.

Ever since I was young, I assumed I would be a journalist. As a student, I wrote for my high school paper and for the local daily (*The Cincinnati Post Times-Star*). I studied journalism in college, and after graduating, I worked on newspapers for five years in New York and four years in Washington, D.C. As a young man, I reached a coveted position in my profession as a manager in the Washington Bureau of Gannett Newspapers (the publisher of *USA Today* and about 80 others). My career seemed to be unfolding with remarkable promise.

It was during my tour of duty in Washington that I became serious about my faith. As I covered the leading issues of the day from the center of the free world, with a White House pass and plenty of access on Capitol Hill, it became increasingly clear to me that our nation's problems weren't political; they were *spiritual*. With each passing moment, I doubted the ability of our government to address the real struggles of the human race. Politics seemed insignificant when compared to the gospel. In a step of faith that surprises me to this day, I left Washington and journalism to study for the ministry at Dallas Theological Seminary. After all, I wanted to be in the heart of God's work in the world.

From my studies at Dallas, I was offered a position at *Christianity Today*, which seemed to perfectly incorporate my training as a journalist and my passion for ministry. I served as news editor and then senior editor at *CT* for five years, covering the life of the church as well as news from "the world." Slowly, I began to experience a restlessness that seemed to echo my earlier disenchantment with Washington. I realized that while the church does have the answers our world so desperately needs, Christian people weren't bringing those answers to bear on the major issues of our day. Certainly we placed a priority in evangelism, but I found Christians ignorant or uninterested in the battle in our culture against the basic truths of our faith—the value of human life, the proper expression for human sexuality, the moral insights of the Scriptures. The gospel seemed more and more significant to politics than I had thought.

These words, attributed to Martin Luther, captured the essence of my concerns:

> If I profess with the loudest voice and clearest exposition every
> portion of the truth of God except precisely that little point
> which the world and the devil are that moment attacking, I am
> not confessing Christ, however boldly I may be professing
> Christ. Where the battle rages, there the loyalty of the soldier is
> proved, and to be steady on all the battlefield besides, is mere
> flight and disgrace if he flinches at that point.

Within evangelicalism, our faith was intact and our churches thriving, but our impact on the nation was imperceptible and the tide of secularism was eating away at the foundations of the church. We had left the salt in the shaker, placed our light under a bushel. While Washington wrestled with our deepest social crises without the guidance of biblical views, Christians had the values but for the most part wouldn't wrestle with the problems. A new burden formed in me—I wanted to help the church recover the moral and intellectual high ground that it had once held in our nation. I wanted to see Christians defending their faith at the very point where it was being attacked, in Luther's words, "by the world and the devil."

As vice president of public policy for Focus on the Family, I now supervise *Citizen* magazine, a monthly issues magazine; *Family News In Focus*, a daily information and analysis radio program; and staff who train people for effective grassroots involvement via state-based family policy councils, seminars, and reliable social research. All of these programs are devoted to informing and equipping Christians to play a decisive role in the moral issues of our times. Its a long way from *The Cincinnati Post Times-Star*, but in many ways, it seems an inevitable outcome to my story. I left the world of politics and culture to serve Christ and found myself taking a stand for Christ in the world of politics and culture.

Perhaps you, like me, planned a course for your life that didn't include social action but found yourself drawn to the great moral issues of our day, wondering how Christians can turn the tide. For several years, I searched for a resource I could recommend to concerned Christians, something that would explain in one volume the root of our social crises, why the Bible calls us to do something about them, and what can be done in the most practical terms. Failing to find one that fit the bill, I commissioned my staff to create the book you are now holding. Whether you are a newcomer to the policy arena or a veteran with many of your own stories to tell, I think you'll find *Reclaiming the Culture* to be the best compilation of answers as to what has gone wrong in our nation, why Christians should care, and precisely what can be done.

This book may represent a bend in the road for you, or it may be a confirmation of a course you've been on for a long time. Either way, I believe it has the power to restore hope, provide direction, and sustain us for effective action over the long haul. The longer I have been a Christian, the more convinced I have become that the gospel does have political implications, that though we are citizens of heaven, we are also called to be exemplary citizens of earth. For in the Lord's Prayer, don't we pray that God's will be done "on earth, as it is in heaven"? *Reclaiming the Culture* will help each of us work toward that end, recognizing that the final answer to our problems will arrive with Christ at His second coming. Till then, may we prove faithful soldiers, defending the truth at the very point it is under attack. This is the way we will confess Christ to our generation.

Reprinted with special permission of King Features Syndicate.

Introduction

Much has been written in recent years about the crisis of the family. Today, families are under great stress and "the family" as the most basic social institution is threatened by turbulent cultural, political, and economic forces. Secularism, self-centered individualism, changing moral values, permissive sexuality, abortion on demand, the prevalence of divorce, increase in child abuse, urban decay, violent crime, drug and alcohol abuse, and unsupportive, if not harmful government policies—these are among the causes and effects that have put families at risk.

What more on this topic can possibly be said? Over the last 20 years, several helpful books have been published, including: *Haven in a Heartless World: The Family Besieged* by Christopher Lasch (1977); *The Battle for the Family* by Tim LaHaye (1982); *The War Over the Family* by Brigette and Peter Berger (1983); *Children at Risk* by James C. Dobson and Gary Bauer (1990); *Culture Wars* by James Davison Hunter (1991); and *The Family Under Siege* by George Grant (1994).

Despite all of the valuable insight and attention that the family is receiving from some of the best minds on the subject, is the family any better off today than it was two decades ago? Are more marriages staying together? Are our neighborhoods safer for children? Do public schools work better? Are our major universities affirming what parents and grandparents know to be right? Is Hollywood producing better movies? Have cable and network television improved their programming? Are government policies more "family friendly"? Is unborn human life protected by law? Are mothers and doctors less inclined to kill the unborn? Generally, have things gotten better or worse for the family in the last 20 years? Is there hope for the family, or should we despair?

As a husband and father of four children, I am profoundly disturbed at the signs of our time. My gut reaction is to "hunker down" and make our home a fortress bunker. In this regard, the old adage "A man's home is his castle" has new meaning for me. While safe and secure from the raging torrent of hostilities all around us, our family could spend time watching "Anne of Green Gables" and "Little House on the Prairie" videos. Then, after the TV is turned off, we could perhaps listen to Focus on the Family's "Adventures in Odyssey" radio program. But as appealing as this kind of response may be, it is unrealistic and unredemptive. As Christian people, we are called to be defenders of faith and family. And this will entail engagement, not isolation.

Our hope for the family should not be placed in the family. That is, "hunkering down" with our families will not save the family. The only hope for the family is in God and His Son Jesus Christ. This book is about that hope. As a divinely established institution dating back to the creation of the world, the family's preservation depends on God. Current attacks upon the family are nothing less than attacks upon the creation ordinances of God Himself. Therefore, integrally related to the defense of the family is a defense of the faith. This book offers a modest "apology" for and reasonable approach to defending faith and family. If the family is to be saved and if American culture is to be restored to goodness, it will be because God has raised up men and women who act justly, love mercy, and walk humbly with Him. This cadre of gentle and respectful citizen Christians will "be prepared to give an answer to everyone who asks . . . the reason for the hope" that they have (1 Pet. 3:15).

◆ ◆ ◆

The first three chapters of this book distill what is important for you to know about why things are the way they are in America today. Then, rather than leave you in "paralysis by analysis," the remaining seven chapters and two appendices offer lucid discussions and practical insights on how to go about changing things for the better. Is Christian social and political involvement biblical? How do you persuade people who disagree with almost everything you believe? What is the role of prayer in social reform? Does Christian character matter? Should you work with other Christians like Baptists, Presbyterians, Episcopalians, and Catholics? How can average people make a difference? What can you do to defend faith and family? Can revival save America? Where can you go for more help? All of these questions and more are addressed in the pages that follow.

Those of us who have worked on this project hope the following pages will stimulate your involvement in the public square. We want to renew your confidence in the positively powerful ideas of the Christian faith. Its simple yet profound ideas like love, mercy, truth, and justice are able to stand against the bad ideas of secularism, relativism, hedonism, and radical individualism that plague our society and fuel its "culture wars." We also desire that this project will help to restore your hope for the future of America. *Reclaiming the Culture* is not an optimistic book, because, as Richard J. Neuhaus has recently stated, "Optimism is merely a matter of optics, of seeing what you want to see and not seeing what you don't want to see." Rather, it is a book about hope. And a hope that is based upon the power of the gospel and the quality of our Christian lives and service is not forlorn, but realistic. With this in mind, let the words of Job comfort us on the hopeful possibilities for our own communities:

> When I went to the gate of the city
> and took my seat in the public square,
> the young men saw me and stepped aside
> and the old men rose to their feet;
> the chief men refrained from speaking
> and covered their mouths with their hands;
> the voices of the nobles were hushed,
> and their tongues stuck to the roof of
> their mouths.
> Whoever heard me spoke well of me,
> and those who saw me commended me,
> because I rescued the poor who cried for help,
> and the fatherless who had none to assist him.
> The man who was dying blessed me;
> I made the widow's heart sing.
> I put on righteousness as my clothing;
> justice was my robe and my turban.

I was eyes to the blind
   and feet to the lame.
I was a father to the needy;
   I took up the case of the stranger.
I broke the fangs of the wicked
   and snatched the victims from their teeth.
   (Job 29:7-17)

Let me offer a word about how to use this book. Not only is *Reclaiming the Culture* a valuable resource for personal enrichment and individual social and political involvement, but it can also be used for instructional purposes. Each chapter begins with a summary statement of the "Big Idea" contained therein and concludes with questions for discussion. This format lends itself to small-group study or use in Sunday school or Christian high school classrooms. Additionally, the last chapter, "A Call to Action" offers practical ideas for organized social and political action in the local church.

Reclaiming the Culture is a product of Focus on the Family's Public Policy Seminars, an educational ministry that seeks to foster the informed, responsible, and effective involvement of Christians in the public square. Consequently, this book is part of the supporting curriculum materials for the seminars. If you would like more information about these educational opportunities, please contact Focus on the Family.

Alan R. Crippen II
Institute for Family Studies
Focus on the Family
Colorado Springs, Colorado

CHAPTER 1

Revolt Against God: America's Spiritual Despair

by William J. Bennett

THE BIG IDEA

With the publication of his best-selling book *The Book of Virtues*, William J. Bennett has become America's leading advocate of public virtue. His experience in national politics as secretary of education and director of drug control policy under the Reagan and Bush administrations has fueled his passion for a national recovery of faith and morality.

In this essay, Bennett assesses the social and cultural condition of American society. What he finds is that America is in a "social regression" that has been induced by a spiritual crisis. *Acedia*, or "an aversion to and negation of spiritual things," is our problem. According to Bennett, America is afflicted by a "corruption of the heart" or "a turning away of the soul."

To face this crisis, Bennett calls for a "social regeneration" that requires taking spiritual and religious matters seriously. Exhorting us not to surrender but to "get mad; and get in the fight," he offers four general prescriptions for America's spiritual-social despair. First, we must not place too much hope in politics, because our moral, cultural, and spiritual afflictions require more than political solutions. Second, public policies must reflect a logical joining of our deepest beliefs about the nature and end of humanity and our legislative agendas. Third, the intellectual and moral purposes of education must be recovered. Fourth, religion must be given a more vital role, because its enervation in both private and public life has "demoralized" society.

"If God does not exist, everything is permissible."
—Fyodor Dostoyevsky

◆ ◆ ◆

My task is to provide an assessment of the social and cultural condition of modern American society. And while many people agree
there is much to be concerned about these days, I don't think people
fully appreciate the depth, or even the nature, of what threatens us.
Therefore, we do not yet have a firm hold on what it will take to better us.
We need to have an honest conversation about these issues.

Not long ago, I had lunch with a friend, a man who has written for
a number of political journals and now lives in Asia. During our conversation, the topic turned to America—specifically, America as seen
through the eyes of foreigners.

He told me what he had observed during his travels: that while the
world still regards the United States as the leading economic and military
power on earth, this same world no longer beholds us with the moral
respect it once did. When the people of the world look at America, he
said, they no longer see a "shining city on a hill." Instead, they see a
society in decline, with exploding rates of crime and social pathologies.
We all know that foreigners often come here in fear—and once they're
here, they travel in fear. It is our shame to realize they have good reason
to fear; a record number of them get killed here.

Today, many who come to America believe they're visiting a
degraded society. Yes, America still offers plenty of jobs, enormous opportunity, and unmatched material and physical comforts. But there's a
growing sense among many foreigners that when they come here, they're
slumming. I have, like many of us, an instinctive aversion to foreigners
harshly judging my nation, yet I must concede that much of what they
think is true.

"YOU'RE BECOMING AMERICAN"

I recently had a conversation with a Washington, D.C., cab driver who
is doing graduate work at American University. He told me that once
he receives his masters degree, he's going back to Africa. His reason?
His children. He doesn't think they're safe in Washington. He told me

he doesn't want them to grow up in a country where young men will paw his daughter and expect her to be an "easy target," and where his son might be a different kind of target—the target of violence from the hands of other young males. "It is more civilized where I come from," said this man from Africa. I urged him to move outside of Washington; things should improve.

But it isn't only violence and urban terror that signal decay. We see it in many forms. *Newsweek* columnist Joe Klein recently wrote about Berenice Belizaire, a young Haitian who arrived in New York in 1987. When she came to America, she spoke no English, and her family lived in a cramped Brooklyn apartment. Eventually, Berenice enrolled at James Madison High School, where she excelled. According to Judith Khan, a math teacher at James Madison, "[The immigrants are] why I love teaching in Brooklyn. They have a drive in them that we no longer seem to have."

Far from New York City, in the beautiful Berkshire mountains where I went to school, Philip Kasinitz, an assistant professor of sociology at Williams College, has observed that Americans have become the object of ridicule among immigrant students on campus. "There's an interesting phenomenon," Kasinitz says. "When immigrant kids criticize each other for getting lazy or loose, they say, 'You're becoming American.' Those who work hardest to keep American culture at bay have the best chance of becoming American success stories."

An article in *The Washington Post* pointed out how students from other countries adapt to the lifestyle of most American teens. Paulina, a Polish high school student studying in the United States, said that when she first came here, she was amazed by the way teens spent their time. According to Paulina:

In Warsaw, we would talk to friends after school; go home and eat with our parents and then do four or five hours of homework. When I first came here, it was like going into a crazy world, but now I am getting used to it. I'm going to Pizza Hut and watching TV and doing less work in school. I can tell it is not a good thing to get used to.

Think long and hard about these words, spoken by a Polish girl about America: "When I first came here, it was like going into a crazy world, but now I am getting used to it." And, "I can tell it is not a good thing to get used to."

Something has gone wrong with us.

SOCIAL REGRESSION

That's a conclusion I come to with great reluctance. During the late 1960s and 1970s, I reacted strongly to the criticisms of America that swept across university campuses. I believe that many of those criticisms—"Amerika" as an inherently repressive, imperialist, and racist society—were wrong then, and they're wrong now. But intellectual honesty demands that we accept facts we would sometimes like to wish away. Hard truths are truths nonetheless. And the hard truth is that something has gone wrong with us.

America is not in danger of becoming a Third-World country; we're too rich, too proud, and too strong to allow that to happen. It's not that we live in a society completely devoid of virtue. Many people live well, decently, even honorably. There are families, schools, churches, and neighborhoods that work. There are places where virtue is taught and learned. But there's a lot less of this than there ought to be. And we know it. John Updike put it this way: "The fact that . . . we still live well cannot ease the pain of feeling that we no longer live nobly."

Reprinted with special permission of North America Syndicate.

Let me outline some of the empirical evidence that points to cultural decline, evidence that while we live well materially, we don't live nobly. Just a few years ago, I released, through the auspices of the Heritage Foundation, *The Index of Leading Cultural Indicators*, the most comprehensive statistical portrait available of behavioral trends over the last 30 years. Among the findings: since 1960, the population has increased 41 percent; the Gross Domestic Product has nearly tripled; and total social spending by all levels of government (measured in constant 1990 dollars) has risen from $142.7 billion to $787 billion—more than a five-fold increase.

But during the same 30-year period, there has been a 560 percent increase in violent crime; more than a 400 percent increase in illegitimate births; a quadrupling in divorces; a tripling of the percentage of children living in single-parent homes; more than a 200 percent increase in the teenage suicide rate; and a drop of 75 points in the average S.A.T. scores of high school students.

Those are not good things to get used to.

Today, 30 percent of all births and 68 percent of black births are illegitimate. By the end of the decade, according to the most reliable projections, 40 percent of all American births and 80 percent of minority births will occur out of wedlock.

Those are not good things to get used to.

And then there are the results of an ongoing teacher survey. Over the years, teachers have been asked to identify the top problems in America's schools. In 1940, teachers identified them as talking out of turn, chewing gum, making noise, running in the hall, cutting in line, dress code infractions, and littering. When asked the same question in 1990, teachers identified drug use, alcohol abuse, pregnancy, suicide, rape, robbery, and assault.

Those are not good things to get used to either.

Consider, too, where the United States ranks in comparison with the rest of the industrialized world. We are at or near the top in rates of abortions, divorces, and unwed births. We lead the industrialized world in murder, rape, and other violent crimes. And in elementary and secondary education, we are at or near the bottom in achievement scores.

Those facts alone are evidence of substantial social regression. But there are other signs of decay, ones that do not so easily lend themselves to quantitative analyses (some of which I have already suggested in my opening anecdotes). What I'm talking about is the moral, spiritual, and aesthetic character and habits of a society—what the ancient Greeks referred to as its *ethos*. And here, too, we face serious problems. For there is a coarseness, a callousness, a cynicism, a banality, and a vulgarity to our time. There are just too many signs of de-civilization—that is, civilization gone rotten. And the worst of it has to do with our children. Apart from the numbers and the specific facts, there's the ongoing, chronic crime against children: the crime of making them old before their time. We live in a culture that at times seems almost dedicated to the corruption of the young, to assuring the loss of their innocence before their time.

This may sound overly pessimistic or even alarmist, but I think this is the way it is. My worry is that people are not unsettled enough; I don't think we're angry enough. We've become inured to the cultural rot that is setting in. Like Paulina, we're getting used to it, even though it's not a good thing to get used to. People are experiencing atrocity overload, losing their capacity for shock, disgust, and outrage.

Not long ago, 11 people were murdered in New York City within 10 hours, and as far as I can tell, it barely caused a stir.

Recently, a violent criminal, who mugged and almost killed a 72-year-old man and was shot by a police officer while fleeing the scene of a crime, was awarded $4.3 million. The decision was met with virtual silence.

During the Los Angeles riots in 1992, Damian Williams and Henry Watson were filmed pulling an innocent man out of a truck, crushing his skull with a brick, and doing a victory dance over his fallen body. Their lawyers then built a successful legal defense on the proposition that people cannot be held accountable for getting caught up in mob violence. ("They just got caught up in the riot," one juror told *The New York Times*. "I guess maybe they were just in the wrong place at the wrong time.")

When the trial was over and those men were found not guilty on most counts, the sound you heard throughout the land was relief. We are "defining deviancy down," in Senator Daniel Moynihan's memorable phrase. And in the process, we're losing a once-reliable sense of civic and moral outrage.

URBAN SURRENDER

Listen to this story from former New York City Police Commissioner Raymond Kelly:

A number of years ago there began to appear, in the windows of automobiles parked on the streets of American cities, signs which read: "No radio." Rather than express outrage, or even annoyance at the possibility of a car break-in, people tried to communicate with the potential thief in conciliatory terms. The translation of "no radio" is: "Please break into someone else's car, there's nothing in mine." These "no radio" signs are flags of urban surrender. They are hand-written capitulations. Instead of "no radio," we need new signs that say "no surrender."

What is so striking today is not simply the increased *number* of violent crimes, but the *nature* of those crimes. It's no longer "just" murder we see, but murders with a prologue, murders accompanied by acts of unspeakable cruelty and inhumanity.

From pop culture, we've heard with our own ears the terrible debasement of music. Music, harmony, and rhythm find their way into the soul and fasten mightily upon it, Plato's *Republic* teaches us. Because music has the capacity to lift us up or bring us down, we need to pay more careful attention to it. It's a steep moral slide from Bach, and even Buddy Holly, to Guns 'n Roses and 2 Live Crew. Not long ago, an indicted murderer, Snoop Doggy Dogg, saw his rap album "Doggystyle" debut at number one. It may be useful for you to read, as I have, some of his lyrics and other lyrics from heavy metal and rap music, and then ask yourself, *How much worse could it possibly get?* And next ask yourself, *What will happen when young boys who grow up on mean streets, without fathers in their lives, are constantly exposed to music that celebrates the torture and abuse of women?*

A lot of criticism is directed at television these days—the casual cruelty, the rampant promiscuity, the mindlessness of sitcoms and soap operas. Most of the criticisms are justified. But that's not the worst of it. The worst of television is the daytime television talk shows, where indecent exposure is celebrated as a virtue. It's hard to remember now, but there was once a time when personal failures, subliminal desires, and perverse tastes were accompanied by guilt or embarrassment, or at least by silence.

Today, such things are a ticket to appear as a guest on the "Sally Jessy Raphael Show" or one of the dozen or so shows like it. I asked my staff to give me a list of some of the daytime talk-show topics from a recent two-week period. They included: cross-dressing couples; a three-way love affair; a man whose chief aim in life is to sleep with women and fool them into thinking he's using a condom during sex; women who can't say no to cheating; prostitutes who love their jobs; a former drug dealer; and an interview with a young girl caught in the middle of a bitter custody battle.

These shows present a two-edged problem to society: The first edge is that some people want to appear on these shows in order to expose themselves. The second is that lots of people are tuning in to watch them expose themselves. That is not a good thing to get used to.

Who's to blame? Here I would caution conservatives against the tendency to blame liberals for our social disorders. Contemporary liberalism does have a lot for which to answer; many of its doctrines have wrought much damage. Universities, intellectuals, think tanks, and government departments have put a lot of poison into the reservoirs of national discourse. But to simply point the finger of blame at liberals and elites is wrong. The hard fact of the matter is that this was not something done to us; it's also something we have done to ourselves. Liberals may have been peddling from an empty wagon, but we were buying.

Much of what I've said is familiar to many of you. Why is this happening? What's behind all this? Intelligent arguments have been advanced about why these things have come to pass. Thoughtful people have pointed to materialism and consumerism; an overly permissive society; the writings of Rousseau, Marx, Freud, and Nietzsche; the legacy of the 1960s; and so on. There is truth in almost all of those accounts. Let me give you mine.

SPIRITUAL ACEDIA

I submit to you that the real crisis of our time is spiritual. Specifically, our problem is what the ancients called *acedia*, which is the sin of sloth. But *acedia*, as understood by the saints of old, is *not* laziness about life's affairs (which is what we normally think sloth to be). *Acedia* is something else; properly understood, *acedia* is an aversion to and a negation of *spiritual* things, which reveals itself as an undue concern for external affairs and worldly things. *Acedia* is spiritual torpor; an absence of zeal for divine things. And it brings with it, according to the ancients, "a sadness, a sorrow of the world."

Acedia manifests itself in mankind's "joyless, ill-tempered, and self-seeking rejection of the nobility of the children of God." The slothful person *hates* the spiritual and wants to be free of its demands. The old theologians taught that *acedia* arises from a heart steeped in the worldly and carnal, and from a low esteem of divine things. It eventually leads to a hatred of the good altogether. With hatred comes more rejection, more ill temper, more sadness and sorrow.

Spiritual *acedia* is not a new condition, of course. It is the seventh capital sin. But today it's in ascendance. In coming to this conclusion, I have relied on two literary giants—men born on vastly different continents, the product of two completely different worlds, and shaped by wholly different experiences—yet writers who possess strikingly similar views and who have had a profound impact on my own thinking. It was an unusual and surprising moment to find their views coincident.

When the late novelist Walker Percy was asked what concerned him most about the future of America, he answered:

> Probably the fear of seeing America, with all its great strength
> and beauty and freedom ... gradually subside into decay
> through default and be defeated, not by the Communist move-
> ment ... but from within by weariness, boredom, cynicism, greed
> and in the end helplessness before its great problems.

And here are the words of the prophetic Aleksandr Solzhenitsyn (echoing his 1978 Harvard commencement address in which he warned of the West's "spiritual exhaustion"):

> In the United States the difficulties are not a Minotaur or a
> dragon—not imprisonment, hard labor, death, government
> harassment and censorship—but cupidity, boredom, sloppiness,
> indifference. Not the acts of a mighty all-pervading repressive
> government but the failure of a listless public to make use of the
> freedom that is its birthright.

What afflicts us, then, is a corruption of the heart, a turning away in the soul. Our aspirations, our affections, and our desires are turned toward the wrong things. And only when we turn them toward the right things—toward enduring, noble, spiritual things—will our situation get better.

Lest I leave the impression of bad news on all fronts, I do want to be clear about the areas where we've made enormous gains: material comforts, economic prosperity, and the spread of democracy around the world. The American people have achieved a standard of living unimagined 50 years ago. We've seen extraordinary advances in medicine, science, and technology. Life expectancy has increased more than 20 years during the last six decades. Opportunity and equality have been extended to those who were once denied them. And, of course, America prevailed in our "long, twilight struggle" against communism. Impressive achievements, all.

Yet even with all of this, the conventional analysis is still that this nation's major challenges have to do with getting more of the same: achieving greater economic growth, job creation, increased trade, health care, or more federal programs. Some of these things are desirable, such as greater economic growth and increased trade; some of them are not, such as more federal programs. But to look to any or all of them as the solution to what ails us is akin to assigning names to images and shadows, it so widely misses the mark.

If we have full employment and greater economic growth—if we have cities of gold and alabaster—but our children have not learned to walk in goodness, justice, and mercy, then the American experiment, no matter how gilded, will have failed.

I realize I've laid down strong charges, a tough indictment. Some may question them. But if my diagnosis isn't right, then someone must explain to me this: Why do Americans feel so bad when things are so economically, militarily, and materially good? Why, amidst this prosperity and security, are enormous numbers of people—almost 70 percent of the public—saying we're off track? This paradox is described in the Scottish author John Buchan's work. Writing a half century ago, he described the "coming of a too garish age, when life would be lived in the glare of neon lamps and the spirit would have no solitude." Here is what Buchan wrote about in his nightmare world:

> In such a [nightmare] world everyone would have leisure. But everyone would be restless, for there would be no spiritual discipline in life. . . . It would be a feverish, bustling world, self-satisfied and yet malcontent, and under the mask of a riotous life there would be death at the heart. In the perpetual hurry of life

there would be no chance of quiet for the soul. . . . In such a bag-man's paradise, where life would be rationalised and padded with every material comfort, there would be little satisfaction for the immortal part of man.

During the last decade of the twentieth century, many have achieved that bagman's paradise. And that is not a good thing to get used to.

In identifying spiritual exhaustion as the central problem, I part company with many. There *is* a disturbing reluctance in our time to talk seriously about matters spiritual and religious. Why? Perhaps it has to do with the modern sensibility's profound discomfort with the language and commandments of God. Along with other bad habits, we've gotten used to not talking about the things that matter most—and so, we don't.

One will often hear that religious faith is a private matter that does not belong in the public arena. But that analysis doesn't hold water—at least on some important points. Whatever your faith—or even if you have none at all—it's a fact that when millions of people stop believing in God, or when their belief is so attenuated as to be belief in name only, enormous public consequences follow. When this is accompanied by an aversion to spiritual language by the political and intellectual class, the public consequences are even greater.

How could it be otherwise? In modernity, *nothing* has been more consequential—or more public in its consequences—than large segments of American society privately turning away from God, considering Him irrelevant, or declaring Him dead. Dostoyevsky reminded us in *Brothers Karamazov* that "if God does not exist, everything is permissible." We're now seeing "everything." And much of it is not good to get used to.

SOCIAL REGENERATION

What can be done? First, here are the short answers: Do not surrender; get mad; and get in the fight. Now let me offer a few somewhat longer prescriptions.

1. At the risk of committing heresy in the eyes of fellow Washingtonians, let me suggest that our first task is to recognize that, in general, we place too much hope in politics. I'm certainly not denying the impact (for good and ill) of public policies. I wouldn't have devoted the past decade of my life to public service—and I could not work at the

Heritage Foundation—if I believed that my work amounted to nothing more than striving after wind and ashes. But it's foolish and futile to rely primarily on politics to solve moral, cultural, and spiritual afflictions.

The last quarter century has taught politicians a hard and humbling lesson: There are intrinsic limits to what the state can do, particularly when it comes to imparting virtue, forging character, and providing peace to souls. Samuel Johnson expressed this (deeply conservative and true) sentiment when he wrote, "How small, of all that human hearts endure, that part which laws or kings can cause or cure!"

King Lear was a great king—sufficient to all his political responsibilities. He did well as king, but as a father and a man, he messed up terribly. The great king was reduced to the mud and ignominy of the heath, cursing his daughters, his life, his gods. Politics is a great adventure; it is greatly important; but its proper place in our lives has been greatly exaggerated. Politics—especially inside-the-Beltway politics—has too often become the graven image of our time.

2. We must have public policies that once again make the connection between our deepest beliefs and our legislative agendas. Do we Americans, for example, believe man is a spiritual being with a potential for individual nobility and moral responsibility? Or do we believe his ultimate fate is to be merely a soulless cog in the machine of state? When we teach sex-education courses to teenagers, do we treat them as if they're young animals in heat? Or do we treat them like children of God?

In terms of public policy, the failure is not so much intellectual; it's a failure of will and courage. Right now we're playing a rhetorical game: We say one thing and do another. Consider the following:

- We say we desire from our children more civility and responsibility, but in many of our schools, we steadfastly refuse to teach right and wrong.
- We say we want law and order in the streets, but we allow criminals, including violent criminals, to return to those same streets.
- We say we want to stop illegitimacy, but we continue to subsidize the kind of behavior that virtually guarantees high rates of illegitimacy.
- We say we want to discourage teenage sexual activity, but in classrooms all across America, educators are more eager to dispense condoms than moral guidance.

◆ We say we want more families to stay together, but we liberalize divorce laws and make divorce easier to attain.

◆ We say we want to achieve a color-blind society and judge people by the content of their character, but we continue to count by race and skin pigment.

◆ We say we want to encourage virtue and honor among the young, but it has become a mark of sophistication to shun the language of morality.

3. We desperately need to recover a sense of the fundamental purpose of education, which is to provide for the intellectual *and* moral education of the young. From the ancient Greeks to the founding fathers, moral instruction was *the* central task of education. "If you ask what is the good of education," Plato said, "the answer is easy—that education makes good men, and that good men act nobly." Jefferson believed that education should aim at improving one's "morals" and "faculties." And of education, John Locke said this: "'Tis virtue that we aim at, hard virtue, and not the subtle arts of shifting." Until about a quarter century ago, this consensus was so deep as to go virtually unchallenged. Having departed from this time-honored belief, we're now reaping the whirlwind. And so we talk not about education as the architecture of souls, but about "skills facilitation," "self-esteem," and being "comfortable with ourselves."

4. As individuals and as a society, we need to return religion to its proper place. Religion, after all, provides us with moral bearing. And if I'm right and the chief problem we face is spiritual impoverishment, then the solution depends, finally, on spiritual renewal. I'm not speaking here about coerced spiritual renewal—in fact, there's no such thing—but about renewal freely taken.

The enervation of strong religious beliefs—*in both our private lives as well as our public conversations*—has de-moralized society. We ignore religion and its lessons at our peril. But instead of according religion its proper place, much of society ridicules and disdains it and mocks those who are serious about their faith. In America today, the only respectable form of bigotry is bigotry directed against religious people. This antipathy toward religion cannot be explained by the well-publicized moral failures and financial excesses of a few leaders or charlatans, or by the censoriousness of some of their followers. No, the reason for hatred of religion is that it forces modern people to confront matters they prefer to ignore.

Reprinted by permission of Tribune Media Services

Every serious student of American history, familiar with the writing of the Founders, knows the civic case for religion. It provides society with a moral anchor—and nothing else has yet been found to substitute for it. Religion tames our baser appetites, passions, and impulses. And it helps us to thoughtfully sort through to "*ordo amoris*," the order of the loves.

But remember, too, that for those who believe, it's a mistake to treat religion merely as a useful means to worldly ends. Religion rightly demands that we take seriously the object of the faith. Those who believe know that although we're pilgrims and sojourners and wanderers in this earthly kingdom, ultimately we're citizens of the City of God—a city which man did not build and cannot destroy, a city where there is no sadness, where the sorrows of the world find no haven, and where there is peace the world cannot give.

PUSHING BACK

In his 1950 Nobel Prize acceptance speech, William Faulkner declared, "I decline to accept the end of man." Man will not merely endure but prevail because, as Faulkner said, he alone among creatures "has a soul, a spirit capable of compassion and sacrifice and endurance."

Today, in the same way, we must decline to accept the end of moral man. We must carry on the struggle—for our children. We will push back hard against an age that is pushing hard against us. When we do, we'll emerge victorious against the trials of our time. When we do, we will save our children from the decadence of our time.

We have a lot of work to do. Let's get to it.

◆ ◆ ◆

This chapter is adapted from Policy Review, *winter 1994, and is reprinted by permission of the Heritage Foundation, 214 Massachusetts Ave., N.E., Washington, D.C. 20002.*

DISCUSSION QUESTIONS

1. What evidence does Bennett present of America's "social regression"?
2. Explain the author's use of the word *acedia*.
3. What does Bennett mean when he says, "We place too much hope in politics"?
4. Bennett calls for public policies that connect "our deepest beliefs and our legislative agendas." Give some examples of existing or proposed policies that do just that.
5. What's your understanding of the primary purpose of education? Is it to teach skills and provide information or to form character and instill virtue?
6. What is religion's role in society?
7. Why does Bennett refuse to accept the "end of man"?

CHAPTER 2

The Public Square: Naked or Sacred?

by Alan R. Crippen II

THE BIG IDEA

Building on William Bennett's call "to return religion to its proper place" in American public life, I will examine the civic case for religion. Starting with a discussion of the impact of secularism on American law and government, this chapter challenges the prevailing assumption that the separation of church and state mandates the separation of religious values from political and legal values.

Citing the writings of the American founders, I assert that religion undergirds a public morality that is necessary for maintaining civil order. For this reason, society needs religion. I will then outline the significant influence of religion in social and political reform movements throughout American history—how religion provided not only moral bearing, but also the meaning of life and purpose for the social order.

Next, this chapter will distill the essence of three major approaches for returning religion to the public square: Christendom, civil religion, and principled pluralism. Favoring principled pluralism, I argue that it is an "affirmative accommodation of America's religious, cultural, and social diversity" that fosters a public forum where religion and religious ideas and values can compete for acceptance on their own merits. I will briefly illustrate how principled pluralism would affect education policy by accommodating religion and parental rights.

> *"Politics and law are not a path to grace and faith.*
> *But are not grace and faith a path to right politics*
> *and right law?"*
>
> —Harold J. Berman

◆ ◆ ◆

In the preceding chapter, one of William Bennett's prescriptions for "social regeneration" was to return religion to its proper place in society. Because religion provides us not only with moral bearing but also with the meaning of life and purpose for the social order, any solution to America's spiritual-social despair must include a prominent role for religion in public life.

There is a civic case for religion at least as old as the American republic. It goes something like this: A democracy without religion is a democracy without morality, and a democracy without morality is an anarchy. In other words, a civil society cannot be sustained without public morality, and morality is rooted in religion; therefore, society needs religion. The advance of secularism, however, has debilitated religion's public role, putting American society in peril.

THE NAKED PUBLIC SQUARE

In the mid-1980s, Richard J. Neuhaus, a Christian intellectual, published *The Naked Public Square: Religion and Democracy in America*.[1] In it, he diagnosed a public square that had become "naked" of religion and religious ideas and values, if not openly hostile to them. According to Neuhaus, the naked public square is the doctrine that America is a secular society, and therefore, religion has no business in public discourse and should be left to private life.

Without a doubt, secularism has fueled the cultural crisis that Dr. James Dobson calls "a great civil war of values," which is nothing less than a "struggle for the hearts and minds of the people . . . a war of ideas."[2] In this conflict, the "secular left" is often pitted against the "religious right" in the all-too-familiar skirmishes taking place in the public schools, courtrooms, city council meetings, and legislatures.

These social and political hostilities are deeply rooted in competing moral visions for America. Though disputes over abortion, homosexual rights, euthanasia, public education, and so on have obvious political manifestations, they are symptomatic of much deeper commitments—secularism versus theism. They are, in fact, worldviews in collision. University of Virginia sociologist James Davison Hunter has called these conflicts "culture wars" for the very definition of America.[3]

Though secularism may not deny the existence of God outright, it does reduce God and religious belief to the irrelevant. Secularism is the dissociation of religion from society, and its effects are particularly evident in law and government. As Harvard University Law School professor emeritus Harold J. Berman observed:

> In the past two generations the public philosophy of America has shifted radically from a religious to a secular theory of law, from a moral to a political or instrumental theory, and from a communitarian to an individualistic theory. . . . Rarely, if ever, does one hear it said that law is a reflection of an objective justice or of the ultimate meaning or purpose of life . . . The radical separation of law and religion in contemporary American thought creates a serious danger for religion—namely, the danger that it will be viewed as a wholly private, personal, psychological matter, without any social or historical dimensions. Jefferson's experiment may be in the process of failing, for though religion is flourishing in America, it is increasingly a "privatized" religion, with little in it that can overcome the forces of strife and disorder in society.[4]

Ever since the 1947 landmark case of *Everson v. Board of Education*, Supreme Court jurisprudence has stretched Thomas Jefferson's metaphor of "a wall of separation between church and state" beyond anything the founders would recognize. And even though those words are not found in the Constitution, in a subsequent decision a year after *Everson*, Justice Hugo Black maintained that "the First Amendment has erected a wall between Church and State which must be kept high and impregnable."[5] Warning against a zeal that would apply so much brick and mortar to Jefferson's metaphor, however, Yale University Law School professor Stephen L. Carter wrote:

> The potential transformation of the Establishment Clause [a part of the First Amendment] from a guardian of religious liberty into

B.C.   by johnny hart

| WHEN THE HIGHEST COURT IN THE LAND IS JUDGED BY THE HIGHEST OF ALL... | THE 'SEPARATION OF CHURCH AND STATE' WILL BE THEIR GRANDILOQUENT SQUALL. | THEY MAY EVEN BRANDISH THE 1st AMENDMENT— ON HIGH—IN THAT HALLOWED HALL, | TO POINT OUT THE PHRASE, BUT DISCOVER—AMAZED— THAT IT AINT EVEN IN THERE AT ALL! |

Used by permission of Johnny Hart and Creators Syndicate, Inc.

a guarantor of public secularism raises prospects at once dismal and dreadful. The more that the clause is used to disable religious groups ... from active involvement in the public square ... the less religions will be able to play their proper democratic role of mediating between the individual and the state.[6]

Yet religiously motivated people of all faiths are disenfranchised by an increasingly secular state that regards religious belief as just a "hobby" on the order of "building model airplanes ... something trivial—and not really a fit activity for intelligent and public-spirited adults."[7]

At the vanguard of the secular left are organizations like the American Atheists, Americans United for the Separation of Church and State, Freedom from Religion Foundation, People for the American Way, and the American Civil Liberties Union (ACLU). An example of their agenda is readily demonstrated by the California ACLU's position on sex education in public schools. In 1988, the California legislature passed a law requiring public schools to emphasize abstinence in public school sex education programs. While the legislation was being debated, the ACLU weighed in on the matter. In a letter to the state Assembly's education committee, ACLU spokespersons Marjorie C. Swartz and Francisco Lobaco wrote:

> It is our position that teaching that monogamous, heterosexual intercourse within marriage is a traditional American value is an unconstitutional establishment of a religious doctrine in public schools. There are various religions which hold contrary beliefs with respect to marriage and monogamy. We believe [this bill] violates the First Amendment.[8]

That paragraph is a striking example of the secularization of law and the "strict separationist" interpretation of the Constitution. It's a radical interpretation of the First Amendment that seeks to exclude religion and religiously informed ideas and values from public policy.

But let's take the ACLU's reasoning to its logical conclusion. Since the Bible forbids murder, does that mean that all statutes against murder are an "unconstitutional establishment of a religious doctrine"? Is the constitutionality of laws against theft, arson, rape, perjury, and fraud to be called into question because those laws are also expressions of the Bible's teaching on morality?

YOU CAN'T LEGISLATE MORALITY?

Those questions invite us to reconsider the notion that "you can't legislate morality." Is there any truth to the idea? Yes, if we mean that it's impossible to change the hearts and minds of people by legislation. Good laws do not make people good. Only social utopians from the left and right believe that government is a cure-all for social ills—that a Democratic or Republican majority is the answer to our moral and spiritual problems. Our hope for social regeneration should never be put wholly in legislative measures, be they Franklin Roosevelt's "New Deal," Lyndon Johnson's "Great Society," or Newt Gingrich's "Contract with America."

But "you can't legislate morality" is more often used to object to the use of religious values in public discourse. In this sense, the phrase carries a completely different meaning. It's now used to mean that religiously informed ideas and values should have no bearing on public policy issues. In the words of former U.S. Surgeon General Joycelyn Elders, "Everyone has different moral standards . . . you can't impose your standards on someone else."[9] In other words, "Who are you to push your moral and religious preferences on everyone else? Your morals are a matter of private choice; to make them into law would be a violation of the separation between church and state."

Is Elders right? Have we reached a time when there can be no national morality? Historically, criminal law was codified and enforced by two basic measurable criteria: (1) Is the behavior wrongful (or immoral); and (2) is it harmful to society (or antisocial)? Unless a crime fit both criteria, it wasn't punishable. But secularism has removed the first criterion by denying the very objective standard by which behavior can be judged good or bad, right or wrong. Everything is now subjective and relative to personal or group preferences. Law, then, divorced from objective morality becomes pragmatic, to be measured by its utility in regulating anti-social behaviors. Law is "simply an embodiment of the ends and purposes of a society at a given point in its history,"[10] to use the words of the late Supreme Court Justice Oliver Wendell Holmes.

If behaviors can no longer be determined to be wrongful, why should anyone be shocked when Elders suggests the decriminalization of illicit drug use? It's no coincidence that our secularization of law coincided with increased crime, increased police requirements, and increased needs for prison space. And all the legislation in the world won't solve the crime problem until we start legislating morality again—in the sense that we recover the idea of right and wrong. To do this, we must recognize the religious foundation of law and public policy, but that won't be possible until religion returns to the public square.

POLITICS AND RELIGION DO MIX: WISDOM FROM THE FOUNDERS

So what exactly is the relationship of religion and morality to politics and law? Neuhaus said, "Because politics is a function of culture and at the heart of culture is morality and at the heart of morality is religion, there is a necessary and unavoidable interaction between politics and religion."[11] In other words, because religion and morality are at the very core of culture, politics is unavoidably and necessarily connected to them.

The Cultural Pyramid

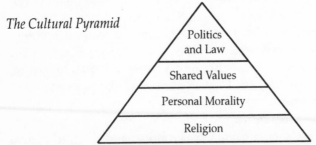

The late Russell Kirk believed religion to be the civilizing element to civilization. Reminding us that at the root of culture is the "cult," or religious worship, he warned that our civilization is in peril: "Our society's affliction is the decay of religious belief. If a culture is to survive and flourish, it must not be severed from the religious vision out of which it arose."[12]

If Kirk was correct (and I'm convinced he was), the survival of American culture requires a recovery of its religious vision. So what were the founders' views on the relationship of religion to public life? Were they strict separationists, as the ACLU and People for the American Way would have us believe? Or did they allow for religious ideas and values to play a role in the governing process? *The empirical historical evidence clearly indicates that the founders of our country were united in believing that religion was essential to the constitutional order.* Let's consult their own words to prove that point.

In his First Inaugural Address, President George Washington said, "We ought to be no less persuaded that the propitious smiles of Heaven can never be expected on a nation that disregards the eternal rules of order and right which Heaven itself has ordained."[13] He believed in an objective moral order of the universe for determining what was right and wrong. Furthermore, in his Farewell Address eight years later, Washington offered the collective wisdom of his life in public service as both soldier and statesman:

> Of all the dispositions and habits which lead to political prosperity, religion and morality are indispensable supports. . . . It is substantially true that virtue or morality is a necessary spring of popular government. . . . Can it be that Providence has not connected the permanent felicity of a nation with its virtue?[14]

Washington believed that religion and morality were the very underpinnings of social order, as well as the fountain of representative democracy. He also believed the nation's happiness and well-being depended on its virtue. If Washington were alive today, would he be sued by the ACLU? Would he be disparaged by People for the American Way?

John Adams, our second president, was probably the most prolific writer of the founders on the relationship of religion and society. A sampling of his thoughts on the subject follows.

> Statesmen, my dear Sir, may plan and speculate for Liberty, but it is religion and morality alone which can establish the principles upon which freedom can securely stand. The only foundation of

a free constitution is pure virtue; and if this cannot be inspired into our people in a greater measure than they have it now, they may change their rules and the forms of government, but they will not obtain a lasting liberty.[15]

We have no government armed with power capable of contending with human passions unbridled by morality and religion. Avarice, ambition, revenge, or gallantry, would break the strongest cords of our Constitution as a whale goes through a net. Our Constitution was made for a moral and religious people. It is wholly inadequate for the government of any other.[16]

Religion and virtue are the only foundations, not only of republicanism and of all free government, but of social felicity under all governments and in all the combinations of human society.[17]

As you can see, Adams shared Washington's conviction that religion and morality were the necessary foundations for freedom and democracy. Even Thomas Jefferson recognized the importance of religion to the social and civil order. The man who used the metaphor "wall of separation between church and state"[18] and is heralded by strict separationists as their canon (and even cannon) wrote:

Let us, then, with courage and confidence pursue our own federal and republican principles . . . enlightened by a benign religion, professed, indeed, and practiced in various forms, yet all of them including honesty, truth, temperance, gratitude, and the love of man; acknowledging and adoring an overruling Providence, which by all its dispositions proves that it delights in the happiness of man here and his greater happiness hereafter.[19]

Can the liberties of a nation be thought secure when we have removed their only firm basis, a conviction in the minds of the people that these liberties are the gift of God? Indeed I tremble for my country when I reflect that God is just; that his justice cannot sleep forever.[20]

Are those the words of a strict separationist? To be sure, Jefferson believed strongly in the institutional separation of church and state at the federal and state levels, but he didn't believe in the separation of political and legal values from religious values. On the contrary, he believed religious values were necessary for the preservation of liberty.

Much the same can be said of Jefferson's successor as president, James Madison, the father of the Constitution and an architect of the First Amendment: "Before a man can be considered as a member of Civil Society, he must be considered as a subject of the Governour of the Universe."[21]

Like the others, Madison believed in the existence of an objective religious and moral order in which the social order must be rooted if a "civil society" were to be achieved and sustained.

Thus, generally speaking, the founders believed that religion provided moral bearing, the meaning of life, and purpose for the social order. They articulated a powerful civic case for religion that seems to have been lost in the twentieth century amidst the onslaught of secularism. Prevailing strict separationist notions of the First Amendment would have impressed them as radical and destructive to democracy.

TWO OTHER VOICES

Further insight into the relationship of religion and morality to politics and law can be gained from Alexis de Tocqueville, a French social scientist who visited America in the early 1800s to study the workings of a bold experiment in the New World—democracy. Regarding the role of religion in the United States, he wrote:

> Religion in America takes no direct part in the government of society, but it must be regarded as the first of their political institutions; for if it does not impart a taste for freedom, it facilitates the use of it. . . . I do not know whether all Americans have a sincere faith in their religion—for who can search the human heart?—but I am certain that they hold it to be indispensable to the maintenance of republican institutions. . . . Religion is much more necessary in the republic . . . it is more needed in democratic republics than in any others.[22]

As Tocqueville observed, religion was the "first" of our political institutions. That was true at the founding of the republic and has been so throughout most of American history. Religion provided the form and norms for exercising political freedom. In Tocqueville's thinking, religion defined the boundaries of democratic freedoms and, in doing so, prevented the degeneration of liberty into license, of community into chaos, of democracy into demagoguery. Because of the vitality of religion in America, we avoided the social anarchy of the French experience in the aftermath of revolution.

More wisdom on the importance of religion to the public square can be gleaned from the American icon Benjamin Franklin. As a participant in the Constitutional Convention in 1787, Franklin made a now-famous proposal for prayer on June 28, when the convention had reached a weeks-long impasse that threatened the entire project:

> Mr. President:
> The small progress we have made after four or five weeks close attendance & continual reasonings with each other ... is ... proof of the imperfection of the Human understanding. ...
> In this situation of this Assembly, groping as it were in the dark to find political truth ... how has it happened, Sir, that we have not hitherto once thought of humbly applying to the Father of lights to illuminate our understanding? ... To that kind Providence we owe this happy opportunity of consulting in peace on the means of establishing our future national felicity. And have we now forgotten that powerful friend? or do we imagine that we no longer need His assistance? I have lived, Sir, a long time, and the longer I live, the more convincing proofs I see of this truth—that God governs in the affairs of men. And if a sparrow cannot fall to the ground without His notice, is it probable that an empire can rise without His aid? We have been assured, Sir, in the Sacred Writings, that "except the Lord build the House, they labor in vain that build it." I firmly believe this; and I also believe that without His concurring aid we shall succeed in this political building no better than the Builders of Babel: We shall be divided by our partial local interests; our projects will be confounded, and we ourselves shall become a reproach and bye word down to future ages. And what is worse, mankind may hereafter from this unfortunate instance, despair of establishing Governments by Human wisdom and leave it to chance, war, and conquest.
> I therefore beg leave to move—that henceforth prayers

imploring the assistance of Heaven, and its blessing on our deliberations, be held in this Assembly every morning before we proceed to business, and that one or more of the clergy of this city be requested to officiate in that service.[23]

I've cited Franklin at length to demonstrate the spiritual aspects of his political thought, including the limits of human reason and the need for spiritual illumination "to find political truth." Franklin placed the security and perpetuation of the republic squarely in the hands of God. Believing that the resolution of the immediate constitutional crisis depended on God's intervening presence, he petitioned for prayer.

It should be clear by now that freedom of religion was never intended by our founders to mean freedom *from* religion. In framing the First Amendment of the Constitution, they envisioned, and even chartered, a more vibrant pluralism—a religious diversity with freedom for faith to compete in the marketplace of ideas. This religious vitality would inform both private and public morality, as well as provide an overall purpose for the social order.

"A CITY UPON A HILL"

Religion has provided a vision for the social order ever since Governor John Winthrop pictured America as "a city upon a hill" in a sermon aboard the flagship *Arabella* while en route to New England in 1630. And like the presidents before him, Bill Clinton borrowed from this heritage in describing his own agenda as a "New Covenant" at the 1992 Democratic National Convention. The obvious Jewish and Christian symbolism of his rhetoric marked the most religious language applied to a presidential candidate's policy agenda in recent history. Regardless of whether one agrees with the objectives of the Clinton administration, the fact is the use of religious language is more than just rhetorical device: It reflects the reality that religious motivations still underlie our discourse in the public square.

Here are Clinton's own words on the relationship between religion and public life:

Sometimes I think the environment in which we operate is entirely too secular. The fact that we have freedom of religion doesn't mean we need to try to have freedom from religion, doesn't mean that those of us who have faith shouldn't frankly admit that we are animated by that faith, that we try to live by it, and it does affect what we feel, what we think, and what we do.[24]

President Clinton was right. Secularism silences religious people in public discourse. Secularism is not neutral but intolerant of and hostile to people of all faiths. It hails a new era in American politics, for it has only been in the last two generations that religious views, and evangelical Christian views in particular, have been shut out of public dialogue.

WHERE WOULD WE BE WITHOUT IT?

It's difficult to imagine the tapestry of American history without the threads of religion. After all, our most significant social reforms were spearheaded by religiously motivated people. During the nineteenth century, the abolitionist movement was organized, financed, and perpetuated by church leaders such as the Rev. Charles G. Finney, the Rev. Lyman Beecher, and Beecher's influential daughter, Harriet Beecher Stowe, author of *Uncle Tom's Cabin*. Their faith in God and vision for His justice in the face of injustice sustained their political efforts through President Abraham Lincoln's emancipation of African-American slaves in 1863.

The religious vision of Frances Willard inspired her in the cause of women's suffrage. As leader of the politically influential Women's Christian Temperance Union (WCTU), her motto was "Home Protection." In those days, home protection involved not only fighting the social evils of alcoholism and the destitution it inflicted on wives and children, but also winning political empowerment for women. The home could not be protected from antifamily government policies until women had a pro-family voice with the right to vote and the political power to achieve reforms in social welfare and education.

Religious vision also motivated William Jennings Bryan, whom Garry Wills of Northwestern University describes as "the most important evangelical politician of this century."[25] According to many historians, Bryan was the most influential figure in the reform politics of America. The "Great Commoner" was his party's presidential candidate three times, a "kingmaker" in the Democratic convention that nominated Woodrow

"THE FIRST DETECTOR IS FOR GUNS AND KNIVES... THE SECOND ONE CHECKS FOR RELIGIOUS MATERIAL!"

Reprinted by permission of Tribune Media Services

Wilson for president, and after the election, Wilson's secretary of state. And perhaps no other American since the founders was as personally responsible for as many constitutional amendments.[26]

Finally, we shouldn't forget that religious vision motivated the civil rights movement. Can you imagine Martin Luther King Jr.'s "I Have a Dream" speech devoid of religious ideals and symbols? King's religious values inspired and defined his understanding of purpose for the social order:

> I have a dream that my four little children will one day live in a nation where they will not be judged by the color of their skin but by the content of their character.... I have a dream that one day every valley shall be made low, the rough places shall be made plain, and the crooked places shall be made straight, and the glory of the Lord will be revealed, and all flesh shall see it together.[27]

Just as it was then, so it is today. Christian people are motivated to achieve justice in the public square by their faith in God. Jesus' great commandments to love God and one's neighbor compel people of faith to seek such things as religious freedom; human rights for the unborn, aged, and oppressed; legal protection for children against pornographers; educational reform; welfare reform; electoral reform; and environmental protection.

Those of the secular left who would deny the so-called religious right a place in American politics because of the "wall of separation" have misinterpreted the First Amendment. In denying religious people the right to express their religiously informed political views, they undermine the fundamental principles of democracy itself. Furthermore, they nullify the religious vision that gives purpose to the social order. Thus, if there's to be any hope of social regeneration, if there's to be any consolation of our community involvement, it must consist of a proper and prominent role for religion in the public square.

A SACRED PUBLIC SQUARE?

Where, then, do we go from here? If religion must be returned to the public square, how can this be accomplished? People of faith often disagree about what form this public role should take. At the risk of oversimplification, there are essentially three options: (1) Christendom; (2) civil religion, or (3) principled pluralism. Let me offer a brief explanation of each.

Backward Christian Soldiers: Christendom Revisited
By *Christendom*, I don't mean the triumphal reign of Jesus Christ on the earth for which all Christians long. Rather, I refer to the efforts of some Christians to impose Christianity on society by force of law. The Christendom option finds articulate expression in T.S. Eliot's book *Christianity & Culture*, in which he argues for a more coherent Christian world. Any Christian with a strong sense of Christ's lordship over all creation will read this book sympathetically.

The Christendom model has historical precedent dating back to the fourth century, when Emperor Constantine made Christianity the official religion of the Roman Empire. Unfortunately, in those earlier times a religious passion for truth led to dogmatism and intolerance, which resulted in the state persecuting "heretics." During the Reformation and continuing into the following century, Protestantism was not only fighting Catholicism, but also itself, as the blood of the Anabaptists so readily testifies. In short, the record of Christendom for promoting social harmony, at least through the Reformation and immediately following, is not good.[28]

That European experience was still fresh in the minds of the American founders when they crafted the First Amendment to protect religious liberty and individual rights of conscience. The United States government was explicitly prohibited from establishing a national church—Reformed, Lutheran, Roman Catholic, or anything else. Rather, organized religions would be supported by the voluntary association of private citizens and perpetuated through the efforts of individual persuasion rather than governmental coercion.

There are Christians today, however, who want to impose Christendom through a radical reform of American government. Their objective is to bring society into conformity with God's laws as revealed in the Old and New Testaments. These "reconstructionists" or "theonomists" (from *theos*, meaning "God," and *nomos*, meaning "law") emanate from some circles of the Reformed Protestant tradition. Unfortunately, and to their discredit, the reconstructionist movement is often characterized by uncharitable and strident tones, which are many times targeted at its own members. Evangelical theologian Carl F. H. Henry recently observed:

> "Christian Reconstructionists['] . . . verbal assaults on those who differ encourage some to wonder whether they would rather take their chances of survival in a radically Shiite society than one run by some Christian theonomists."[29]

But there are "kinder and gentler" advocates of the Christendom option. These people are often inspired by the openly evangelical faith of such American founders as John Witherspoon, Patrick Henry, Roger Sherman, John Jay, and Oliver Ellsworth. They're animated by the knowledge that Christian principles and values were presupposed or even articulated in documents like the colonial charters, the Declaration of Independence, state constitutions, and national actions like the appointment of chaplains to the Congress and the military, and the proclamation of days of fasting and thanksgiving.

Such people believe America's basic social consensus was Christian in its early days and, therefore, should be Christian again. The long-standing absolute separation of church and state should be ended in favor of more church-state collaboration for promoting justice and a national morality. The public school system should have the "Christian coloration" that its founders, Benjamin Rush and Horace Mann, envisioned it to have. Advocates of the Christendom option point to current European models of church-state relations in countries such as England and Switzerland.

Some Christendom advocates believe the U.S. Constitution is entirely too secular and must be amended to explicitly acknowledge the authority of Jesus Christ. Organized in 1864 and existing up to the present day, the National Reform Association has promoted a rewording of the preamble of the Constitution as follows:

> Recognizing Almighty God as the source of all authority and power in civil government, and acknowledging the Lord Jesus Christ as the Governor among the nations, His revealed will as supreme law of the land, in order to constitute a Christian government. . . .[30]

Early in the organization's history, nationally recognized leaders like the Rev. Charles G. Finney and U.S. Supreme Court Justice William Strong lent their enthusiastic support to this measure. In 1874 and again in 1896, members of the House Judiciary Committee discussed this proposed amendment. Even as recently as 1954, the Senate Judiciary Subcommittee on Constitutional Amendments held hearings on the "Christian Amendment," as it later came to be called. However, all these efforts to achieve a Christian nation by constitutional amendment were unsuccessful.

Is the Christendom option a valid approach to restoring a public role for religion? For several reasons, I think not. First, it has not retarded the advance of secularism in modern Europe. Even with the special legal and political status afforded to Christianity by many European countries, secularism has become the prevailing worldview on the continent. There's no evidence to suggest that constitutional and legislative measures to Christianize America will fare any better.

Second, the Christendom option fails to accommodate pluralism. Our society has many different components—ethnic, religious, linguistic, and racial. In the last century, America has experienced an explosion of diversity—so much so that it seems the well-known metaphor of America as the great melting pot of the world is no longer adequate. The idea that immigrants dissolve into a monolithic "American" culture is just not accurate. Immigration in the nineteenth and early twentieth centuries broke up the Protestant cultural dominion when Irish and Italian Catholics and eastern European Jews forever transformed the landscape of American ethnicity and religion.

But now, American pluralism extends beyond Protestant-Catholic-Jewish consensus to include almost all the world's religions. For the first time in our history, minority faiths boast significant numbers. Hindus, Buddhists, and Muslims are now a vibrant part of America's religious landscape. For example, a public elementary school in Paterson, New Jersey, with a student population of 1,146 students, is 46.5 percent Muslim.[31] Paterson is named after Senator William Paterson, who worked with Representative James Madison on the congressional conference committee that drafted the final wording of the First Amendment. Could Paterson, Madison, or any of the other founders ever have envisioned the pluralistic society we have today? Probably not.

As a social reality that's here to stay, pluralism forces all Americans to ask, *How do we live together with our deepest differences, especially when they're religious in nature?*

Christendom would answer the question by favoring Christianity above all other religions, because of its majority status. But is that a just solution for believers of minority faiths? Would an Islamic republic be in order if Islam were the majority religion in America? The imposition of religious faith by force of law, be it Christianity, Islam, or the worship of Chnemu-Ra, is not the way to restore a public role for religion.

"Give Me That Old-Time 'Civil' Religion"

While Christendom maintains that Christianity is the national religion, civil religion—the second option—celebrates a more generalized, common religion, the "American Way of Life," which incorporates the ideas, values, and behaviors common to all Americans. Civil religion is not a new idea but one that dates back to the ancient world. And in the eighteenth century, French philosopher Jean-Jacques Rousseau coined the term "civil religion" in his book *The Social Contract*. Rousseau maintained that because "no state has ever been established without having religion for its basis," the state should establish a civil religion, or a "purely civil profession of faith," in order to cultivate "sentiments of sociability without which it is impossible to be either a good citizen or a faithful subject."[32]

Rousseau's civil religion is a politically expedient and benign theism with only four dogmas: (1) the existence of God, (2) the life to come, (3) the reward of virtue and punishment of vice, and (4) the exclusion of religious intolerance. All other religious doctrines and ideas are unnecessary for the maintenance of the social order and are, therefore, outside the purview of the state. Citizens may freely hold other doctrines in addition to this core of belief.

Civil religion allows the authority of law to be supported by a transcendent law, or "higher law." After all, Thomas Jefferson and the other signatories of the Declaration of Independence located the legitimacy of the new nation in this concept of transcendent authority when they wrote of "Laws of Nature and Nature's God."

Perhaps the words of former President Dwight Eisenhower best epitomize American civil religion: "Our government makes no sense unless it is founded in a deeply felt religious faith—and I don't care what it is."[33] After being moved during a sermon by the Rev. Peter Marshall's successor, the Rev. George M. Docherty, at the New York Avenue Presbyterian Church on February 7, 1954, President Eisenhower led the charge for amending the Pledge of Allegiance to include "one nation under God." Two years later, "In God We Trust" became the official motto of the United States, and the U.S. Senate Subcommittee on Constitutional Amendments held hearings on the proposed "Christian Amendment."[34]

What about the merits of reviving civil religion? Certainly, it acknowledges a transcendent reality that challenges secularism and its effects on law and government. Civil religion also accommodates pluralism to the extent that it doesn't force a particular religion on anyone. In this manner, it safeguards individual consciences from coercion by a state-imposed religion. Or does it?

Evangelical sociologist Os Guinness has described civil religion as "the bedeviling factor," for it's a confusing of the American creed with the Apostles' Creed, resulting in a semi-religious nationalism. Guinness warns, "Those religious believers who continue to advocate and press for civil religion in the face of contemporary realities will either fail and find their efforts ineffective or else succeed and find them idolatrous."[35]

For Christians and Jews, the moral obstacle to clothing the naked public square with civil religion is the first commandment: "You shall have no other gods before me" (Ex. 20:3). Civil religion is idolatry. It's not an authentic religion but a false one that any devout Christian, Jew, or Muslim must reject for conscience's sake.

That's why a school prayer amendment that would simply reinstate the New York State Board of Regents' prayer or any other form of state-mediated prayer is unacceptable.[36] Though a constitutional amendment restoring students' First Amendment rights to all forms of religious expression is now necessary and welcome, the regents' nondescript, nondenominational, and nonsectarian prayer to a lowest-common-denominator deity revives civil religion. To the devout believer, an idolatrous religion is no better than no religion, because neither option is believed to be true. Any solution for restoring a public role for religion must accommodate *authentic* religion and its claims of truth.

"Back to the Future" with Principled Pluralism

As Richard Neuhaus points out in his book, a naked public square can never really be naked, because when the public square is devoid of religion, secularism assumes the role of religion. On the other hand, a sacred public square would impose Christianity or civil religion on all citizens, thus violating a proper institutional separation of church and state, as well as freedom of conscience for many. Clearly, the public square must be neither naked nor sacred, but more accommodating of the vibrant pluralism that is America.

America "*was* in its guts Christian, for Christianity *shaped* the society and the individuals who lived in it," as Terry Eastland of the Ethics and Public Center has pointed out.[37] That fact is both inspiring and depressing. It's inspiring to learn our nation has a great spiritual heritage that helped shape its culture, laws, and government. Yet it's also depressing to realize that the marble statues and biblical inscriptions on granite in the nation's capitol, statehouses, courthouses, and Ivy League universities are virtually all that remain of Christian civilization. Rather than being symbols of a present reality, those things are monuments to a largely forgotten past. We now live in a "post-Christian" America. The Judeo-Christian ethic no longer guides our social institutions. Christian ideals and values no longer dominate social thought and action. The Bible has ceased to be a common base of moral authority for judging whether something is right or wrong, good or bad, acceptable or unacceptable.

In this situation, principled pluralism accommodates the reality of pluralism without compromising conviction. It recognizes the fact of a post-Christian America and looks to a pre-Christian world—the world of Jesus and the apostles—for direction on how to live. In this sense, principled pluralism can be said to go "back to the future."

In New Testament times, various ethnic, racial, and religious groups composed the Roman Empire. Then, like today, pluralism was a social reality. How did Jesus, the apostles, and the early Christians engage their culture? They resorted to persuasion—to winning hearts and minds with the truth of Christian ideas. Their confidence in the truth allayed any fears of opposition, and their ability to persuade others (through the power of the Holy Spirit) reformed ancient society and helped build Western civilization.

Our modern inability to persuade others of the truth has contributed to the demise of Western civilization. So it would seem that we have come almost full circle: from a pre-Christian, to a Christian, to a post-Christian era. We can only hope that in God's providence, our post-Christian era is prelude to a pre-Christian one leading to a flourishing Christian culture. If we're to accomplish that, what must we do? Lawrence Burtoft will address how we can recover the art of persuasion in chapter 5. But let me address the need for a public forum that allows us the opportunity to persuade others with the positively powerful ideas of the Christian faith.

Principled pluralism envisions a society like your living room—a safe and comfortable place where you and your neighbor can have coffee over a lively and civil discussion about your deepest differences in the hope of changing her mind on the issues. She, of course, will be attempting to change your mind as well. But if we believe in the power of truth, why should we fear such a forum?

Principled pluralism seeks to create a free marketplace of ideas. Rather than enforcing a naked public square or imposing a sacred one, principled pluralism accommodates authentic religious belief. It seeks to responsibly apply the founders' vision of *e pluribus unum* ("out of many, one") to our current social setting by calling for an affirmative accommodation of America's religious, cultural, and social diversity. It recognizes that God's creation contains a variety of human institutions, such as family, school, church, and state, as well as various groups of people with rights to organize churches, schools, political parties, and even labor unions to promote their way of life. Principled pluralism seeks a commonwealth of free families, free schools, and free churches in a free state. It would guard the rights of all people of faith, be they Christian, Jew, Muslim, Hindu, Buddhist, or atheistic secularist.

Confidence in the truth affirms principled pluralism, because it presupposes that we can understand, reason, and be persuaded of right and wrong, meaning, and purpose. Principled pluralism offers our society a public square in which competing truth claims can be treated with respect, debated, and then embraced or rejected. In this forum, tolerance and civility are necessary, not as ultimate values or ends, but rather as means to an end—the finding of ultimate truth amidst conflicting truth claims.

A religious passion for truth need not lead to intolerance. To the contrary, a commitment to exclusive truth claims makes tolerance essential, as German theologian Wolfhart Pannenberg explained:

> While the truth of God's revelation is indeed ultimate, our understanding of that truth is always provisional and will remain so until the end of history (1 Corinthians 13:9-12). This distinction is of utmost importance because it yields the imperative of tolerance ... tolerance is not against the truth; it is truth that makes tolerance imperative.[38]

Tolerance is a religious virtue, especially for Christians. Jesus' teaching of the parable of the weeds established it as a biblical principle.[39] In that passage, the servants are commanded not to pull up the weeds (i.e., nonbelievers) in the field because they may end up harming believer and nonbeliever alike. Judgment is reserved for God alone, as Jesus later explained. At the end of the age, His harvesters, or angels, will weed the kingdom of nonbelievers.

As we've seen, the naked public square has actually enforced secularism as the only framework for public-policy debate. Secularism has become the only "ground rules" for the conduct of public business. One prime example of this is public education. In the interest of maintaining "neutrality" toward religion, our schools have become "religion-free zones"; in fact, the schools have become agents of a secularist understanding of life. In the public school, American families are confronted with a near government monopoly that, at least tacitly, undermines their religious understanding of life.

When no room is made for religion in our democracy's schools, secularism is established by default. But secularism is a cosmology, a nontheistic worldview, or philosophy of life. In other words, secularism is a functional religion, and even the U.S. Supreme Court has recognized it as such.[40] Why, then, should secularism be the only "ground rules" for public discourse? Why has Supreme Court jurisprudence favored secularism over religion in its decisions of the last 50 or so years? In 1963, Justice Potter Stewart admonished the Court that "a refusal to permit religious exercises [in public schools] thus is seen, not as the realization of state neutrality, but rather as the establishment of a religion of secularism."[41]

Principled pluralism, on the other hand, offers a more just approach. It affirms that American society is made up of peoples with deep differences that are often religious in nature. It suggests that the answer to living together is not to trivialize our differences or regulate them to private spheres of "religious" and family life, but rather to recognize that these beliefs animate us in public life (even public schools) as well as in private. In a democracy, there can be no right not to be offended. The free exchange of ideas (including religious ones) mandates tolerance—the religious rights of other people to follow the dictates of their consciences.

Principled pluralism affirms that it's wrong to censor a public high school valedictorian because she wants to speak about the importance of Jesus Christ in her life.[42] Nor is it right to refuse a student permission to write a research paper on "The Life of Jesus Christ" because the paper involves religion when the topic is otherwise appropriate.[43] Equal rights means equality under the law for people of all faiths and no faith. Equal rights also means that when a secular viewpoint is permitted in the public square, a religious viewpoint should also be allowed. True government neutrality mandates that the government should show no preference for religion or secularism. To deny benefits or otherwise discriminate against any person because of the religious character of their speech, ideas, motivations, or identity is a violation of human rights.[44]

To continue with the example of public education, a principled pluralist approach would demand some dramatic policy reform. It would offer a cafeteria of schools. Families would have a range of choices from which to pick the one that best fits their religious beliefs and child's learning needs.

Because principled pluralism recognizes a diversity of religious worldviews, educational philosophies, and methodologies, it affirms parental rights in education. This is in keeping with the United Nations' Universal Declaration of Human Rights, which proclaims, "Parents have a prior right to choose the kind of education that shall be given to their children."[45] The United Nations' International Covenant on Economic, Social, and Cultural Rights is even more specific on the right of parents to "ensure the religious and moral education of their children in conformity with their own convictions." This right can be exercised by parents choosing "schools, other than those established by public authorities."[46] Parental rights, in turn, imply the right of citizens "to establish, where practicable, educational institutions based on a common culture, language or religion, provided that there shall be no discrimination on the ground of race,"[47] as the Republic of South Africa recognizes now that it begins to deal justly with its ethnic, racial, and religious pluralism.

But in contrast, the poor, working-class, and even most middle-class families in the United States don't have the real freedom to choose something other than a nontheistic governmental education for their children. Economic realities and an unjust tax burden deny them this right. Yet tuition vouchers, tax credits, flexible charter schools, and other creative policy ideas would give all parents greater choice. Simple justice and equality of opportunity require that tax moneys should be distributed fairly to all children regardless of where they're schooled. For education to be truly public, religious majorities and minorities must be accommodated, as well as the secularist minorities.

In restoring a public role for religion in American society, we must affirm that the public square should be neither naked nor sacred, but rather truly representative of America's pluralism. This includes not only Christianity, but all the world's other major religions as well. Like it or not, these religions inform personal morality, the meaning of life, and purpose for the social order. In this situation, Christians must articulate an approach to public discourse that engages their ideas in a principled and persuasive way.

Love of neighbor must govern our motivations and methods of political and social involvement, as well as the goals and outcomes of our laws and public policies. As followers of Jesus Christ, this approach is our greatest responsibility and opportunity in the public square. We need to articulate a common vision for the common good of all people, not just Christians. We must seek justice for every citizen. Our love should lead us to public policies and practical social programs on our neighbors' behalf.

In short, principled pluralism would be a most effective way to restore a public role for religion.

DISCUSSION QUESTIONS

1. What is the civic case for religion?
2. What is secularism, and how has it affected American government and law?
3. Explain the relationship of religion and morality to politics and law.
4. How do you think the American founders would respond, if they were alive today, to groups like the American Civil Liberties Union and People for the American Way?
5. What role has religion played in America's social and political reform movements? What is religion's role in the pro-family movement today?
6. Describe the major differences between Christendom and principled pluralism as approaches for restoring religion to the public square.
7. How does principled pluralism demand educational policy reform?

CHAPTER 3

The Train Wreck
of Truth and Knowledge

by Greg R. Jesson

THE BIG IDEA

According to Greg R. Jesson, Christians who desire to reach their neighbors for Christ and to respond to the many social crises presently afflicting America must begin by understanding the times. As a society, we have lost confidence in the availability of moral truth. Consequently, those who claim to have it are held suspect. Americans are confused about moral and social issues because they no longer believe in a firm foundation of reality. Convinced as many are that truth is relative and reality is in the "eye of the beholder," as a people we vacillate from uncertainty to rigid and irrational dogmatism.

Jesson demonstrates that the disastrous grip of moral relativism is devastating American families and culture. The bottom-line consequence of this view is that there are no abiding values, principles, or practices that can serve as objective standards for ordering our personal and political lives. It becomes your morality versus my morality, and what is "right for you" may be "wrong for me."

A failure to recognize the fundamental importance of these ideas will destine our responses to failure, for they will be woefully inadequate to the present crisis. On the other hand, if we do grasp the power of these ideas and realize that bad ideas can bear only so much reality before they collapse, we shall see the current predicament as a grand window of opportunity. Into this present darkness we can shine the bright light of truth.

"Turning and turning in a widening gyre
The falcon cannot hear the falconer;
Things fall apart; the centre cannot hold;
Mere anarchy is loosed upon the world,
The blood-dimmed tide is freed, and everywhere
The ceremony of innocence is drowned;
The best lack all conviction, while the worst
Are full of passionate intensity."

—W.B. Yeats, "The Second Coming," 1921

◆ ◆ ◆

Never before in the history of the world have so many people believed in so little. The current cultural collapse reveals itself daily in everything from skyrocketing crime that staggers the mind in its frequency and depravity, to music, film, and art that celebrate the destruction of life and beauty, to an increasing inability of many to live beyond their own overwhelming needs and center their lives on commitment, sacrifice, and love. Of course, every culture has gone through its tasteless and troubling times, but those that survived were able to draw on some inherent personal integrity and corporate character that seems strangely distant and unavailable to us.

Ironically, our culture is ever increasing in information but daily decreasing in moral insight and wisdom. The family is immediately impacted by these shifts in knowledge. Many have abandoned their moral and common-sense bearings, for increasing numbers are incapable of deciding if the traditional family should be scrapped, if heterosexual relationships should be preferred over homosexual relationships, if abortion is even a moral question, and if lifelong commitments and sacrificial love are meaningful in the twentieth century. The modern family has become, in the view of many, merely an economic unit that agrees to cohabitate for the purposes of paying bills and watching television.

Many harbor the fear that our culture has slid downhill too far beyond the point of no return. The barbarians are inside the gate and we have no option but to witness, in thousands of evening news broadcasts, the gradual, irrevocable dismantling of life as we know it. As William Bennett remarked:

For there is a coarseness, a callousness, a cynicism, a banality, and a vulgarity to our time. There are too many signs of de-civilization—that is, civilization gone rotten. . . . We live in a culture that at times seems almost dedicated to the corruption of the young.[1]

THE POWER OF IDEAS

How did we get to this place where fear, foolishness, pain, and loss seem to affect every corner of life? What happened to the American culture? Why do your neighbors think as they do? Contrary to many accounts that trace this cultural shift to the removal of prayer from public schools or to the advent of MTV or to the election of President Clinton or to the downfall of President Nixon or to the turbulent 1960s, the real cause for our present condition is far closer to each person than any of these events.

Life turns on ideas. Human choices simply reflect the ideas that people hold. The ideas that each person believes deep within his or her heart and mind concerning happiness, freedom, God, love, responsibility, death, suffering, and a thousand other issues determine what every human life is about.

As John Stuart Mill observed, "Ideas are not always the mere signs and effects of social circumstances; they are themselves a power in history." This sentiment was echoed by the historian Christopher Dawson, coming from a very different perspective than Mill, when he said:

> I do believe that it has been on the plane of ideas that the process of the secularization of culture began, and that it is only by a change of ideas that this process can be reversed. It has always been the weakness of the Anglo-Saxon tradition to underestimate the influence of ideas on life . . . and the result of this error has been that many Christians in England and America never realized the existence of culture until the culture of the age had ceased to be Christian.[2]

To miss this insight is to miss everything. We often tell people to live up to their ideals, but the simple matter of fact is that everyone always does. What we do reveals what ideas and ideals are driving our lives. Our homes, neighborhoods, cities, countries, and cultures are but the physical manifestations of our ideas, assumptions and beliefs. Nothing has more practical consequences, for good or evil, than ideas. Jesus changed the world by first presenting ideas—but so did Hitler.

If we are to understand our neighbors, country, and world, then we must come to grips with the powerful cultural transformation to which Dawson refers. If Western culture has ceased to be motivated by Christian ideals, it is because the fundamental ideas percolating within the lives of people in that culture are fundamentally incompatible with Christianity.

TRUTH THROWN IN THE GUTTER

The paramount component of any worldview is its claim to the possibility and extent of knowledge that is available to the common person. A curious and unprecedented feature of the contemporary worldviews, often represented in both the university and the ordinary person on the street, is that truth, about more than one's immediate experience, is forever beyond our grasp. Each person is marooned within their own experiences and never able to rise above their merely personal opinions.

In the past, full-blown skepticism was safely cloistered and tolerated in the philosophical lecture halls of the universities, but it has now poured out into the general culture, swamping the traditions and norms of the past. What was utterly unthinkable just a generation ago is today commonplace. Yet this brave new world has not brought an upsurge of happiness. The monument of our age is the pathetic daytime television talk show, celebrating the pooling of ignorance and dedicated to every person having the right to be a deplorable, decadent fool. Only those who claim to know anything about how people should live are reprimanded as judgmental, intolerant, and wrong. Television talk shows are the social equivalent of barbarians sacking ancient cities.

But every person must grapple with the issues of truth and knowledge. As it turns out, not everything is true, and truth is not just a matter of personal opinion, and merely trying to make that claim will always contradict the very claim itself. Notice how silly it sounds to say, "Nothing is true" or "Truth is just personal opinion." But are not these statements claimed to be true in a way that is being denied by the statements themselves? It is like saying, "This sentence is false." But if the sentence is false, then it is true, and if it is true, then it is false. Truth, like reality, can't be denied without serious problems following.

Allan Bloom raised the problem of truth and issued a stinging indictment of the university in his book *The Closing of the American Mind*, which claimed:

> There is one thing a professor can be absolutely certain of: almost every student entering the university believes, or says he believes, that truth is relative.[3]

This is the crucial mark of our times. It is not always clear what people mean when they say that truth is relative, but this much is clear—there is no set of objective, independent facts that exist whether or not anyone ever believes in them. Relativism really means that the standards, assumptions, and beliefs that one group or culture has are "true" for that group but might be "false" for another group. The important point here is that mere acceptance of ideas is as far as anyone can go. You can never find out what is really true, what really exists.

To say that there is objective truth is to say that just because someone sincerely believes they are right does not make them right. Mistaken belief is possible. The only thing that would ever make anyone right is if their belief corresponds with some objective fact. On this account, it is possible for everyone in the world to believe something and to be wrong. Similarly, it is possible for nobody to believe something which is in fact true. Since beliefs and reality are independent, they do not always match. As the renowned philosopher of mathematics Gottlob Frege said:

> The thought, which we express in the Pythagorean Theorem is . . . true independent of whether anyone takes it to be true. It needs no bearer. It is not true for the first time when it is discovered, but is like a planet which, already before anyone has seen it, has been in interaction with other planets.[4]

The upshot here is that the claim "truth is relative" just means that there is no independent truth. For example, just because I believe I have a full tank of gas in my car does not make that belief true. My belief is true if the tank is actually full of gas, and my belief is false under all other circumstances—that's why people run out of gas. Just because you believe you have gas in your car will not push your car one inch farther down the road.

When people abandon truth, all they are left with are personal feelings expressed in indignant and self-justifying language. William James, the Harvard psychologist and philosopher, remarked at the turn of the century, "A lot of people think they are thinking, when all they are really doing is just rearranging their prejudices."[5] When truth is abandoned, there is nothing left to base life on except merely pragmatic concerns. We are left with phrases such as, "I just personally believe it" or "That's the way I feel, so that's the end of it."

Not long ago, researcher George Barna polled Americans and asked them to respond to this statement: "There is no such thing as absolute truth; two people could define truth in totally conflicting ways, but both could still be correct." Sixty-seven percent agreed. Within three years, that figure had risen to 72 percent.[6] Concerning morality, 71 percent agreed that "there are no absolute standards that apply to everybody in all situations."[7] Of course, people are sometimes confused in responding to polling questions; nonetheless, these figures reveal a profound crisis of truth in our times.

Around the same time as the Barna poll, the *Los Angeles Times* surveyed 3,583 people concerning abortion. Sixty-one percent said abortion is morally wrong, with most saying it is murder—but 74 percent of the same group said it should remain legal.[8] This is a group of people who believe that some forms of murder should be legal. Thomas Huxley once said, "Logical consequences are the scarecrows of fools and the beacons of wise men." Once people abandon truth, they are often quite comfortable living with conflicting and contradictory beliefs, because there are no independent facts that matter.

HOW DID WE GET HERE?

As the ship of Western culture has navigated across the treacherous and turbulent waters of the past few centuries, it has drifted gradually, often imperceptibly, but certainly off its previous course. What pushed Western culture so far off course? If we misunderstand the causes, inevitably we will miscalculate what the possible solutions could be. Kenneth Clark remarked in his momentous study, *Civilisation*:

> What happened? It took Gibbon six volumes to describe the
> decline and fall of the Roman Empire, so I shan't embark on that.

But thinking about this almost incredible episode does tell one something about the nature of civilisation. It shows that however complex and solid it seems, it is actually quite fragile.[9]

The crucial ideas that have affected our culture are not limited to the artistic, theological, philosophical, or scientific realms. The crucial divide, the most profound set of ideas, concerns the nature of truth and knowledge. This cuts across all disciplines. Is there truth out there, waiting to be discovered, which does not depend upon our mind, culture, or background? In just a few generations, we have shifted from a culture that held truth to be objective to one which holds that truth is mere subjective experience. The objective-subjective distinction transcends all other ideas and raises the central issue of life: Is there anything to base our opinions on besides our feelings? Can truth be known?

At the foundation of Western culture lies the profound thought of Plato, Aristotle, and the biblical writers. Of course, these three disagreed on many things, but all were radical as they held that reality, as it is in itself, is knowable. Plato and Aristotle launched sustained and rigorous critiques of the entrenched skepticism and sophism of their day, while the biblical writers insisted that it is possible to know what God and morality are truly about. Their views might be pictured as follows:

PLATO, ARISTOTLE, AND THE BIBLICAL WRITERS

KNOWLEDGE

1. God
2. The soul
3. Values
4. What other people think, feel, perceive
5. The real world of science

BLIND FAITH

1. Nothing

The point is that Plato, Aristotle, and the biblical writers were utterly convinced that knowledge of reality was available to humanity and was a necessary prerequisite to live a rational and meaningful life. They were confident that nothing had to be accepted on mere blind faith. The biblical writers held that biblical faith is most certainly not blind faith. This was the worldview that launched the entire Western world. All of the art, literature, philosophy, political thought, theology, and science was rooted in the common notion that there is a reality waiting to be known as it is in itself. Knowledge of each of these realities could be demonstrated by evidence, proof, and argument. By the seventeenth and eighteenth centuries, however, this notion was being undermined and finally uprooted by a group of philosophers called the empiricists.

It is here where the vast avalanche of Western culture began. The massive snowpack of knowledge shifted just a fraction of an inch, but once it began, an avalanche would sweep over the traditions and institutions of the past 20 centuries. Empiricism maintains that knowledge is sense experience. Sounds simple enough. Aristotle warned long before that "The least deviation in the truth is later multiplied a thousand fold."[10] Knowledge, according to the empiricists, must be sense experience, and if something cannot be seen, heard, felt, tasted, or smelled, then it is not an object of knowledge. David Hume, the most radical and consistent of the empiricists, asks, "What is the nature of evidence which assures us of any real existence and matter of fact beyond the present testimony of our senses?"[11] For Hume, nothing does, and nothing could ever tell us about reality beyond our own experience.

EMPIRICISM: SEVENTEENTH AND EIGHTEENTH CENTURIES

KNOWLEDGE	BLIND FAITH
1. The real world of science	1. God
2. Other people	2. The soul
	3. Values

What was, in the past, a possible object of knowledge, for the empiricists, has shifted over to objects of mere blind faith. You may believe that God, the soul, and values exist, but that is simply blind and forever unprovable faith. If all knowledge is strictly limited by sense perception, then as Hume pointed out, we have no knowledge of our soul, or even that we exist:

> For my part, when I enter most intimately into what I call myself, I always stumble on some particular perception or other, of heat or cold, light or shade, love or hatred, pain or pleasure. I never can catch myself at any time without a perception, and never can observe any thing but the perception.[12]

Again Hume, in his characteristically witty style, claims:

> If we take in our hand any volume; of divinity or school meta-
> physics [descriptions of reality] ... let us ask, "Does it contain
> any abstract reasoning concerning quantity and number? [Is it
> quantifiable?] No. Does it contain any experimental reasoning ... ?
> [Science] No." Commit it then to the flames; for it can contain
> nothing but sophistry and illusion.[13]

Empiricists rarely notice that the above statement contains no quan-
tifiable information, nor is it based upon experimental reasoning, so, on
its own account, it should be "committed to the flames." Thus Hume.

Immanuel Kant, who claimed to have been "awakened from his
dogmatic slumbers" by the thought of Hume, saw clearly where empiricism leads. Kant said:

> It still remains a scandal to philosophy ... that the existence of
> things outside of us ... must be accepted merely on faith, and
> that, if anyone thinks good to doubt their existence, we are
> unable to counter his doubts by any satisfactory proof.[14]

Unhappily, Kant tried to solve these problems by going further into
the ideas and structures of the mind, for although his whole purpose was
to oppose empiricism, he was committed to the basic empirical assumption that we do not have access to independent reality as it is in itself.

Herein lies the heart to so much of the contemporary world:
Knowledge is denied if the object in question is not experienced. And
since you don't go looking for God, the soul, or values like you go looking for your car keys, these cannot be objects of knowledge and must be
accepted, if at all, on blind faith. However, empiricism, like uranium, is
unstable and would inevitably degenerate—into relativism.

If knowledge is sense experience as the empiricists held, and if
different groups of people experience the world in different ways, which
seems obvious, then the next logical step in the understanding of
knowledge is relativism. Truth and thus knowledge are dependent on
what groups of people happen to believe, so one set of things may be
true in one society or group and a different set may hold in another. The
possibility of the whole community being mistaken is ruled out.

Reprinted by permission of Tribune Media Services

Relativism just means that truth must always be considered relative to a society, whether it consists of the believers in a particular religion, the holders of a certain scientific theory, the members of a tribe, or any other identifiable group. Relativism can be represented as follows:

RELATIVISM

KNOWLEDGE	BLIND FAITH
1. The "world" as my group sees it	1. God
2. Group values	2. The soul
	3. Universal values
	4. The real world of science

Notice that as knowledge is reduced, blind faith is increased. One mark of much contemporary thought is not that God, the soul, and values are rejected, but rather they can only be accepted as objects of blind faith. If no one can have access to the way reality is, then belief in God, the soul, and values is acceptable only so long as no truth claims are made.

According to relativism, it is impossible to conceive of an independent reality that is knowable. Reality is simply what groups of people hold it to be, and as different groups have different conceptions of it, there must be different realities. This is somewhat troublesome, for it seems to be incoherent to claim that there is no such thing as reality but only realities.

Nevertheless, relativism has been particularly popular in the social sciences, where different cultures are studied. However, relativism is itself a teetering position, for the same insight that lead from empiricism to relativism pushes us from relativism to subjectivism. If it is obviously true that different groups of people perceive the world differently, then is it not just as obvious that different individuals in those groups can perceive the world differently? Relativism finally collapses into subjectivism.

The subjectivist holds that what is right or wrong, and true or false, is determined by each person. What I think is true is true for me, and what you think is true is true for you. Protagoras claimed in Athens in the fifth century B.C. that "Man is the measure of all things" and that "Anything is to me as it appears to me, and is to you as it appears to you."[15] Subjectivism is just a more radical relativism, which claims truth never rises higher than any individual's experience. Subjectivism can be represented as follows:

SUBJECTIVISM

KNOWLEDGE
1. My feelings

BLIND FAITH
1. God
2. The soul
3. Values
4. The real world of science
5. What other people think, feel, perceive

Subjectivism places all truth within the mind of each individual, maintaining that there are no standards of truth beyond personal feelings or thoughts. Therefore, no point of view is any more justified that any other—"anything goes." There is no distinction between *being* right and *believing* you are right. All we are left with is our feelings, our personal convictions. Any claims beyond one's immediate and private experience is nothing but blind, unwarranted belief. This is exactly what is involved when people say, "Well, that may be true for you, but it's not true for me. You have your thoughts and I have my thoughts, and who are you to place your standards, values, and truths on me?"

Hilary Putnam, the distinguished Harvard philosopher, illustrates the profound effect of ideas, as he intensely opposes relativism and subjectivism but can't quite escape their gravitational pull. In his article "Philosophers and Human Understanding," Putnam ironically claims:

> The correct moral to draw is not that nothing is right or wrong, rational or irrational, true or false, and so on, but . . . that there is no neutral place to stand, no external vantage point from which to judge what is right or wrong, rational or irrational, true or false. But is this not relativism after all?[16]

If we misunderstand this shift and try to ameliorate the suffering of people and offer insight to our culture without understanding the subjective turn, we will simply not be communicating to the modern mind. Relativism and subjectivism are not just abstract, philosophical points of interest. Rather, they have filtered down into every sphere of contemporary life. The values portrayed in art, music, the media, and peoples' personal lives are the result of denying an objectively existing independent reality and centering the world around each person's personal perceptions. All other tragic shifts in our culture are the result of the loss of truth. Without truth, there is nothing but personal feelings, and no amount of wishful thinking, creative myths, nor clichéd traditions can prevent the inevitable cultural collapse we have been witnessing for the last generation.

There is no great mystery why our cultural discussion, on serious issues, is so polarized and bogged down in personal aspersion and condemnation. When the center ground of truth is abandoned, and when individual beliefs are raised to the status of truth, no one is able to see when they are wrong, and all that is left is to "rearrange our prejudices."

THE SEEDS OF RELATIVISM
AND SUBJECTIVISM BEARING FRUIT

Ideas reveal themselves in the lives of those who hold them. If we have just lived through the most cataclysmic train wreck in Western civilization, we should expect immediate and practical consequences. Every person and every culture must struggle with the ultimate issues of love, death, God, good and evil, suffering, and meaning. Six areas concerning ultimate issues affected by the subjective turn will briefly be explored.

1. Love and Sexuality

Two of the deepest and most powerful concepts in the human heart, love and sexuality say much about who we are (either male or female), where we come from, our longing for love in the present, and how we relate to the future—through children.

Love and sexuality are some of the first casualties of the subjective turn, as their value, purpose, and context are devoid of any guidelines whatsoever. When an individual life or culture collapses, the first areas to unravel are love and sexuality, because they go so deep to the human heart. If nothing is more deeply intertwined in the human heart, then in the midst of the loss of truth, sex loses all its content, dignity, and beauty. For without truth and knowledge, sex becomes just another betting chip in the grand poker game of life. As T.S. Eliot remarked, "In the twentieth century we are obsessed with turning roses into weeds."

The entertainer Madonna epitomizes this contemporary view of sexuality with her acerbic phrases such as "boy toy," "like a virgin," "material girl," and "justify my love." She flaunts a view of love and sexuality in her book Sex that has pathetically drifted light years from the unconditional love presented by the apostle Paul in 1 Corinthians. The objective view, realizing the immense power of sex for both good and evil, made sex absolutely dependent on love and refused to allow love to be defined as anything less than unconditional, unfailing, and sacrificial commitment. "Love never fails," so if it does fail, it is not love. In the subjective turn, the meaning of love, and everything else, is determined by each person's individual feelings and circumstances. Love becomes lust, sex, something you fall into and out of and mere convenience. This is echoed in Tina Turner's disheartening rhetorical question, "What's love got to do with it [sex]?" Her point is, nothing at all. Once all content is stripped away from sex and love, all that is left is our feelings, and no one should be surprised to discover that the compass needle of their feelings almost always points to the magnetic north of themselves.

The subjective turn and the eventual heyday of hedonism have left an entire generation unloved, used, and abandoned. For an ever-increasing number of people, Jesus' words "Greater love hath no person than he lay down his life for his friend" are so beyond their experience that they are almost inconceivable. Many, now beyond their most attractive and alluring years, are fearfully aware that they have never truly loved or been loved by another, and thoughts of genuine and whole-hearted love are almost too painful to consider.

2. Good and Evil, Right and Wrong

The subjective turn quickly undermines objective morality, for the only standards available are one's own unpredictable feelings. The moral fulcrum has been lost. Under such circumstances people will do what is right only if it is to their benefit, and as soon as right and personal feelings diverge, morality gets thrown out.

The objective view of ethics holds that what is good and evil, right and wrong is set and endures whether anyone knows or does what is good. For example, it is always wrong to intentionally take the life of an innocent human being. Today, the subjective view is accepted as self-evident. The objective view of ethics has been almost completely abandoned in our time, and therefore, it is little wonder why the front page of the newspaper is daily filled with tragic and hopeless stories of life without standards.

When Dr. Joycelyn Elders still held the position of surgeon general, she was asked if it is immoral for people to have children out of wedlock. Her response is telling: "No, everyone has different moral standards. . . . You can't impose your standards on someone else."[17] This is consistent with her advocating condom distribution to teens and the legalization of drugs. As one reporter noted, "It is difficult to imagine a more succinct expression of . . . moral relativism."[18]

Dr. Elders has confused objective ethical standards with imposing ethical standards. From the fact that there are objective mathematical truths, say addition, it does not follow that these truths will be *imposed* on anyone. However, what does follow is that to deviate from those mathematical truths simply means one is wrong. Dr. Elders seems to be implying that since "everybody has different moral standards" nobody could ever be morally wrong. This seems indisputably preposterous and dangerous.

It is impossible to avoid the ultimate issues of good and evil, right and wrong, for each of us must make decisions on how to live our lives. Aristotle put the ethical question this way: What are the conditions under which human beings flourish? How can humans live up to their highest potential and experience the truly good life? Aristotle was convinced that most have missed the ethical life when he said:

To judge from the lives that men lead, most men, and men of the most vulgar type, seem (not without some ground) to identify the good, or happiness, with pleasure; which is the reason why they love the life of enjoyment. . . . Now the mass of mankind are evidently quite slavish in their tastes, preferring a life suitable to beasts. . . .[19]

Jesus uses a similar approach to ethics as Aristotle when, in the Sermon on the Mount, He describes the truly good life as one founded on faith, hope, and love and thus freed from the slavish, self-consumed, and groveling ways of this world. Aristotle, Plato, and the biblical writers would be utterly shocked by our contemporary subjective culture and find it to be the perfect prescription for unabridged individual and corporate disaster.

Chuck Colson, in his book *Against the Night*, recounts a meeting of college educators that took place at Harvard in the fall of 1987. Frank Rhodes, president of Cornell, said, "We need to pay real and sustained attention to students' intellectual and moral well-being." The audience gasped, and one student stood up to challenge Rhodes: "Who is going to do the instructing and whose morality are we going to follow?" The audience applauded, affirming that the heckler had posed an unanswerable question. President Rhodes sat down, unwilling or unable to respond.[20]

Hilary Putnam is unquestionably one of the most influential philosophers of the twentieth century. He has been at Harvard University his entire academic career, and has persistently sought to chart a middle course between moral knowledge and relativism. Although interesting, Putnam has continually been pulled back into relativism and subjectivism. He wrote:

We must come to see that there is no possibility of a 'foundation' for ethics, just as we have come to see that there is no possibility of a 'foundation' for scientific knowledge, or for any other kind of knowledge.[21]

Later, Putnam claims that ethical judgments are "something that we ultimately judge by the 'seat of pants' feel."[22] Contrast this subjective view of ethics with the objective view of ethics given by C.S. Lewis during World War II in his essay, "The Poison of Subjectivism":

"Here comes Congressman Blotts with more silly suggestions!"

Reprinted by permission of Tribune Media Services

Everyone is indignant when he hears the Germans define justice as that which is to the interest of the Third Reich. But it is not always remembered that this indignation is perfectly groundless if we ourselves regard morality as a subjective sentiment to be altered at will. Unless there is some objective standard of good, over-arching Germans, Japanese and ourselves alike, whether any of us obey it or not, then of course the Germans are as competent to create their ideology as we are to create ours. . . . Unless the measuring rod is independent of the things measured, we can do no measuring.[23]

In the midst of the subjective turn in ethics, it should be no surprise that ethical education in America has been a dismal failure. The experiment with "values clarification," which was in vogue in the 1970s, is now widely recognized as woefully inadequate in the formation of moral character in our youth. Values clarification was an implicit affirmation of relativism and subjectivism, for educators strove to be "value neutral" by not imparting moral knowledge but merely assisting students to clarify some reasons why they held whatever values they happened to hold. Don Whatley, president of the Albuquerque Teachers Federation, summed up this failed social experiment when he wrote, "We have seen tremendous evidence that we are raising a generation of amoral youth—young people who have no fundamental sense of what is right and what is wrong." The values clarification movement "didn't clarify anything but produced a pervasive notion that anything you can justify is okay to do no matter how much it hurts others."[24]

Valiant efforts have been made to affirm virtues such as respect, responsibility, trustworthiness, caring, justice, fairness, civic virtue, and citizenship. However, without moral knowledge, they appear to be *ad hoc* social constructions fabricated to restrain cultural collapse. In the context of relativism and subjectivism, the question can always be asked, under pressure, "Why should I be respectful, responsible, and caring if it does not benefit me?" Further, holding abstract virtues is a long way from wrestling with the concrete ethical problems of life involving sexuality, work relationships, and character.

3. The Meaning of Life

Irving Singer, a professor at the Massachusetts Institute of Technology, recently wrote a book entitled *Meaning in Life: The Creation of Values*.[25] He does not claim that there is an objective meaning of life, rather each person must create his or her meaning in life. Singer's title is a one-line commentary on our culture. There is no intrinsic purpose or goal to life.

Singer and others have substituted objective meaning by creating their own subjective meaning on the basis of what anyone happens to feel at any particular moment. Once the subjective turn is made, there are no objective standards to determine the meaning of life, and therefore, nothing but personal feelings and interests to evaluate how life should be spent. If someone devotes his entire life to collecting comic books, who are you to say that his life is not as meaningful as Winston Churchill's was? As the French atheistic, existentialist philosopher Jean-Paul Sartre remarked:

> I'm quite vexed that that's the way it is; but if I've discarded God the Father, there has to be someone to invent values. You've got to take things as they are. Moreover, to say we invent values means nothing else but this: life has no meaning.[26]

It is not difficult to ascertain the meaninglessness that people experience in their lives. More and more seem incapable of handling the anxiety, stress, and loneliness of life void of objective intrinsic meaning.

If life has no intrinsic meaning, then neither do people. Meaning and value must be derived from human decision. Since 1973, by fiat of the United States Supreme Court, a preborn child does not have an intrinsic right to life; his mother must decide to grant that right and thereby christen it with value. If, for example, a baby is born with spina bifida, the meaning and value of its life has in some areas been made dependent upon achieving a sufficient score by means of the mathematical formula, $QL = NE \times (H+S)$: Quality of life (QL) is determined by natural, physical, and intellectual endowment (NE) multiplied by the sum of the contribution from home, family, and society (H+S). When this policy was adopted in Oklahoma, it was babies born into poor families who tended to have the lowest "quality of life" scores and therefore were "allowed" to die.[27]

Such is life in a world intoxicated by relativism and subjectivism. All issues of value, meaning, and purpose will be determined by our feelings, desires, and interests. Anyone who cannot promote their interests and feelings will be run over by the powerful.

4. Reality and Truth

The subjective turn voraciously attacks reality and truth, and leaves nothing but nonsense. The comedian George Carlin once said wryly, "Reality—what a concept!" Or as the poet William Blake said, "As for me I prefer dreams, straight past the North Star will do."

Philosophical squabbles and fine distinctions aside, truth and reality objectively exist—they are real things. The subjective turn ventures to make reality and truth a function of the experience of each person. So we seek for insight without truth, and wisdom without reality. So much education, from grade school to university, attempts to avoid truth with the substitutions of socialization and the politically correct.

Reality is a set thing, and how any of us feels about it has no effect on how it is. Shakespeare said, "If horses were dreams then beggars could ride." Since horses are not dreams, beggars must walk or take public transportation.

"True for me" and "reality for me" mean nothing more than I believe it, but believing does not make truth. If I sincerely, but mistakenly believe that I have a million dollars in the bank, my belief does not make it true. If you can't balance your checkbook on your subjective feelings, then you certainly can't live your whole life that way or build a just and compassionate society on mere mercurial feelings.

5. God and Religion

The greenhouse of relativism and subjectivism has had a profound warming effect on the fertile ground of spiritual aspirations and religion. The icy atheism of the past has thawed, but fewer and fewer are really interested in whether or not a particular religion is true, and therefore, everything that contradicts that particular religion is false. Since relativism and subjectivism both deny that universal objective knowledge is possible, every religion is equally "valid," and none could ever be criticized as being false.

The pedestrian pronouncement that "Nobody can prove the existence of God" is often seen as axiomatic, yet few have taken the trouble to seriously study the issue. The point is this: Once relativism or subjectivism are adopted, arguments, evidence, and proofs are irrelevant, because there is no truth to be discovered. In the subjective turn, religion and every other important issue in life is relegated to personal subjective feelings—beyond dispute, discussion, and correction.

So, for example, not too long ago Shirley MacLaine announced that she is god. But don't worry, not wanting to sound too presumptuous, MacLaine also assures each of us that we can be god also.[28] The New Age movement has been one of the most influential religious movements of our time and was hatched out of the relativism of the 1960s. Since God is not objectively knowable, belief in God (or gods or goddesses) is always filtered through each person's experience.

This moves far beyond atheism, because the subjective turn denies that there is any truth to the matter whatsoever. At best, the truth concerning God is forever beyond our grasp. Our only option is to wander through the giant supermarket of religions and spiritual beliefs guided only by a shopping list that merely reflects individual desires and feelings. If you don't find anything to your liking, there is nothing to prevent you from creating your own religion. And who is to say it is not just as "valid" as Jewish or Christian traditions?

6. Tolerance

Tolerance is one of the great buzz words of our time. However, it is rarely defined carefully and therefore results in confusion. To be tolerant can mean that every human being should be treated as a human being and permitted to enjoy his or her own opinion on any issue. This kind of tolerance is perfectly compatible with intense, respectful discussion and debate over what is true.

However, in the context of relativism and subjectivism, tolerance is valued above everything, for disagreement and debate are perceived as unloving, condemning, and threatening. If no one has a "God's eye view" of reality, every opinion is just as justified (or unjustified) as any other opinion. Under such circumstances, we must tolerate and respect every opinion as being just as reasonable as every other opinion. Without truth, every opinion must be respected just as every taste must be respected. If I don't like pistachio ice cream, how could anyone tell me that I am wrong? With relativism and subjectivism, all opinions are no more objective than personal feelings and tastes.

Allan Bloom clearly conveyed where this all leads in *The Closing of the American Mind*:

> The danger university students have been taught to fear from absolutism is not error but intolerance. . . . The true believer is the real danger. The study of history and culture teaches that all the world was mad in the past; men always thought they were right, and that led to wars, persecutions, slavery, xenophobia, racism, and chauvinism. The point is not to correct the mistakes and really be right; rather it is not to think you are ever right at all.[29]

Tolerance, in the context of relativism and subjectivism, just means that no opinion should ever be criticized since truth and falsity are necessarily excluded. This is an attempt to be compassionate and loving, but without knowledge, love and compassion are meaningless. What can it mean to do "good," refrain from "evil," and do no "harm" when each term is defined by each individual? Compassion without truth is empty and in the end is not compassionate.

"Politically correct" means nothing more than what is currently in vogue and what is accepted by the prominent universities, political liberals, and movie stars. Intellectual inquiry should be concerned to be correct in reference to reality and shouldn't care less what is politically correct, fashionable, or chic.

Jesus taught that truth incorporated in life is freeing. This does not just refer to religious truth but to all truths. If you don't know the truth of turn indicators, lane changes, and freeway on-ramps, your Sunday drive across town will be an unforgettable trip. If you don't know the truths of sexuality (I'm not referring to the mechanics), your life will be a complete disaster. If you don't know the truths of relationships, acceptance, and forgiveness, you will end up in this world alone. Without truth, life entangles us in endlessly complex and heartbreaking problems that are beyond solutions since life is beyond truth.

Unhappily, there is now no sphere of human existence in our culture that is left unscathed by relativism and subjectivism. That snow-pack that shifted just a fraction of an inch when knowledge was identified with sense experience has gathered momentum and swept away over 20 centuries of tradition and thought. Yet there is hope, for life is relentless and ideas that fail to correspond to reality are revealed to be hollow and empty. Life vindicates truth.

THERE IS HOPE: REALITY HAS LIMITS

Albert Einstein once said, "The main difference between stupidity and genius is that genius has limits." Reality has limits and those who would ignore or contradict it discover those limits, often in surprise and suffering.

Consider one of the most prevailing ideas of the 1960s: "free love." What did life reveal about that? It would be difficult to find a single person in America who believes that anything is free. The last 30 years have taught us that love is never free; it will cost you everything you are, everything you have, and everything you ever hope to be. A generation of broken hearts, children born without fathers, and more than 20 sexually transmitted diseases have taught us that "free love" is hollow and spurious.

What about no-fault divorce? It was hailed by feminists just 10 years ago to be a panacea for women trapped in bad marriages. Unfortunately, it has produced a whole new impoverished class in our society: single mothers and their children. No-fault divorce, ignoring responsibility and unfaithfulness, resulted in the "feminization of poverty." The same has been discovered about "no-harm divorce." Dr. Judith Wallerstein, in her provocative book *Second Chances*, clearly demonstrates the continual disastrous effects of divorce on children. Research, across the board, shows that the traditional loving, two-parent family provides the most positive environment for the growth and nurture of children.[30]

The 1980s produced another social delusion: You can have it all. Years later, it is amazing that many Americans have anything at all. Commitments to spouse, friends and children were often jettisoned in an unabashed quest for self-fulfillment and personal happiness. Economic prosperity has proven not only fragile, but also empty for those who found it. And personal happiness proved not only illusive, but also lonely for those who thought they had it.

Relativism, subjectivism, and the policies and lifestyles that express those views are bottoming out. Our culture is in desperate need of ideas that match reality and work. More importantly, individuals long and cry for ideas that work. A tremendous opportunity exists to reach out and help people by providing truth in love, compassion, and humility.

At the turn of the century, G.K. Chesterton said, "The Christian ideal has not been tried and found wanting. It has been found difficult, and left untried." Hope lies not in following the pathetic, weary path of relativism and subjectivism, but in a rediscovery of God's truths revealed in this world concerning the ideal conditions for human fulfillment. Helen Keller, though blind and deaf, sensed that "Everyday God puts thousands of things in our hands to do with as we will, then He moves silently on His way."

There is hope for humanity—there is always hope. This hope is not centered on our capacity to transform ourselves and our culture, rather it is centered on the availability of truth in this world. We are offered the possibility of discovering and experiencing the profundity of reality over delusion, of truth over falsehood, and of goodness over evil. Above all, the hope of this world is centered on the fact that God has not abandoned us and still offers love, forgiveness, and wisdom. This is the good news in the midst of the train wreck of truth and knowledge—it is news worth sharing and worth living.

DISCUSSION QUESTIONS

1. Why are ideas more influential than people, countries, or historical events?
2. What is the difference between relativism and subjectivism?
3. Give additional examples of the "subjective turn" in the areas of:

(1) love and sexuality; (2) good and evil, right and wrong; (3) the meaning of life; (4) reality and truth; (5) God and religion; and (6) tolerance.
4. How can your children, church, and friends learn to understand the times and the power of ideas?
5. What are the central ideas that were influential in your upbringing and education? How have these ideas affected your life?

CHAPTER 4

A Biblical Case for Social and Political Involvement

by John Eldredge

THE BIG IDEA

For most of the twentieth century, evangelical Christians have been exiles to social and political involvement. The American aphorism that "religion and politics don't mix" has been unwittingly embraced by far too many Christians. But times are changing and now it can be said that evangelicals are "no longer exiles" to the political scene. Evangelical groups are active in local, state, and national politics. Political scientists, pollsters, and the news media have attributed election outcomes to the increasing influence of Christians. Political leaders consult with evangelicals on proposed legislation about human rights (including the most fundamental right to life), religious liberty, parental rights, education, taxation, public funding of the arts, welfare reform, and other issues.

Is this kind of involvement by citizen Christians good? Should Christians care about these concerns, let alone get actively involved with them? Are these kinds of activities warranted by biblical teaching? John Eldredge believes that Christians should be involved in these areas of social concern. He makes a "biblical case" for involvement based on the Christian principles of love and justice, as well as the nature of government as established by God.

*"The more profoundly one is concerned about heaven,
the more deeply one cares
about God's will being done on earth."*

—J.I. Packer

◆ ◆ ◆

Should Christians be socially and politically active? Efforts to shape government policy, reform the entertainment industry, create better schools and communities—do endeavors like these have any place in the Christian life? Are they forbidden, merely to be tolerated, or duties to which we are called? The Christian community has debated these matters for years. The future not merely of society but of the Christian witness *to* society waits on the church to come to a biblical conclusion.

I have tried to distill the essence of the historical Christian perspective in the following three points, seeking an answer from the Scriptures to this question: Why should Christians be socially and politically involved?

I. A CHRISTIAN VIEW OF LOVE
AND COMPASSION COMPELS US.

Let us begin with a point of agreement: We are commanded to love our neighbors as ourselves.[1] Jesus gave this command extraordinarily high priority, making it second only to loving God with our whole being. Scripture calls it the "royal law."[2] So then, how do we fulfill this mandate? The question was posed to Christ, and His illustrative response is what we call the Parable of the Good Samaritan, found in the Gospel of Luke, chapter 10.

> A man was going down from Jerusalem to Jericho, when he fell into the hands of robbers. They stripped him of his clothes, beat him and went away, leaving him half dead. A priest happened to be going down the same road, and when he saw the man, he passed by on the other side. So too, a Levite, when he came to the place and saw him, passed by on the other side. But a Samaritan, as he traveled, came where the man was; and when he saw him, he took pity on him. He went to him and bandaged his wounds, pouring on oil and wine. Then he put the man on his own donkey, took him to an inn and took care of him. The next day he

took out two silver coins and gave them to the innkeeper. "Look after him," he said, "and when I return, I will reimburse you for any extra expense you may have."

Several guiding principles can be derived from this rich story.

Loving Our Neighbor Is Practical Business.

The love of the Samaritan for the victimized traveler was more than mere sentiment. Rather, the Samaritan took action; he intervened. "He took pity on him" and he "went to him." It is not enough to simply say to someone in distress, "God loves you. I'll pray for you." In fact, James renounces empty acts of so-called spirituality:

> Suppose a brother or sister is without clothes and daily food. If one of you says to him, "Go, I wish you well; keep warm and well fed," but does nothing about his physical needs, what good is it? (James 2:15-16)

Love must be expressed in tangible acts of relief to the actual sufferings of real people. The late Francis Schaeffer often remarked that "man is not just a soul to be saved." Throughout his published works, Schaeffer placed a great emphasis on the biblical vision of humanity, and with good reason. Scripture teaches that God is concerned about the physical, emotional, and social needs of humankind. Take a careful look at the parable of the sheep and the goats in Matthew 25:

> When the Son of Man comes in his glory, and all the angels with him, he will sit on his throne in heavenly glory. All the nations will be gathered before him, and he will separate the people one from another as a shepherd separates the sheep from the goats. He will put the sheep on his right and the goats on his left.
>
> Then the King will say to those on his right, "Come, you who are blessed by my Father; take your inheritance, the kingdom prepared for you since the creation of the world. For I was hungry and you gave me something to eat, I was thirsty and you gave me something to drink, I was a stranger and you invited me in, I needed clothes and you clothed me, I was sick and you looked after me, I was in prison and you came to visit me. . . .

I tell you the truth, whatever you did for one of the least of these brothers of mine, you did for me." (Matt. 25:31-36, 40)

This sober passage reveals that Christ is quite concerned about our life here and now, not just hereafter. What have the sheep done that they are welcomed into eternal life? They have engaged in practical ministry to people's physical, emotional, and social needs. In contrast, the goats are eternally condemned for failing to meet those needs. British theologian John Stott says, "Therefore if we truly love our neighbors, and because of their worth, desire to serve them, we shall be concerned for their total welfare, the well-being of their soul, their body and their community. And our concern shall lead to practical programs. . . ."[3]

What About Evangelism?

Ministering to temporal human needs is not a substitute for evangelism; it is a partner to it. Skeptics of Christian social and political action point to the shortcomings of the "social gospel" movement as reason for rejecting this type of ministry. Around the turn of the century, many mainline Protestant churches in the United States adopted a theology that made social reform equivalent to salvation. According to the proponents of the social gospel, man needed to be saved not from sin but from political oppression. In response, evangelical churches overreacted to this grave mistake by focusing on evangelism to the exclusion of social action.

In 1982, the Lausanne Committee for World Evangelization and the World Evangelical Fellowship sponsored a conference in Grand Rapids, Michigan, to bring social action and evangelism into biblical balance. They drafted a report calling for the integration of these two areas of ministry, convinced that they are "like the two blades of a pair of scissors or the two wings of a bird."[4] The one does not work well without the other. The report demonstrated three ways in which social responsibility and evangelism are related.

♦ "First, *social activity is a consequence of evangelism*." That is, our salvation should result in social responsibility. Paul wrote in Galatians 5:6 that "faith works through love." James says, "I will show you my faith by my works." Titus 2:14 tells us that Christ came not only to "redeem us from all wickedness," but also "to purify for himself a people that are his very own, eager to do what is good." Similarly, Ephesians 2:10 teaches that Christians are "created in Christ Jesus to do good works, which God prepared in advance for us to do." Thus, the writers of the *Grand Rapids Report* noted that "Good works cannot save, but they are an indispensable evidence of salvation. . . . Social responsibility, like evangelism, should therefore be included in the teaching ministry of the church."

♦ "Secondly, *social activity can be a bridge to evangelism*. It can break down prejudice and suspicion, open closed doors, and gain a hearing for the gospel. . . . If we turn a blind eye to the suffering, the social oppression, the alienation and loneliness of people, let us not be surprised if they turn a deaf ear to our message of eternal salvation."

♦ "Thirdly, *social activity not only follows evangelism as its consequence and aim, and precedes it as a bridge, but also accompanies it as its partner*." In His own ministry, Jesus went about "teaching and preaching" and also "doing good and healing. Both were expressions of His compassion for people, and both should be of ours. . . . Thus evangelism and social responsibility, while distinct from one another, are integrally related in our proclamation of and obedience to the Gospel. The partnership is, in reality, a marriage."[5]

Love demands action, and a biblical understanding of human needs requires action not only to save souls, but for the temporal welfare of those souls. The history of Christian missions is the story of men and women who understood that they were sent not only to bring the good news of eternal life, but also to demonstrate the blessings of that life in ministry here on this earth.

Social action can be traced from the time of the Apostles. . . . Concern was never limited to relief. The itinerant missionary carried with him a bag of medicines, new or better seeds and plants, and improved livestock. Nevius introduced the modern orchard industry into Shantung. The Basil missionaries revolutionized the economy of Ghana by introducing coffee and cocoa grown by families and individuals on their own land. James McKean transformed the life of Northern Thailand by eliminating its three major curses: smallpox, malaria, and leprosy. Wells and pure water often came through the help of missionaries. Industrial schools were stressed through the 19th century, and industries were established. In addition, the missionaries were constantly the protectors of the native peoples against exploitation and injustice by government and commercial companies. . . . They played a very important part in abolishing forced labor in the Congo. . . . They fought fiercely for human rights in combatting opium, foot-binding, and exposure of girl babies in China. They waged war against widow-burning, infanticide, and temple prostitution in India. . . .[6]

Frankly, when our Christianity fails to address all aspects of life, it appears to the world too trivial to be true. Therefore, our love must find practical expression.

Love Is Going to Cost Us Something.
Let us be honest—we just do not want to be inconvenienced. If we could look beneath all the objections people raise to Christian social and political action, I think we would find the universal human preference to simply be comfortable. This is no judgment; it is a personal confession. But I have a strong suspicion that I am not alone.

The reason the priest and the Levite would not even come near the beaten man was for fear of becoming "unclean." According to the Jewish Law, to touch a corpse would make a person impure, sullied, ceremonially defiled in the eyes of God. It would have required a period of religious "cleansing" during which they could not perform their professional duties. And what might have been worse to their minds, they would have been unwelcome in Jewish society for a time. They were important people with important things to do; they simply could not be inconvenienced.

Jesus says that if your religion keeps you from helping people in distress, you've missed the point entirely. We must be willing to risk our reputation and inconvenience ourselves if we are going to love as God calls us to.

II. A CHRISTIAN VIEW OF JUSTICE REQUIRES IT.

Every social issue has a human face. This is the basis for a Christian understanding of social action. Represented in the statistics we read in our newspapers and the reports we hear on the nightly news are the lives of real people. Pornography, abortion, racism, homosexuality, poverty—these are not "political" issues; they are human issues that have become politicized.

Most Christians would agree with everything I have said thus far. We know we ought to love our neighbor as ourselves, and we know that love must have practical ramifications. Where the tension usually arises is when the issues are "controversial." Feeding the poor, sheltering the homeless, helping the less fortunate—there is little debate that Christians should do these things. It is when an issue becomes "political" that the church becomes a house divided.

The *Grand Rapids Report* may be helpful on this point. The drafters included the following table to clarify the difference between social *service* and social *action*.[7]

SOCIAL SERVICE	SOCIAL ACTION
relieving human need	removing the causes of human need
philanthropic activity	political/economic activity
seeking to minister to individuals and families	seeking to transform the structures of society
works of mercy	the quest for justice

Reprinted by permission of Tribune Media Services

Social *service* is the area of agreement, where the church can remain free from controversy. On the issue of abortion, for example, supporting the work of a crisis pregnancy center would fall under social service. Soup kitchens, hospices, and recovery groups for the sexually abused would be other examples. Like the good deeds of the Samaritan, these are all "works of mercy."

Social *action*, on the other hand, represents activity often derisively labeled "political," and by implication off-limits for the Christian. Campaigns to overturn abortion laws or shut down clinics would fit under this category. So would issues such as school choice, civil rights, and religious liberty. They are concerned with "the quest for justice."

While these distinctions are helpful, they are also artificial. In the long run, it is neither logical nor consistent to seek to love our neighbor with mercy while ignoring or minimizing the importance of justice. Stott uses slavery as an example. The harsh treatment of individual slaves might have been eased through social service, but the suffering would have continued on a massive scale unless slavery was abolished through social action.[8] Government sanction of slavery cries out for justice. Likewise, while we seek to minister to women and children by providing abortion alternatives, we should also seek to protect the rights of the unborn through law.

Another way of looking at the relationship is reducing the *demand* for abortion through social service, but for the same very reasons we should seek to reduce the *supply* through social action. If accidents keep occurring at an unregulated intersection, then what is needed is not more ambulances but a traffic light. As it has been said, "An ounce of prevention is worth a pound of cure."

Mercy *and* justice go hand-in-hand in our efforts to love our neighbor. "He has showed you, O man, what is good. And what does the Lord require of you? To act justly and to love mercy and to walk humbly with your God" (Micah 6:8). In order to fulfill the Golden Rule, we must seek justice for all people in the public square.

But Who Is My Neighbor?

Let us return to the parable of the Good Samaritan. Jesus picks a Samaritan—not a member of the Jewish religious elite—as the hero of the story. In fact, the priest and Levite are examples of failure. His choice would have outraged His listeners. The Jews despised the Samaritans; they were considered "outsiders." In a stinging rebuke of prejudice, Christ makes it clear that we are to love all people, not merely those in "our group."

Christianity is not a special interest group. Scripture does urge us to give special attention to our fellow Christians, but not to the exclusion of all others: "Therefore, as we have opportunity, let us do good to all people, especially to those who belong to the family of believers" (Gal. 6:10). Every person bears the image of God, giving them a dignity that does not depend on race, gender, age, education, ability, or social status. Further, this inherent dignity persists no matter how corrupt they may now appear.

> It is a serious thing to live in a society of possible gods and goddesses, to remember that the dullest and most uninteresting person you talk to may one day be a creature which, if you saw it now, you would be strongly tempted to worship, or else a horror and a corruption such as you now meet, if at all, only in a nightmare. All day long we are, in some degree, helping each other to one or other of these destinations. It is in the light of these overwhelming possibilities, it is with the awe and the circumspection proper to them, that we should conduct all our dealings with one another, all friendships, all loves, all play, all politics. There are no *ordinary* people.[9]

From Abraham through Israel to the church, God's plan has always been to raise up a people not just whom He can bless, but who will *be* a "blessing to all nations."[10] Christianity is not a special interest group.

III. A CHRISTIAN VIEW OF GOVERNMENT ASSUMES IT.

Webster's Dictionary defines politics as "the art or science of government." Given the respect the Bible accords to government, why has the church shied away from politics? There are many reasons, but foremost among them is the confusion surrounding the New Testament teaching on civil government. One scholar who has looked deeply into the relationship of Christians to the state is the theologian C.E.B. Cranfield.[11] He makes these observations from the following passages:

Mark 12:13-17
During the time of Christ, the nation of Israel was governed by Rome. The Israelites were deeply divided over whether and how they should

cooperate with the Roman authorities. Some advocated revolution; others thought appeasement was the wiser route. In this story, the Herodians (a group of appeasers) attempt to force Jesus to takes sides in this controversy by asking if it is proper to pay taxes to the Roman government. At Christ's request, one of them produces a Roman coin and Christ says, "Render to Caesar what is Caesar's and to God what is God's." Christ not only handles this political trap masterfully, He also lays the foundation for a political philosophy. The Romans required worship of Caesar as a sign of political support. Christ makes it clear that worship belongs to God alone (many early Christians were martyred over this issue), but He also makes it clear that there are godly obligations toward our governors. The word "render" carries a sense of duty or obligation. Christ commands His hearers to do their duty to civil government, and in the United States that means participation in the political process. Those of us who live in a democratic republic *are* Caesar.

But why this sense of obligation? The fact that the Jewish questioners produce a Roman coin is essential to the story. Those taking advantage of the amenities of Caesar's rule are obligated to help pay for them. As citizens of our country, we benefit from its economic prosperity, its political order, its public safety, transportation, educational opportunities, and so forth. We are obligated to our government.

Romans 13:1-4
God has established government, and service to the state as part of our debt of gratitude. Romans 13 does not appear in a vacuum. It is merely a continuation of an exhortation that starts with chapter 12, an exuberant call for us to love, give, bless, and serve others. Why? This attitude of service wells up out of a deep sense of gratitude for all that God has done and is doing for us, His people (chapters 1-11). Further, God's purpose in establishing government is limited and specific: to reward good behavior and punish evil. Why should God be so concerned that government function well? Magnificent light is shed on this in 1 Timothy.

1 Timothy 2:1-4
Paul exhorts Timothy to have the church pray for their government officials. Why? So we might live peaceable and godly lives and so that the gospel might go forth. When government restrains chaos, conditions are best for preaching the gospel, and God desires that all people be given the

opportunity to repent and be saved. This is why government is essential. What stronger motivation could there possibly be for the Christian to ensure that government works well?

Unfortunately, a superficial reading of these three passages has led many Christians to conclude that we must accept whatever form of government we have and submit to whatever actions our rulers take. This is a deeply mistaken reading of the text. Scriptural examples abound in which God's people opposed authority when their human leaders violated the law of God.

Acts 5:29

The principle set forth in this passage is quite clear: When government violates the will of God, it is our duty to oppose it. Part of the act of submission is to hold our government accountable to a higher law, the law of God. Remember Shadrach, Meshach, and Abednego (Daniel 3)? How about Rahab (Joshua 2) or the Hebrew midwives (Exodus 1)? They are all examples of limited submission. It is interesting to note that Charles Finney, the great nineteenth century evangelist still revered today for his work in revival, taught his followers that Christians have a moral duty to oppose government when government fails to do the will of God.[12] Many of Finney's converts were instrumental in the abolition of slavery. The state is not supreme, and it is the role of the church to hold the state to a higher standard.

There is so much more that could be said to build the case for Christian social and political involvement. Once we have agreed that the church should be involved, there are plenty of questions as to when, where, and how.[13] But I hope this will suffice to lay the foundation. Love helps where people hurt, and politics often hurts people deeply. As Stott reminds us, "So if we truly love our neighbors, and want to serve them, our service may oblige us to take . . . political action on their behalf."[14]

DISCUSSION QUESTIONS

1. What would you say to those who claim Christians should not be socially and politically involved because the Christian faith only concerns our relationship with God?
2. Why are some Christians reluctant to "get involved"?

3. How can we bring social and political involvement and evangelism back into proper balance?
4. At what point should the Christian resist the authority of civil government?
5. Are compassion and justice ever at odds with each other when it comes to social action?

CHAPTER 5

Principled Persuasion: Making Your Case in the Public Square

by Lawrence F. Burtoft

THE BIG IDEA

Nothing is more obvious in darkness than light—even a small light. A single candle will illuminate an otherwise pitch-black room. Such is the power of goodness and truth in the face of apparently overwhelming falsehood and social corruption. Therefore, argues Lawrence F. Burtoft, American Christians living at the end of the twentieth century have every reason to consider the present difficulties not only as a cultural *crisis*, but more importantly, as a *chairos*, a moment of unprecedented opportunity to show forth the brightness of truth.

The great challenges facing Christians engaged in today's social issues are best met through *the art of principled persuasion*. However, it is an unfortunate fact that much Christian involvement has lacked in persuasive power. This deficiency can and must be corrected. And to do so requires only that Christians return to their roots. Jesus is the shining example of persuasive power, and His approach is no better summed up than by the apostle Paul's phrase, "speaking the truth in love."

As Burtoft says, "To speak truth requires understanding. To do so in love requires respect." Thus, under the heading of these two essential requirements—understanding and respect—he develops six principles of persuasion applicable to any and all attempts to convince others of the justness and goodness of one's position.

> *"Civility, which I take to be a strong virtue*
> *and not simply wimpishness, requires that we not try to cram*
> *our beliefs down anybody's throats,*
> *whether we be Christian or non-Christian or even anti-Christian.*
> *But that we all try to articulate as persuasively*
> *as we can what it is that we believe,*
> *of course in the hope that others will be persuaded."*
> —Richard John Neuhaus

◆ ◆ ◆

These days of darkness are also days of opportunity. If you listen carefully you will hear the sound of bad ideas shattering on the hard surface of reality. Those are bad ideas whose day has passed. Unfortunately, hundreds and thousands of people suffered, and continue to do so, because of those ideas. And there are quite a few others still at large, wreaking havoc: safe sex, euthanasia, abortion on demand, condom distribution in public schools, and many others. Ideas like these are what make the days dark. But what makes them days of opportunity is the power of light—of good ideas and good people—to pierce and dispel the darkness. It can be said another way: Our cultural crisis is at the same time a cultural *chairos*.[1]

CRISIS AS *CHAIROS*: THE WINDOW OF OPPORTUNITY

The apostle Paul encouraged the Christians under his care with this exhortation:

> Be very careful, then, how you live—not as unwise but as wise, making the most of every opportunity, because the days are evil. (Eph. 5:15-16)

The Greek word here translated as "opportunity" is *chairos*, a term used in the New Testament to describe moments in history that are pregnant with possibility. Paul was no "pie-in-the-sky" optimist. He recognized that "the days are evil." All the more reason, he concluded, for Christians to live wisely, not missing any opportunity to bear witness to the truth about Jesus Christ.

Jesus said of Himself, "I am the light of the world" (John 8:12). Amazingly, He also said, "You are the light of the world. A city on a hill cannot be hidden" (Matt. 5:14). Of course, our light is wholly dependent upon His. He is "the true light that gives light to every man ..." (John 1:9). As Christians concerned about our culture (as all should be), we must ask ourselves, "How can I make the most of the opportunity that is before me to shine as Jesus would? How can I best treat the present crisis as a *chairos* and focus my beam into the present darkness?"

It needs to be said and said continually: The first task of every Christian is to be like Jesus. We are to give ourselves wholly to the pursuit of Christlikeness. This is not the place to expand on the issue of discipleship. Suffice it to say that if every American who had claimed to be a Christian had lived a life conformed to the One whom they call Lord, the days would never have gotten as dark as they are now. What is more, the days will only get darker unless Christians follow the exhortation of Peter:

> For this very reason, make every effort to add to your faith goodness; and to goodness, knowledge; and to knowledge, self-control; and to self-control, perseverance; and to perseverance, godliness; and to godliness, brotherly kindness; and to brotherly kindness, love. For if you possess these qualities in increasing measure, they will keep you from being ineffective and unproductive in your knowledge of our Lord Jesus Christ. But if anyone does not have them, he is nearsighted and blind, and has forgotten that he has been cleansed from his past sins.
>
> Therefore, my brothers, be all the more eager to make your calling and election sure. For if you do these things, you will never fall, and you will receive a rich welcome into the eternal kingdom of our Lord and Savior Jesus Christ. (2 Pet. 1:5-11)

As we discuss how best to present the light of truth, about how to argue persuasively for policies that reflect the values we cherish, we would do well to remember often the words of Ben Jonson: "A good life is a main argument." We dare not urge in public life what our private lives deny.

A TIME TO PERSUADE

When it comes to confronting the many forms of evil in our day, there are as many possibilities as there are Christians. Each one of us is a unique blend of personality, experience, gifts, and resources. Also, God calls different people into different fields of concern. Social and political involvement is one of these, and even this field is itself diverse in issues and approaches.

Having said that, however, we must acknowledge that there are better and worse ways to combat these issues. Clearly, some responses to evil are themselves evil. The most glaring example of this would be the murder of abortion providers. As evil as the abortion industry is, these murders cannot be tolerated by Christians.

Quite apart from their immorality, such responses fail to reach their goal. They do not, in general, persuade people of the justness and rightness of the pro-life position. Doubtless they accomplish the exact opposite by suggesting hypocrisy and hatred, rather than wisdom and compassion. Yet persuasion is what is needed more than anything else in the abortion debate. As James Davison Hunter has written:

> No matter what happens in courts and legislatures, the abortion issue will not disappear until we somehow reach a greater consensus with respect to the standards of justice and goodness our communities will abide by. If there is to be an abortion law that is politically sustainable over the long haul, then, the fundamental task must be one of moral suasion.[2]

What is true about abortion holds for every significant social issue of our day. Purely political or legislative answers will be insufficient if they are not supported by a broad cultural consensus. One of the greatest challenges before Christians today is to make the case for just public policies in such a way that a majority of Americans will embrace the moral values on which the policies are based. Without such a consensus, we are like salmon, constantly swimming upstream, against the flow, to spawn and die.

There really is only one way to gain a cultural consensus on behalf of Judeo-Christian values: convincing a majority of Americans of the truth, goodness, and beauty of those values. In other words, people need to be persuaded that living according to those values is the safest and surest way to their own well-being.

A FORGOTTEN ART

Unfortunately, persuasion is something of a lost art within American Christianity. Os Guinness put it this way:

> Despite the fact that communication is at the heart of the Christian view of the Godhead and the gospel, and a politics of persuasion is one of America's greatest legacies from the First Amendment, most Christian contributions to public life are strikingly persuasionless. They rely on protest, pronouncements and picketing, but without a recovery of principled persuasion.[3]

Picketing an abortion clinic can have important and positive results, not the least of which is saving human lives. But such activities have had little effect in swaying society as a whole, where a majority still support fairly liberal abortion practices.[4]

Rational persuasion does not hold the place it once did in our culture. Few today change their minds as a result of considering, in any sensible and reasonable way, the evidence and arguments for a position. Few, indeed, compared to those who are moved by feelings stirred by images manipulated by the mass media gurus. Advertisement has in large measure replaced tough thinking and honest discussion.

So it is no wonder that there exists massive misunderstanding as to just what persuasion is and how it works. Simply put, persuasion is just where the heart and mind are transformed through reasons, evidence, and experience. Life runs on ideas, and it is by means of persuasion that the ideas in anyone's mind are challenged, questioned, and transformed. Chairman Mao said, "Persuasion comes out of the barrel of a gun." He was deeply mistaken. People can be made to do all kinds of things through force and intimidation, while remaining unpersuaded in heart and mind.

Guinness pointed out that "communication is at the heart of . . . the gospel." It is to be remembered that Christianity gained its foothold in the Roman Empire not by means of coercion but persuasion. Thus we are repeatedly told in the Book of Acts that Paul was busily engaged in the ministry of persuasion.[5] The church desperately needs to reclaim a vision of persuasion as the primary means for bringing people to a knowledge of God and a knowledge of truth in general.

When Paul and other early Christians sought to persuade their contemporaries to become followers of Christ, they did so by means of argumentation. Indeed, that is precisely what the Greek word for "persuade" means: to convince by means of argument. So Paul writes:

> We demolish arguments and every pretension that sets itself up against the knowledge of God, and we take captive every thought to make it obedient to Christ. (2 Cor. 10:5)

The heart of an argument is the attempt to convince another of the truthfulness or rightness of one's own claims, based upon the reasons set forth in the course of the argument. It is, in effect, a duel of ideas. If Christians are to be persuasive in the public square, they will do so by becoming adept with ideas. *The future of America depends upon people committed to truth and goodness persuading others, by their life and their logic, to be committed themselves.*

THE PRIORITY OF PRUDENCE

Os Guinness mentioned a particular kind of persuasion—*principled* persuasion. From a Christian perspective, there are many different approaches to persuasion, not all of which are acceptable. Of those that are acceptable, not all are as appropriate and productive for achieving the desired goals. What was a prudent and useful approach in one age may, because of either the prominence or absence of certain ideas, be unsuitable in another. We need to be as the sons of Issachar in ancient Israel, who were men "who understood the times and knew what Israel should do" (1 Chron. 12:32).

It is essential to recognize the moral and spiritual changes that have taken place in America over the last 200 years. "It would be a dreadful mistake for us to assume that our culture is a predominantly Christian one," warns R. C. Sproul.[6] Our involvement in the social issues of today must take this change into consideration. Thus, the first principle of persuasion is *prudence*. As Proverbs 8:5 tells us, "You who are simple, gain prudence; you who are foolish, gain understanding." If we do not attain and exercise this virtue, there is little hope that our voices will be heard or understood.

THE GREAT PERSUADER

Jesus, of course, was a master of prudence—and persuasion. The two go together. In the words Dallas Willard, a philosophy professor at the University of Southern California, "Jesus knew what to do and when to do it." He understood His times and His audience, and He always had the right word for the right moment. There is no better model for our own persuasive activities than His.

One of the first things we notice about Jesus' attempts at persuasion is that He was not always successful. In spite of the great multitudes that listened to Him and who were astonished at His teachings and miracles, precious few were around at the end. Most of the religious leaders were unconvinced; indeed, they were outraged. Many people were, in one way or another, like the rich young man who turned down Jesus' invitation to "Follow me" (Matt. 19:22). The same is true for Paul and other New Testament figures: Despite their clear, logical, and impassioned presentations of the facts concerning Jesus, many listeners were not persuaded. So why be concerned with persuasion? Because those who were convinced turned the world upside down. The same thing can happen today.

To engage in principled persuasion is not necessarily to win every argument and convince every school board. The *emphasis* must be on *being principled*, not on winning. We can plant and we can water, but it is God who gives the increase.[7]

Whether it's in evangelism or social action, we must attempt to follow in the footsteps of "the Great Persuader." In Ephesians 4:15, Paul speaks directly to the matter:

> Instead, speaking the truth in love, we will in all things grow up into him who is the Head, that is, Christ.

Notice that "speaking the truth in love" is directly related to maturing as a Christian ("grow up into . . . Christ"). And if there was ever a time when there was a need for mature Christians, it is now. So what does "speaking the truth in love" mean in practice? What principles flow from this basic theme?

Reprinted by permission of the Colorado Springs Gazette Telegraph

THE PRINCIPLES OF PERSUASION

To speak truth requires understanding. To do so in love requires respect. These are the two essential requirements for anyone seeking to be persuasive, and they are the basic forms of the principles of persuasion.

Principles of Understanding
Jesus was persuasive because people recognized that He spoke with authority. He knew what He was speaking about. He possessed insight. As Matthew 7:28-29 says:

> When Jesus had finished saying these things, the crowds were amazed at his teaching, because he taught as one who had authority, and not as their teachers of the law.

The reason that He could *proclaim* the truth in such a way that people were "blown out of their socks" was because He *possessed* the truth. He understood people and their problems, and He knew what life was about and how wrongs could be made right. His authority was grounded in understanding.

Next to love, there is nothing so important as understanding. The wise Israelite, King Solomon, recognized this: "Wisdom is supreme; therefore get wisdom. Though it cost all you have, get understanding" (Prov. 4:7). Whatever persuasive authority we have must come from our understanding. If we possess insight, people will recognize that we have something to say. Otherwise they will ignore us, as they should.

Being persuasive, then, demands a serious commitment to three principles for gaining and giving understanding. Before we can speak the truth with conviction, we must first *seek the truth*. Only then, after we have done our best to equip ourselves with the best information and understanding, should we speak. And when we speak, we do not say everything there is to say; we *speak the relevant truth*, presenting the facts that are appropriate to the moment and to the issue at hand. As the discussion continues, we must be careful to remain open to a fuller understanding of the facts. We must be receptive to new information, especially to that which corrects our misunderstandings. In other words, we must do our best to *stay open to the truth*.

As these three principles of understanding are foundational, let's examine each more fully.

1. Seek the Truth.

Before you *speak* the truth, *seek* the truth. In order to convince others, you must be able to demonstrate that the facts and good reasoning support your position. But you cannot show what you do not know. Unfortunately, this does not stop some people. As Donald P. Shoemaker, chairman of the Social Concerns Committee of the Fellowship of Grace Brethren Churches, bemoans:

> One of my biggest frustrations is how Christians act without fact. *Truth must always come before social action.* But what we often see is action based on half-truth, hearsay and rumor.[8]

We cannot expect to be convincing if we are not perceived to be credible. And credibility is born of the hard work of studying the issue thoroughly, doing your homework, and checking your facts.

Unfortunately, as former U.S. Senator William Armstrong knows too well, Christian activists often fail to be prepared. "It is important that Christians know what they are talking about," Armstrong said. "All too often, even now, they don't and that undermines their credibility."[9] Armstrong points out how ludicrous it would be for someone not trained in medicine to stand up and talk about brain surgery, yet some Christians are guilty of almost the same thing:

> You'll find people who ... know nothing about economics, yet feel well-qualified to discuss the flaws and defects of the free enterprise system. Such persons generally end up being ignored. So if people really want to have influence, they've got to know what they're talking about.[10]

It has been said that Christians need to "wise up" before they "rise up." And there is no wisdom without information and understanding. These, in turn, require time, trouble, and determination. For example, you may be convinced that your local school board's plan to distribute condoms to high school students is pathetically wrongheaded. Your pastor has preached a fiery sermon against the proposal, your spirit has been stirred, and you are ignited for action. He pointed out that condom distribution is a bad idea because it actually encourages promiscuity. And you believe it!

But do you *know* it?

Can you point to research data that backs up your belief? If not, your chances of being persuasive before the school board are greatly diminished. It is one thing to stand up and say "No!" in clear and unmistakable terms. It is quite another to be able to present, in a cool and logical manner, the basis for your protest. It requires that you not only gather information, but that you *check those facts*. Unfortunately, Christians have often failed to do this and have been responsible for spreading false information.

The classic example of this involves the over 20 million letters that the Federal Communications Commission received protesting Madalyn Murray O'Hair's attempt to ban all religious broadcasting. This baseless rumor has been circulating since 1974! It would cost so little time and money to find out the truth, but millions of people simply did not make the effort. The result of such irresponsible action is that Christians pay a higher price in public opinion. In this case, John Murray, president of

American Atheists, concluded that Christians' gullibility proved that "religious people really don't want to pay attention to facts. They want to push what they would like to be the case, not what actually is the case."[11]

We must beware of the temptation to believe merely because we want to believe. As Friedrich Nietzsche said, "Convictions are more dangerous enemies of truth than lies." This is particularly true when it comes to convictions about policies with which we disagree. Our tendency is to accept as fact anything which will discredit the opposition, while being far too easy on ourselves and our arguments. Phillip Johnson, a law professor at the University of California at Berkeley, speaks to this issue:

> Something I always try to teach my law students is that people tend to be uncritical when they evaluate arguments for their own side. It's very important to know the difference between good and bad arguments for your own position, so that you don't make the bad ones.[12]

Of course, ferreting out truth from falsehood involves time, effort, and determination. This is why the ministry of persuasion is not for the slothful. It is also why so few are effective persuaders, as Johnson points out in regard to people who reject the idea of creation:

> Most people are intellectually lazy. They don't want to wrestle to get the truth. They want to be satisfied they've already got it. So one of the things those people will do is say, "Well, I heard X make an argument for creation that was ridiculous. So now I know for sure there's nothing in that position." You don't want to make it easy for them to rest in that attitude, and *we do make it easy when we give bad arguments.*[13]

So take the time to be informed. Find out what organizations are dealing with your issue of concern. Read widely on both sides of the debate. Don't take things at face value. Know your opponent's position as well as your own. Check and double-check sources. And when it comes to sources, here are three guidelines to follow when possible: Use original sources, use multiple sources, and avoid anonymous sources. It is not enough to claim "They say . . ."; someone is liable to ask you who "they" are. The more solid your information, the stronger your argument.

The bottom line is this: If the problem is important enough to set right, then the facts are important enough to get right. The effort spent in research, fact-checking, and self-criticism is well worth it.

2. Speak the Relevant Truth.

Because our goal is persuasion, we are concerned not only to *have* understanding ourselves, but to *impart* it to others. Gathering facts is where we must begin; then we must communicate them. It is not enough for us to understand. The point is to help others do the same. Here is where we face another temptation. When it comes to gaining insight, if our weakness is doing too little, in our communication we often do too much.

Jesus warned His followers of the danger of superabundant confabulation ("having a big mouth"): "Do not give dogs what is sacred; do not throw your pearls to pigs. If you do, they may trample them under their feet, and then turn and tear you to pieces" (Matt. 7:6). Jesus was not experiencing a lapse of civility. He was not calling some people pigs and dogs, or suggesting that we ought to identify our opponents as such. Rather, He was using a common truth about these animals to illustrate a crucial truth about people and about persuasion.

Dogs could care less about "sacred" or "holy" things. I once ministered in a church where this was obvious. We met in a school auditorium that did not have air conditioning. In the summers, we would open the side doors to let in a breeze. This also let in the neighborhood cats and dogs. Do you suppose they acted any differently inside than they did outside? Of course not. The fact that a "holy" meeting was going on in the auditorium made absolutely no difference to them.

If you go to a pig farm and seek to impress the residents with a string of the finest cultured pearls an oyster can offer, and you are standing between a hungry pig and a pile of corn husks, you will soon discover that Jesus knew exactly whereof He spoke.

What is the point? In the same way that it is useless (and even dangerous) to give holy things and pricey pearls to dogs and pigs, so it is unhelpful and unwise to try to give people what they cannot, or will not, receive. At best it falls on deaf ears; at worst it enrages them and hardens them even more. Paul's admonishment that we are to speak the truth does *not* require that we speak *all* the truth *all* at once. People cannot use (though they can abuse) what they cannot receive.[14]

Grant Jensen produced television advertisements for the successful campaign against the pro-euthanasia Initiative 119 in Washington State in 1991. His observations are worthy of notice:

> There are a lot of people who want to put burdens on campaigns that campaigns cannot carry. If you're lucky, you can let people know what the issue is about and get across your theme. If you expect to get out there and change their value systems and beliefs, you're adding burdens the campaign just cannot handle.[15]

We must not miss the significance of this truth for our engagement in social issues. There is always more that could be said than should be said. We need to distinguish between *all* the facts and the *relevant* facts. Discerning Christians realize that the problems in America are far bigger than any particular proposal before the county commission or any initiative that is before the voters. It does little good to rail against "secular humanism" when the issue is school-based health clinics. As Francis Schaeffer said, "If you demand all or nothing, you'll get nothing every time."

This is not to say that Christians should not be concerned with value systems and beliefs. Such matters are at the heart of evangelism and the ministry of the church. However, when it comes to specific social issues and policies, relevance to the moment is of singular importance.

So after you have done the hard work of seeking the truth and you are ready to speak the truth, make sure it is relevant truth. As Solomon wrote, "There is a time for everything, and a season for every activity under heaven . . . a time to tear and a time to mend, a time to be silent and a time to speak" (Eccl. 3:1,7).

A final point on relevancy. It is difficult to identify what is relevant to your audience without understanding how they think and what they mean by their use of language. It is possible to use the same words while meaning different things. Therefore, it is critical that we understand what people mean when they are for or against something. We must do our best to distinguish between apparent and real differences and disagreements. This, in turn, requires that we follow the advice of James: "Everyone should be quick to listen, slow to speak and slow to become angry" (1:19). For it is in listening that we come to understand those we wish to understand us.

3. Stay Open to the Truth.

The most careful search for truth does not guarantee 100 percent accuracy. Our best intentions aside, we will make mistakes. Only God knows enough to be error-free. We do not have that option. Shakespeare was right: "To err is human." But it is also human to be able to detect—and correct—many of our mistakes.

There is a sense in which persuasive arguments are like chains— they are only as strong as their weakest link. This is particularly true when addressing persons who are strongly opposed to your position. They are looking for the slightest chink in your factual or logical armor. When they find it, they will focus their whole arsenal at that one point. Mark Crutcher, a pro-life activist who teaches Christians how to articulate the pro-life position, points out the danger involved in using inaccurate information:

> If you make an argument based on [a false quote], and somebody finds out that the quote is inaccurate, then you've lost them. It may be that you speak to somebody for an hour, and you make one factual error like that, and everything else you've said in the entire hour is totally accurate, but you've lost every bit of it now.[16]

Thus it is essential that we stay open to the truth. We need to be correctable, especially by our critics. As the Greek philosopher Antisthenes said, "Pay attention to your enemies, for they are the first to discover your mistakes." It is quite difficult, if not impossible, for us to detect all the errors in fact and logic that we commit. Humility will allow us to admit this and recognize our tendency to overestimate the strength of our own arguments. Ben Jonson was right: "To make arguments in my study and confute them is easy, where I answer myself, not an adversary."

We need to be receptive to criticism. In 1992 Focus on the Family began placing a full-page ad called "In Defense of A Little Virginity" in newspapers around the country. The ad was critical of condom distribution programs and cited statistics demonstrating the folly of such programs. It was not long before letters to editors began appearing, attacking the ad. Some of these were critical of our interpretation and presentation of the social research, claiming that we were intentionally misrepresenting the facts and that the data did not support our assertions. How did we respond?

Since it would be futile to counter the accusations regarding our intentions, there were really only two options. We could haughtily and self-righteously defend ourselves with a response such as, "Pardon us, but you apparently don't realize who we are. We're Focus on the Family, and we don't make mistakes!" The course we took was quite different. We went back, checked our sources, and discovered that one or two of our claims did overstate the facts. They were not grievous errors and did not, when corrected, undermine our main argument. Instead, the ad is now stronger because of our willingness to stay open to the truth and to receive criticism, even from our opponents.

Christians, of all people, should be open to correction. If we understand our relationship with God correctly, we know that our hope does not lie in being right all the time; it resides in the goodness of His grace. If we make a mistake, we acknowledge it, correct it, and move on, grateful for the opportunity of getting a firmer grip on the truth.

It helps to remember what we are asking others to do, which is essentially to consider that they may be wrong. We should lead the way in having this attitude of humility before the truth. Oliver Cromwell exhorted his opponents in the British Parliament, "I beseech thee in the bowels of Christ, consider that ye may be wrong!" As James Nuechterlein comments, such an admonishment is as fitting for ourselves as those we desire to sway.[17] In this sense, staying open to the truth is another form of "doing to others what you would have them do to you." We can never do wrong in doing that.

We come now to the second category of principles of persuasion, those having to do with the way we think about, and treat, those whom we are seeking to influence.

PRINCIPLES OF RESPECT

Seeking the truth and speaking the relevant truth are two important ways in which we can maximize understanding. But there is more to persuasion than simply discovering and dishing out data. Few, if any, are persuaded by those whom they do not respect. And one of the surest ways of gaining the respect of others is by granting it—abundantly and consistently.

Treating people with respect is not first and foremost a pragmatic principle; it is a moral and theological one. Respect is not right because it "works"; it is right whether or not it works. Jesus commanded us to treat others in just that manner whereby we ourselves wish to be treated.[18] Why? They deserve it. They deserve respect for two main reasons: creation and redemption. First, they are indelibly stamped with the image of God in which they were created. Second, they are part of the world for whom Christ died.

It just so happens that respecting people can be quite persuasive. Not always, but often. Mark Patinkin is not a Christian, as far as I know. He is a columnist with the *Providence Journal* who also hosts a Sunday morning television show. Several years ago, he featured a program dealing with school prayer and God in the schools. His audience was composed of more than 50 evangelical Christians. He expected the worst. Going into the program, he had some preconceived ideas of what these folks, whom he called "religious crazies," would be like: "wild-eyed, fire-and-brimstone sorts; stern-looking Puritans wagging fingers and thumping Bibles."[19]

By the end of the show, however, he had changed his mind. Why? Because the Christians not only communicated their concerns, they also conveyed respect. This allowed Patinkin to understand their point of view—and even to *sympathize*. Here are some of the reasons he gave:

- "What made me sympathize is that they weren't trying to force their own views."
- "After the show, several parents gave me articles about America's moral decline. They didn't do it dogmatically; they only wanted me to understand. And I did."
- "I still think there are religious crazies out there. But I won't be using that term as sweepingly. What I saw in the audience was something very different—people who simply care deeply about their children and their faith, and want to protect both."

What took place that Sunday morning was a case study in principled persuasion. Those Christians clearly "spoke the truth" about their concerns and did so in a way that brought about not only understanding, but *sympathetic* understanding. And this was facilitated in large part by the fact that they treated Patinkin with respect. That is, they also spoke the truth "in love." The result was noteworthy. While not convincing Patinkin on every point, they gained his respect and changed his perception of evangelical Christians. But the effect was not limited to one individual. There was also the viewing audience that observed their demeanor and presentation and the readers of the editorial that Patinkin wrote telling of the encounter.

Although he would not have described it in these terms, Patinkin's reaction is reminiscent of the response of the Jewish leaders to the witness of Peter and John:

> When they saw the courage of Peter and John and realized that they were unschooled, ordinary men, they were astonished and they took note that these men had been with Jesus. (Acts 4:13)

This is, after all, the most significant thing that can be said of us. And ultimately, it is the most persuasive.

There are three essential principles of respect with special significance for engaging in the public debates concerning social issues.

1. Don't Demonize, Equalize.

No doubt, we are in a serious cultural conflict. There are battles to be fought and far-reaching victories to be won. In the midst of such a moral and spiritual upheaval, it is natural to cast one's opponents as sinister and inhuman. This, however, is not an option for Christians. It is not an option, but it is a temptation, as the words of Paul remind us:

> For our struggle is not against flesh and blood, but against the rulers, against the authorities, against the powers of this dark world and against the spiritual forces of evil in the heavenly realms. (Eph. 6:12)

The "powers of this dark world" and the "forces of evil in the heavenly realms"—these are the real enemy. The people we engage in debate and seek to persuade are as much objects of the enemy's evil intentions as we are. This is a truth that, in the midst of heated debates, is all too easy to forget. But we dare not forget, lest we be guilty of "aiding and abetting the enemy."

We must not demonize our opponents, for the fact is, they are not demons. Nonetheless, to treat them as such can have the effect of driving them—as well as those who are neutral on a particular issue—away from the Light and further into darkness. And it does our own souls no good either. Far better, we should see others as our brothers and sisters in the larger human family, of which we are all a part. This is what I mean by "equalize." Like it or not, we are all in this mess together and, theologically speaking, we share much in common: We are all the objects of a common enemy; we are all a part of the world for which Christ died; and we are all the objects of God's undying concern. This is what it means to be a part of society—any society.

Our attitude toward those with whom we disagree must not be one of moral superiority. We can believe that we are right without believing we are righteous, and certainly not "more righteous than thou." We are far more likely to be heard when others sense that we are treating them as equals in the debate.

The story is told of Queen Victoria and her husband, Prince Albert. Early in their marriage they had a fairly heated argument, with Albert stomping out of the room and locking himself in his private apartment. Victoria stormed after him and furiously knocked upon his door. "Who's there?" called Albert. "The queen of England, and she demands to be admitted." There was silence from inside the room, and the door remained locked. Victoria again pounded upon the door, with Albert responding as before: "Who's there?" The reply was the same, "The queen of England." The door remained shut. After several more volleys of fruitless knocking came a pause. Then there was a gentle tap. "Who's there?" The queen replied, "Your wife." The prince at once opened the door.

If we would have the doors of understanding opened to us, we would do well to treat people with the respect due equals. To respect my neighbor is to love my neighbor in a most fundamental way. It is also one of the surest ways to gain a hearing. As the author Rabindranath Tagore wrote, "He who wants to do good knocks at the gate; he who loves finds the gate open."

Practically speaking, this means that we do not argue *ad hominem* ("against the person"). Except in cases in which a person's character is the issue, such as a candidate for public office, the content of our presentations should focus on the issue and the relevant facts. What the school board superintendent may or may not have included on last year's income tax is altogether irrelevant to the content of the sex education curricula. Not only is it irrelevant, it is ethically inappropriate to bring this kind of issue up in a public forum dedicated to public matters. Remember, the "golden rule" is always applicable, *especially* in the area of social involvement where the stakes are high, tempers flare, and civility is rare.

2. Don't Dogmatize, Civilize.

To be respectfully persuasive—or persuasively respectful—requires that we esteem highly the right of others to *consider* what we have to say, not merely concede to it. Recall that one of the characteristics of the Christians that so impressed Mark Patinkin was presenting their concerns in a way that wasn't dogmatic. To speak dogmatically involves a spirit and tone of intolerance, along with a stubborn insistence that the other accept, without question, what you are saying. Such rigidity reeks with the stench of insolence, pride, and self-righteousness.

There are really two agendas to which we must attend when engaged in public debate. There is the immediate issue at hand, and there is the more basic and far-reaching matter of the atmosphere that our conduct helps create. When we "dogmatize," we "de-civilize" the public square. The air becomes acrid with dissension and bitterness. In essence we are saying, "There is no room in this place for any disagreement." Or worse, "All who oppose us are unworthy of respect."

Because so much of current public discourse is marked by this kind of interaction, the need is great for Christians to do all they can to promote civility. Civility is respect at work. Without it, genuine persuasion is impossible. Coercion, yes; persuasion, no. Richard John Neuhaus has put it well:

> Civility, which I take to be a strong virtue and not simply wimp-ishness, requires that we not try to cram our beliefs down any-body's throats, whether we be Christian or non-Christian or even anti-Christian. But that we all try to articulate as persuasively as we can, what it is that we believe, of course in the hope that others will be persuaded.[20]

What this means in practice is that we give others the freedom to hear what we have to say, to consider it, and then either accept or reject it. To do less is simply uncivil. Our concern is with our conduct, not the short-term outcome of our argument. We do well to cultivate the attitude prescribed by Paul:

Do nothing out of selfish ambition or vain conceit, but in
humility consider others better than yourselves. Each of you
should look not only to your own interests, but also to the
interests of others.[21]

Principled persuasion entails a consideration of others that is free
from a need to "win." Winning is not the primary concern; speaking the
truth in love holds first place.

3. Don't Compromise, De-Biblicize.

Whenever I talk to Christians on the subject of being persuasive, I warn
them about the use and abuse of the Bible. I stress that, given the great
changes our culture has undergone, the Bible no longer functions, socially,
in the same way as it did in the past. When the American founders were
forming the nation, the primary written authority from which they drew
their ideas was the Bible. Indeed, the Bible was the most frequently cited
book in American political literature between 1760 and 1805.[22] It was
widely recognized as authoritative in moral and legal matters, because the
culture of the day was "Christianized," under the sway of the ideas,
values, and principles of the Bible. The Bible *functioned* as an authority in
public because most Americans believed it was authoritative.

But in the "post-Christian" culture of late twentieth-century America,
the consensus regarding biblical authority that held 200 years ago is
largely absent. This is due in part to secularization, in part to the current
legal understanding of the separation of church and state, and in part to
the increased religious pluralism of American society. The bottom line
is that we must presume our opponents do not consider the Bible authoritative in public debates on social issues.

To acknowledge this does not imply compromise on either our view
of the Bible or its teachings. It does *not* mean that the Bible is no longer
relevant. It is as relevant as ever. It simply must be used in a different
way. Trying to persuade the city council to reject a gay rights ordinance
by quoting from Romans will most likely be ineffective, not because the
Bible is inaccurate in its appraisal of homosexuality, but because it is no
longer recognized as authoritative on matters of public concern.

The same precaution must be taken with Christian terminology. As
members of the "household of faith," we share a common religious
language by which we communicate to one another essential truths about

God, faith, salvation, sanctification, and other matters of spiritual significance. In addition, much of our moral reasoning is based upon this Christian thought and language, as it should be. So when we speak about social issues of ethical significance, it is understandable that we would do so in familiar terms. Unfortunately, the terms are not familiar to large portions of Americans, at least not as appropriate language for discussing public policy concerns. The counsel of C.S. Lewis is well-heeded:

> What we need to be particularly on our guard against are precisely the vogue-words . . . of our own circle. . . . These are, of all expressions, the least likely to be intelligible to anyone divided from you by a school of thought, by a decade, by a social class.[23]

When engaged in debate over controversial issues, understanding is all-important. If we intend to be persuasive, we must first be understood. We must speak in a language that communicates our ideas in ways easily comprehended. In short, we must trade in a currency the bank recognizes if we want credit for our rhetorical deposits.

There is also the problem of the negative connotations that "Christianese" carries for people. Like Mark Patinkin's preconceptions of "religious right" Christians, people have ideas (mostly unfavorable) about people who quote the Bible and use words like "repent," "abomination," and "fornication." These negative connotations have the effect of closing ears and hardening hearts to the substance of what we are trying to communicate.

It may help to realize that the content of the Bible is true, not simply because it is in the Bible, but because it corresponds to the way things are. The reason that monogamous marriage is morally superior to polygamy is not only because the Bible says so, but because that specific sexual and familial arrangement is by far the most conducive to human well-being. The Bible does not condemn homosexual behavior arbitrarily, but because such behavior is personally and socially destructive. In other words, it is wrong and that is why the Bible prohibits it.

One implication of this is that we are free to argue for and against various policies on bases other than the Bible. We certainly ought to be biblically informed on the issue of concern. But when it comes to making a case for a certain policy or practice, we need not—and probably should not—do so by quoting from the Bible.[24]

The Washington State euthanasia initiative mentioned earlier provides a pertinent example. Dr. Robin Bernhoft, who was president of Washington Physicians Against 119, understands the significance of speaking in a biblically responsible way that is at the same time persuasive. Talking of his group's strategy, he comments:

> We recognized early on that people don't want to hear about the sixth commandment, "Thou shalt not murder." But people will listen to the logical consequences of the violation of a commandment.[25]

Beware also of overusing certain phrases, such as "traditional values," which can become mere buzzwords that complicate rather than illuminate the discussion. Besides, something is not necessarily good or right simply by being "traditional." Slavery, after all, was a traditional family value for large numbers of Americans, even Christians. Being traditional did not change the immorality of the practice. We should be careful to define our terms. When speaking of values such as monogamous marriage or premarital virginity, instead of always referring to them as "traditional values," we might talk about "time-tested standards," "enduring moral values," or even "person-friendly values."

There is still much mileage to be gained from emphasis upon the common moral language of virtue and value. Focusing on such virtues as civility, honesty, responsibility, courage, kindness—and upon public values such as justice, decency, and equality—can carry substantial persuasive power.

We do not truly respect people if we are insensitive to the effect of what we say. There can be no persuasion where there is no communication, and no communication as long as we speak in a "foreign language." We easily recognize the rudeness (not to mention the foolishness) of the person who fails to communicate with one who does not speak the same language, so merely speaks louder. Too often, however, this is what Christian attempts at persuasion amount to. We must do better if we expect to be genuinely heard in the public square.

THE PLACE OF PASSION AND "PRINCIPLED COERCION"

Do not misunderstand and assume that by advocating principled persuasion I am recommending the abandonment of passion and politics.

Goodness will not advance without a strong dose of both in the great social debates of our time.

By passion, I mean the forceful communication of deeply felt beliefs. Without it few persuasive arguments will achieve their goal. The great social issues of our day are not merely intellectual contests; they cut to the heart and soul of every person. Arguments in defense of the voiceless unborn, for example, ought to reflect the urgency for which every effort to protect the innocent calls.

Let us not forget that passion is at the heart of *compassion*. If we truly care for the people whose lives are being ravished by the many social problems of our day, we will pursue our attempts at persuasion with an emotional honesty that reflects our heartfelt desire for justice and righteousness.

Sadly, more and more in America there seems to be an inability on the part of the citizenry to follow involved arguments. This does not mean that we should not think through our positions carefully, seeking to establish our arguments on the best data available, buttressed by careful reasoning. It does mean, however, that few people will respond merely on the basis of a well-reasoned argument. A picture is still worth a thousand words, and an impassioned plea, appropriately presented, can make an impression that will linger a long time after the premises and conclusions have faded from memory.

This brings us to the topic of politics and politicians. Both suffer from an unfortunate, though sometimes deserved, reputation of being strong on passion but weak on principle. While many are certainly well-motivated, it is naive to think that our public servants will always act on the basis of facts and right reason. What are we to do when, in spite of our best attempts to present the truth coherently and clearly, we encounter an ear deafened by the press of special interests and political game-playing? The answer is, play the game as well, and play the game well. This does not necessitate compromising our most fundamental values, but it does involve what has been called "principled coercion."

Principled coercion involves the recognition that self-interest is a powerful motivator and that when a public official is unpersuaded by our arguments, he will often be all ears to the threat of personal political defeat. There is a place for picketing, for politicking, and for pressuring.

Jesus counseled us to be "shrewd as serpents, and harmless as doves" (Matt. 10:16). To be "harmless as doves" speaks to both our motivation and our explicit behavior. We need to do all that we can to assure that our words and actions are in keeping with the spirit and example of Christ, whose primary goal was human redemption and well-being. We are still called to "speak the truth in love," even when we are speaking the hard realities of political pressure. It is not against the tenets of love to stand up for that which is right, nor to hold accountable politicians who are sworn to serve the public good. If the only thing that will move a legislator to vote against a bill to fund abortions is the prospect of political failure, then so be it. We are not responsible for his motives; we are responsible to do all that we can to promote the social good.

Jesus did not hesitate to utilize the fear of negative consequences to motivate people. Witness His many warnings regarding hell, condemnation, and judgment. Fear is a low-level motivator from a moral perspective, but it can serve moral ends. A politician who is not persuaded by a rational, even passionate, argument may come around when he senses that public sentiment is against him and a job search looms on the horizon. While it is doubtful that "principled coercion" can bring about a change of heart, it can bring about a change of vote. The culture war won't be won on such change alone, but a vote in favor of truth and justice is an important step in the right direction.

There is nothing contradictory between the concepts of principled persuasion, passion, and political pressure. We must simply remember to maintain our principles, discipline our passions, and recognize both the realities and limits of politics.

There is much more that could be said about principled persuasion. However, what has been discussed above is basic. As our fundamental concern is to represent Christ in all that we do, we have no choice but to do our best to "speak the truth in love." To do so requires understanding and respect, both on our part and on the part of those we hope to persuade. I have identified six principles that should mark our persuasive efforts:

Principles of Understanding	Principles of Respect
Seek the Truth	Don't Demonize, Equalize
Speak the Relevant Truth	Don't Dogmatize, Civilize
Stay Open to the Truth	Don't Compromise, De-Biblicize

As I wrote at the beginning of this chapter, to put these principles into practice is no guarantee of success. We should value them, and our social action should exemplify them, not because they work, but because they are right. Ultimately, we depend not on the superiority of our arguments, but upon the sovereign goodness of our God. Our persuasive abilities are limited. This fact should drive us to our knees.

DISCUSSION QUESTIONS

1. What is the significance of the word *chairos* for the Christian response to the crisis of our time?
2. Why is persuasion an essential factor in Christian social involvement?
3. Place the following in order of importance: persuasion, prudence, principles. Why do you give them this order of priority?
4. In what way is Jesus a model for persuasion?
5. What are the two basic elements of principled persuasion? Why are these so essential?
6. Choose a contemporary issue for discussion. How would you apply the six principles of persuasion?

CHAPTER 6

Partnering with God: The Centrality of Prayer

by John Eldredge

THE BIG IDEA

In this chapter, John Eldredge warns that without prayer as the basis, hopes for social reform are tenuous at best. He says: "We need to be careful not to trust in our ability to make a compelling case for traditional values." Any lasting social reformation will ultimately depend upon God. Prayer allows us the privilege of partnering with God to accomplish His will "on earth as it is in heaven."

Using the prayer of Nehemiah, which preceded the successful campaign to rebuild the walls of Jerusalem in the aftermath of Israel's captivity, Eldredge identifies three principles for the proper *posture* of effective prayer: (1) We must have a confidence in God's desire and ability to intervene; (2) We must confess our own culpability; and (3) We must petition on the basis of our relationship with God.

Eldredge then turns to the question of *what* to pray for. By examining Micah 6:8 and 1 Timothy 2:1-3, he argues that there are five basic virtues that are God's will for every society: justice, mercy, righteousness, peace, and humility. Eldredge goes on to show how the application of these virtues would change the debate over abortion and racism. He concludes this chapter by recommending a model of prayer from *The Book of Common Prayer*.

> *"I have been driven many times upon my knees*
> *by the overwhelming conviction that I had nowhere else to go."*
> —Abraham Lincoln

◆ ◆ ◆

For the Christian, prayer must play the central role in any program of social reform. There are at least three reasons this is so. First, societies have a destiny as much as do individuals. Scripture is replete with reminders that cities and cultures are in the hands of the One who "rules over the nations." Witness the specific plans God had not only for Lot, but for Sodom *as a city.* Joseph certainly had a God-ordained destiny, but so did Egypt *as a nation.* The situation we face at the end of the twentieth century is nothing less than the unraveling of the social order. As Christians, we have a responsibility to work for the good of our society.[1] But we need to be careful not to trust in our ability to make a compelling case for traditional values or outwit our opponents to secure lasting restoration of our communities without God's assistance. Whether and when our society will be restored rests on the providence of God, and it is to Him we must turn for guidance and help. The Scriptures tell us that apart from Christ, we accomplish nothing of lasting value.[2]

Second, our desire to see society restored in justice and truth inevitably comes down to the individual men and women who make up society. The battle in which we are engaged is for hearts and minds. We certainly have our part to play, and play it we must. But in the final analysis, only the Spirit of God can change the soul of man.[3] A change of heart on a scale large enough to change the direction of society is what is meant by revival and reformation. Such events simply cannot be engineered, though they may be sought after with great passion.

Third, as Paul reminds us, our ultimate struggle for what is right and good is not against mere mortals, but "against the spiritual forces of evil" (Eph. 6:12). The subject of spiritual warfare cannot be sufficiently addressed in this book.[4] For our purposes here, it should suffice to highlight two biblical imperatives on the topic: (1) Satan and his minions of fallen angels are to be taken as real and powerful beings; (2) much evil in the world is spurred on by the pernicious activities of these evil personalities.[5] It would be utter foolishness to confront "evil personified" in our own strength. Therefore, we must give prayer its proper place in any program of social reform. And so we find the Bible calls for the same:

> If my people, who are called by my name, will humble themselves and pray and seek my face and turn from their wicked ways, then will I hear from heaven and will forgive their sin and will heal their land. (2 Chron. 7:14)

> Also, seek the peace and prosperity of the city to which I have carried you into exile. Pray to the Lord for it, because if it prospers, you too will prosper. (Jer. 29:7)

> I urge, then, first of all, that requests, prayers, intercession and thanksgiving be made for everyone—for kings and all those in authority, that we may live peaceful and quiet lives in all godliness and holiness. This is good, and pleases God our Savior. (1 Tim. 2:1-3)

Not only does the Bible call for prayer in social reform, many stories model it as well. When Nehemiah heard what had happened to his beloved country, how beaten down Jerusalem was, how overrun with real and deep problems, the first place he went was not to the king of Babylon but to the King of kings. "When I heard these things, I sat down and wept. For some days I mourned and fasted and prayed before the God of heaven" (Neh. 1:4). Before Nehemiah embarked on one of the greatest social reform programs of the Old Testament, he prayed. So, too, when Daniel and his colleagues faced a desperate governmental crisis, they prayed (see Dan. 2:12-18). When the New Testament lays out the program for local church activity, prayer for government and society is at the top of the list (see the above passage, 1 Tim. 2:1-3). Regardless of whatever else we may believe about the church's responsibility regarding social action, surely we can agree that prayer for our communities, government, and leaders is a mandate for the Christian personally and the church collectively.

TEACH US TO PRAY

How then should we pray about the sorry condition of our culture and the myriad social problems we face? Calling down fire from heaven may seem an attractive option to some, but Christ squelched that approach when suggested by His disciples.[6] Perhaps we can learn something of the key to Nehemiah's success by looking at the nature of his prayer.

> O Lord, God of heaven, the great and awesome God, who keeps his covenant of love with those who love him and obey his commands, let your ear be attentive and your eyes open to hear the prayer your servant is praying before you day and night for your servants, the people of Israel. I confess the sins we Israelites, including myself and my father's house, have committed against you. We have acted very wickedly toward you. We have not obeyed the commands, decrees and laws you gave your servant Moses. Remember the instruction you gave your servant Moses, saying, "If you are unfaithful, I will scatter you among the nations, but if you return to me and obey my commands, then even if your exiled people are at the farthest horizon, I will gather them from there and bring them to the place I have chosen as a dwelling for my Name." They are your servants and your people, whom you redeemed by your great strength and your mighty hand. O Lord, let your ear be attentive to the prayer of this your servant and the prayer of your servants who delight in revering your name. Give your servant success today by granting him favor in the presence of this man. (Neh. 1:5-11)

Nehemiah affirmed his belief in God's desire and ability to intervene in his deteriorating community.

We can pray with the assurance that God cares more about our communities than we do. In the book of Jonah, God compels the reluctant prophet to go and preach to the citizens of Nineveh, a pagan nation and longtime enemy of Israel. We remember that Jonah didn't want to go; that's why he wound up in the belly of the fish. But do you recall *why* the prophet didn't want to preach to this city? "I knew that you are a gracious and compassionate God, slow to anger and abounding in love, a God who relents from sending calamity" (Jonah 4:2). Jonah knew God's gracious heart, and he didn't want Him to forgive his enemies, the Ninevites. Indeed, revival broke out in Nineveh after Jonah preached a one-line sermon! "When God saw what they did and how they turned from their evil ways, he had compassion and did not bring upon them [the Ninevites] the destruction he had threatened" (3:10). Jonah is angry (he says, "I knew it!"), and God confronts his selfish attitude by reminding him that He loves *all* people, not merely the nation of Israel (4:11). As Robert Frost observed, "After Jonah, you could never trust God not to be merciful again."[7]

We can also pray with the assurance that God is more than able to change the direction of nations as well as individuals. God answered Nehemiah's prayers by providing, through the king of Babylon, all the resources necessary for rebuilding Jerusalem. Nineveh experienced a national revival following Jonah's visit, and it remained a prosperous city for many years. Scripture and human history both contain ample evidence that "the nations are like a drop in a bucket" (Isa. 40:15) and that "the Most High is sovereign over the kingdoms of men and gives them to anyone he wishes" (Dan. 4:17). Chapters 38–41 of the book of Job ought to remove any shadow of a doubt that the One who created heaven and earth and sustains them still is able to restore any society. With Job, we can say, "I know that you can do all things; no plan of yours can be thwarted" (Job 42:2).

Nehemiah confessed his own sins, those of his ancestors and those of his countrymen.

We can pray with honesty and humility. Confession is a vital part of effective prayer. Christ taught us that before we set out to correct others, we should begin by taking a good, hard look at our own lives: "First take the plank out of your own eye, and then you will see clearly to remove the speck from your brother's eye" (Matt. 7:5). This is as true on the societal level as it is on the individual level. Listen to the order of prayer that God gave to Israel for their social restoration: "If my people, who are called by my name, will humble themselves and pray and seek my face and turn from their wicked ways, then will I hear from heaven and will forgive their sin and will heal their land" (2 Chron. 7:14). While this specific *promise* was uttered to a theocratic nation (i.e., a nation under the direct rule of God) several thousand years ago, the *principle* remains today. Personal as well as corporate repentance precedes social reform.

The Welsh Revival of 1904-5 resulted in remarkable social reform. Nearly two thirds of the country professed faith in Christ, and as a result, crime nearly disappeared, illegitimacy dropped by 50 percent, and drunkenness plummeted. It all began in a single church with a sermon urging the people of God to repent and seek His face. Evan Roberts, the young seminarian who preached that sermon, had four simple points: (1) You must put away any unconfessed sin; (2) You must put away any doubtful habit; (3) You must obey the Spirit promptly; and (4) You must confess Christ publicly. The ensuing revival was compared to "an earthquake . . . a tornado, predicting far-reaching social changes."[8] Are we willing to acknowledge our own complicity in the evils of our society? Can we admit that we have played a part in our nation's decline, if not by what we have done, then certainly by what we have left undone?

Nehemiah affirmed his relationship with God and asked Him to intervene.

We can pray with confidence that our prayers are heard with sympathetic ears. Our access to God through prayer is based on our restored relationship with Him. Jesus said we are more than mere servants—we are His friends (see John 15:15-16). It is on the basis of this intimate relationship that Jesus encouraged us to pray. We come to Him as partners, colaborers in the advance of God's agenda on earth. As Augustine said, "Without God, we cannot, and without us, He will not." This provides us with boldness and confidence to bring our concerns for our society before the One who created human society, who shares our concerns and upon whom we depend for the success of our reforms. "Let us then approach the throne of grace with confidence, so that we may receive mercy and find grace to help us in our time of need" (Heb. 4:16).

THY WILL BE DONE

These same ingredients found in Nehemiah's prayer are also found in what has come to be known as "the Lord's Prayer": Relationship as the basis for prayer, confession as essential, and confidence in God's desire and ability to intervene. (Actually, the prayer might better be referred to as the "disciples' prayer," for Christ gave it to us as a model for how we ought to pray!) Jesus taught us to pray that God's will "be done *on earth* as it is in heaven" (see Matt. 6:9-13, emphasis added). The apostle John assures us that "if we ask anything according to [God's] will, he hears us" (1 John 5:14). How then can we pray for our communities and nation with the confidence that we are in accordance with God's will?

When Paul calls for prayer for the nation, he indicates two virtues which are God's will for society: Peace and righteousness.[9] Micah 6:8 gives us three more: "He has showed you, O man, what is good. And what does the Lord require of you? To act justly and to love mercy and to walk humbly with your God." Certainly, there are many, many more guidelines from Scripture to help us pray for our communities. But these five will go a long way—justice, mercy, righteousness, peace, and humility.

Consider what a restoration of justice might do for the abortion debate. Surely, the Lord is an advocate of the unborn child as much as He is an advocate of the women and men involved. Justice would ensure that abortion laws would reflect the Golden Rule, that we would treat others as we would want to be treated. Needless to say, it would mean dramatic changes from our current policy of abortion-on-demand, which ignores the rights of the children and their fathers, and victimizes women. Any change in policy would require peace in what has become the most polarized social battle of our times. Peace in turn comes from humility.

Racism is another social evil crying out for justice. What would the Golden Rule look like when applied to racial issues? Remember that we are seeking objective justice, not justice as a particular group defines it. During the 1930s and '40s, the Nazis defined justice as whatever was in the best interest of the Third Reich. Needless to say, it was not justice for the Jews. We face our own modern counterfeits. Some conservatives tend to emphasize personal responsibility as the remedy for racial inequity, implying that simply by working hard minorities can overcome years of social ostracism. But they neglect the significant influence of oppressive laws and institutions, such as the Jim Crow laws that treated African-Americans as second-class citizens. Many liberals err by emphasizing institutional evils to the exclusion of personal responsibility, as if mere policy changes will lift the economic status of the underclass. Biblical justice would restore to every person equal *opportunity*, regardless of race. The *outcome* will be determined by what each individual does with that opportunity. In other words, society ensures justice; personal righteousness determines the result for the individual. Because of our nation's checkered past, racial reconciliation (peace) will require not only justice and righteousness, but also humility and mercy (forgiveness).

These virtues are desperately needed in our nation at this time. Their absence is at the center of all our social ills. We also know they are at the heart of God's desire for every society, so we can begin by praying for a recovery of justice, mercy, righteousness, peace, and humility. The following prayers for the nation contained in *The Book of Common Prayer* are given here as a model for you and your church as you seek to establish prayer as the foremost and ongoing discipline in your quest for social reform.

> *O Lord our Governor, whose glory is in all the world; We commend this nation to thy merciful care, that being guided by thy Providence, we may dwell secure in thy peace. Grant to the President of the United States, and to all in authority, wisdom and strength to know and to do thy will. Fill them with the love of truth and righteousness; and make them ever mindful of their calling to serve this people in thy fear.*[10]
>
> *Lord God Almighty, in whose name the founders of this country won liberty for themselves and for us, and lit the torch of freedom for nations then unborn: Grant that we and all the people of this land may have grace to maintain our liberties in righteousness and peace.*
>
> *Lord, you have made all the peoples of the earth for your glory, to serve you in freedom and in peace: Give to the people of our country a zeal for justice and the strength of forbearance, that we may use our liberty in accordance with your gracious will.*
>
> *Almighty God, who created us in your own image; Grant us fearlessly to contend against evil and to make no peace with oppression; and that we may reverently use our freedom, help us to employ it in the maintenance of justice in our communities and among the nations, to the glory of your holy Name.*
>
> *Bless all who, following in the steps of Christ, give themselves to the service of others; that with wisdom, patience, and courage, they may minister in His name to the suffering, the friendless, and the needy; for the love of him who laid down his life for us. Deliver us in our various occupations from the service of self alone, that we may do the good work you give us to do in truth and beauty and for the common good.*
>
> *O God, most merciful Father, make us modest and humble, strong and constant. Graft in our hearts the love of your name; nourish us with all goodness; and bring forth in us the fruit of good works.*

Through Jesus Christ our Lord, who lives and reigns with you and the Holy Spirit, one God for ever and ever. Amen.[11]

If the people of God, individually and collectively, did nothing else but pray for their communities, nation, and leaders in a sustained and earnest manner, there is no telling what changes would follow. But history gives us a clue. Nearly every great movement of social reform has come as a result of spiritual revival, and nearly every revival was born of prayer. Social reform, spiritual revival, and prayer are deeply intertwined in God's work through His people in the world. In the next chapter, I will demonstrate this in the lives of two remarkable men.

DISCUSSION QUESTIONS

1. Why is prayer such an important part of any campaign to improve society?
2. What priority has your church given to prayer for the nation?
3. Was the discussion around Nehemiah's prayer helpful in clarifying the proper posture for your own prayer life?
4. How can we pray with confidence when it comes to social reform? What are the general principles we know are God's will?
5. Choose one or two issues as the subject for your own prayers this week. Apply the five virtues that have been discussed (justice, mercy, righteousness, peace, and humility).

CHAPTER 7

Profiles of Courage:
The Lesson of Character

by John Eldredge

THE BIG IDEA

"We're faced with insurmountable opportunities." Pogo, the comic strip character, humors us with this observation that seems so appropriate to the plight of American society. One does wonder if we really can reclaim the culture.

Can it be done? Is social reform possible in these times, and if so, what kind of person does God use to change society? Using stories from the lives of British parliamentarian William Wilberforce and the Old Testament prophet Daniel, John Eldredge envisions the character traits needed to be a truly effective Christian social reformer in a "post-Christian" age.

He argues that, indeed, it can be done. However, aspiring activists need certain essential qualities: Love, rather than anger and hatred; faith, rather than fear and doubt; and hope, rather than desperation and despair. The lesson in all of this is that character matters. Eldredge concludes his chapter with an engaging discussion on hope.

"Of all that was done in the past,
you eat the fruit, either rotten or ripe.
And all that is ill you may repair if you walk together in humble
repentance, expiating the sins of your fathers;
And all that was good you must fight to keep with hearts
as devoted as those of your fathers who fought to gain it."
—T.S. Eliot

◆ ◆ ◆

The preceding chapters have attempted to outline what has gone wrong in our society and what is needed to turn things around. Several questions remain: Can it be done? Has it ever been done before against the seemingly insurmountable obstacles we face today? What kind of person does God use to change the world—or at least their little part of it?

Yes, it can be done, for it *has* been done before against far greater obstacles. And God's requirements aren't stiff by the world's standards. Jesus turned the world upside down in the first century with a pretty rag-tag group—fishermen, prostitutes, tax collectors, and even a political zealot or two. The issue God seems most concerned with is *character*. Let us look at two men whose lives serve as inspiring examples of faithfulness in the public square. From them we can learn something about what is required of us if we are to be used of God in the struggle for our communities.

WILLIAM WILBERFORCE

If ever there was a change that led to further change, a radical individual conversion that prompted radical national and social transformation, it was that of William Wilberforce. His life is a stirring and instructive precedent for the task we face as followers of Christ in our own time.[1]

Few social issues have ever rivaled the African slave trade of the eighteenth century. It was an evil of tremendous proportion. Sailors said that the stench could be smelled across a mile of open ocean. Five hundred men, women, and children, shackled two and two, lying chest to back in the bowels of the ship, surrounded by their own waste and vomit. Torn from their families and homes, prisoners of commerce, the slaves were shipped to the West Indies and the American colonies. Nearly half died on the journey; in addition to disease, ship captains reported that many simply died of broken hearts. Those who survived were consigned to a lifetime of brutal labor.[2]

It was also an entrenched evil. During its heyday, nearly two-thirds of the British economy depended on the slave trade. This gave virtually every citizen a stake in it, one way or another. Many were direct investors; others depended on the success of family investments. In England, it was simply referred to as "The Institution," and no one dared challenge it. The great political moralist Edmund Burke thought of introducing a bill for the abolition of the trade, but he gave up the idea as "insurmountable." The slave traders owned a majority of seats in parliament, and the crown was supportive of their cause.

Furthermore, the British culture was unsympathetic. Eighteenth-century English society was surprisingly wicked. The upper classes were made up largely of selfish, pagan hedonists. High society was, as one historian called it, "one vast casino" in which fortunes were won and lost in a single night. Government officials had no qualms about appearing drunk in the House of Commons. Even the Church of England was corrupted by greed and political influence.

Those at the top of society built their lifestyles on the misery of the masses. Highwaymen terrorized the countryside. Women labored in the coal mines. Children, many under seven years old, were employed in the cotton mills 15 hours per day. Cheap gin was the primary means of escape for the poor. Twelve percent of all deaths in London were attributed to alcohol. Townsfolk regularly complained of being kept awake by the screams of victims of assault and rape.

Clearly, whoever was going to combat the British slave trade would have to possess more than mere political influence. The champion of this cause would face a hostile government, a decadent culture and an apathetic church.

When he entered parliament at the age of 21, William Wilberforce was considered to be a candidate for the next prime minister. A Cambridge graduate, he was popular, witty, charming, a brilliant debater, and a member of all the right clubs. The world was his oyster. But he was a most unlikely candidate for a moral reformer. Wilberforce loved the casinos and the life of careless privilege. By his own admission, "My own distinction was my darling object."

Furthermore, he was a man of slight stature; barely five feet tall, he had to stand on a table to deliver a speech. His health was poor. There was nothing about Wilberforce to set him apart as a great spiritual leader.

But then something happened that changed the course of history: Wilberforce became a Christian. And God laid on his heart "two great objects," the abolition of the slave trade and the reformation of English manners (what we today would call moral values).

Against tremendous odds and at the risk of his own life, Wilberforce not only led the successful campaign for the abolition of the slave trade, but his work to reform the moral life of England shaped the character of that nation for more than a century. As Os Guinness has observed:

> If Wilberforce had not succeeded and Britain had proceeded to build its nineteenth-century colonial empire in the earlier way, Africa would have been turned into one gigantic slave farm. The Holocaust would have been small by comparison. . . . More than any other person, Wilberforce blocked the course of that monstrous possibility. All the same, these achievements were neither easy nor quick—they took Wilberforce an entire lifetime. He made his commitment to Christ and to these two master objectives when he was in his early twenties. The suppression of the slave trade alone took 20 years. Full emancipation took 50 years and Wilberforce heard that he had finally won only a few days before he died.[3]

Through it all, it was his character that sustained Wilberforce in his mighty struggle. He was a man of dogged perseverance, a virtue that flowed out of his remarkable spiritual life. He wrote in his diary:

> This perpetual hurry of business and company ruins me in soul if not in body. More solitude and earlier hours! I suspect I have been allotting too little time to religious exercises, as private devotion and religious meditation, Scripture-reading, etc. Hence I am lean and cold and hard. I had better allot two hours or an hour and a half daily. Surely the experience of all good men confirms the proposition that without a due measure of private

devotions the soul will grow lean. But all may be done through prayer—almighty prayer, and why not? For that it is almighty is only through the gracious ordination of the God of love and truth. O then, pray, pray, pray!

Wilberforce was anything but "lean and cold and hard." His campaign to free the slaves was driven by love and brotherly kindness; in fact, his slogan on behalf of the Africans was, "Am I not a man, and a brother?" But his spirituality didn't result in a sober pietism; Wilberforce had a lively sense of humor, which he used to good effect. On more than one occasion, during fierce debates in the House of Commons, Wilberforce diffused a tense moment with a joke at his own expense.

But at least Wilberforce lived during the time when Western civilization considered itself Christian. For all its corruption, the Anglican church was still the official church of England, and the Bible was still regarded as the moral standard. We live in what has been called a "post-Christian" age, a pagan culture increasingly hostile to our faith. Are there any other precedents we might look to for inspiration?

DANIEL

In 605 B.C., Jerusalem became a vassal city of the Babylonian Empire. King Nebuchadnezzar demanded not only the submission of Palestinian cities, but also the procurement of able young men to be removed to Babylon for future government service within the Empire. Among the number selected from Jerusalem was a bright young man named Daniel. Exiled from his homeland and the city of his God, Daniel not only lived the rest of his life in the capital of a profoundly pagan nation, but he also served the system as a government official.

We can see in Daniel's situation many of the challenges we face. Babylon outranks Hollywood and Washington, D.C. as a synonym for debauchery; in the book of Revelation the city is used as a metaphor for ultimate iniquity, the "mother of prostitutes and of the abominations of the earth" (17:5). Like most cosmopolitan centers today, Babylon was filled with political corruption, unbridled sensuality, and flagrant idolatry. Religion was fashionable, but faithfulness to the one true God wasn't. Not surprisingly, Daniel's personal ethics were at constant odds with the culture around him. Shortly after his arrival, he was confronted with his first temptation to compromise. It was a matter as seemingly insignificant as what to have for lunch. A devout Hebrew, Daniel held deep convictions about what he believed God wanted him to eat—and what was forbidden. The standard Babylonian fare for the Jewish captives was not very "kosher." Daniel chose then and there to maintain his personal integrity, and God rewarded him for it.

On other occasions, Daniel and his friends were victims of religious persecution far more serious than contemporary scuffles over whether public school children can sing "Silent Night." For insisting on worshipping God and only Him, Daniel and his friends were threatened with grisly torture and death. Conniving public officials tried to frame him. Irrational monarchs demanded the impossible of him under penalty of execution. He could have found ways to compromise. Or he could have lost his head. Literally.

In spite of the odds, Daniel not only maintained his personal integrity and his public witness, he did it without abandoning his post. He didn't flee to the wilderness; he didn't retreat to the Jewish ghetto in Babylon. Because "he was faithful, and no negligence or corruption was to be found in him," and since he possessed "an extraordinary spirit, knowledge and insight, interpretation of dreams, explanation of enigmas, and solving of difficult problems," Daniel rose to a position of extraordinary social influence. He was a statesman in the court of two successive kings, holding under them the second highest office in the land. Like all of us, Daniel had his ups and downs; he fell out of favor at times and spent many a lonely night in prayer. In spite of the opposition, Daniel lived to a ripe old age, shining as a star in a darkened society. God ranked Daniel with Noah and Job as one of three great men of all time.[4]

Like Wilberforce, Daniel was a man of profound character. He, too, was sustained by his rich spiritual life; it was his custom to pray three times each day. The angel Gabriel told him that in heaven, he was "highly esteemed." He was a faithful counselor, administrator, and friend. When he rose to power under Nebuchadnezzar, Daniel petitioned the king to promote his three friends Shadrach, Meshach, and Abednego as well. His remarkable integrity was acknowledged by friend and foe alike. When his enemies set out to frame him, they said, "We will never find any basis for charges against this man Daniel unless it has something to do with the law of his God." Power tends to corrupt, but unlike many who enjoy the perquisites of high office, Daniel held those fringe benefits

Reprinted with special permission of King Features Syndicate

lightly. After his friend Nebuchadnezzar died, Daniel apparently fell out of favor in the new court. Wicked King Belshazzar offered to restore him to power, but Daniel sensed temptation. He told the king, "keep your gifts for yourself and give your rewards to someone else." The Marine Corps motto fits him well—*Semper Fidelis* ("always faithful").[5]

CHARACTER MATTERS

Both Daniel and William Wilberforce prove that it is possible to be "*in* the world but not *of* it."[6] Christians can impact society while remaining faithful to God. But if we desire to speak for God in the public square, our lives must reflect in growing measure the same qualities demonstrated by Daniel and Wilberforce. The first issue is one of *motive*. We need to ask ourselves why we are involved or, more often than not, why we aren't.

Love Versus Anger and Hatred
In Romans 12, the apostle Paul tells Christians, "Love must be without hypocrisy . . . never return evil for evil to anyone . . . do not be overcome by evil, but overcome evil with good." Because of the positions they took on the critical moral issues of their times, both Daniel and Wilberforce were controversial figures. People mocked them and spread rumors

about them. Wilberforce's enemies tried to discredit him as a wife-beater (being single at the time, it lacked a certain credibility). At one point, he was the most hated man in England. Daniel was framed by jealous colleagues. But you never see either of these men lash out and respond in anger. They were graceful under pressure.

The only way they could do this was because both were motivated and sustained by their deep love of God and neighbor. This is the foremost reason we should want to become involved in the "civil war of values."[7] Yet many Christians today appear to be motivated more by anger and hatred than by love. In Matthew 24, Jesus warns us about this:

Nation will rise against nation, and kingdom against kingdom. There will be famines and earthquakes in various places. All these are the beginnings of birth pains. Then you will be handed over to be persecuted and put to death, and you will be hated by all nations because of me. At that time many will turn away from the faith and will betray and hate each other, and many false prophets will appear and deceive many people. Because of the increase of wickedness, the love of most will grow cold, but he who stands firm to the end will be saved.

Like Daniel and Wilberforce, we will face hard times. As this tired, old world winds to its troubled conclusion, things will get worse. In the face of mounting opposition, evil, and general mayhem, Jesus warns that the love of most people will grow cold. He isn't talking about those who *do* evil; rather, Jesus is warning Christians not to forget the foremost commandment: To stand firm in our love. This is precisely why He chastises the church at Ephesus:

I know your deeds, your hard work and your perseverance. I know that you cannot tolerate wicked men, that you have tested those who claim to be apostles but are not, and have found them false. You have persevered and have endured hardships for my name, and have not grown weary. Yet I hold this against you: You have forsaken your first love. (Rev. 2:2-4)

Love is the mark of the Christian, our purpose for being, our deepest longing, and our primary witness to the world. If we get involved in public debates for the wrong reasons, or in getting involved become so overwhelmed by evil that we grow cold, all our efforts will be for nothing. This is precisely what the apostle Paul was trying to drive home in 1 Corinthians 13. This great man of God stated plainly that no matter how impressive were his spiritual gifts, his service for Christ, or testimony to the world, without love it would have been empty and meaningless. Permit me to adapt this passage to our present discussion:

> If I am the most articulate defender of truth and morality,
> full of penetrating insights and clever soundbites,
> but refuse to submit all of it to love, I am nothing.
> Worse, I am irritating, a polarizing noisemaker.
>
> If I grasp all the research, expose all the lies,
> and have the courage to stand alone for righteousness
> against the most extreme radicals,
> but refuse to submit all of it to love, I am nothing.
>
> If I spend my own life savings
> and even die for the cause,
> but refuse to submit all of it to love,
> I have accomplished absolutely nothing.

Among Wolves: The Need for Cunning

There are two errors we can fall into in this whole question of love. The first error is to justify an unloving attitude by arguing: "This isn't church, this is politics—we're not witnessing, we're standing for righteousness." But surely we cannot say we are standing for righteousness and dismiss the highest ethic of all! If love is indeed the greatest virtue, we ought to be more aghast at violations of love than anything else.

The second error is the idea that love requires that we speak only greeting-card sentiments to everyone we meet. Opponents of Christian social action often speak of our need to "maintain the good reputation of our church." But Christ said that something is deeply wrong when "all men speak well of you" (Luke 6:26). Others insist that we "shouldn't judge." But love is often best served by strong words of rebuke, as evidenced on more than one occasion by our Lord Himself. How, then, do we know when to speak and when to hold our tongue? And when we speak, should it be softly or firmly? We need to be more than loving (never less); we must be cunning as well.

In Matthew 10:16, Jesus says, "I am sending you out like sheep among wolves. Therefore be as shrewd as snakes and as innocent as doves." In one sentence, Christ lays out the necessary requirements for our success in the world: innocence and shrewdness. Innocence speaks to our *ethics* (the highest principle of which is love), and shrewdness speaks to our *methods*. These two are not contradictory, though at times we feel they may be in tension with one another. For those seeking to be shrewd, love sometimes seems an impediment, secondary to winning the fight. But love is not a synonym for naiveté; it is a fundamental commitment to another's well-being. Love provides a North Star. Quite simply, it is the Golden Rule: Treat others as you would like to be treated. For those seeking to be loving, shrewdness smacks of deception. But shrewdness is not a synonym for dishonesty; it is a recognition of the need for wisdom and prudence as we seek the best for others. Loving well, in a fallen world, requires more than good intentions. Sometimes, in order to seek the best for others, we will need to take a less than direct route.

King Nebuchadnezzar was a hard man to get along with. He had a dream that troubled him deeply, and he desperately wanted someone to interpret it. However, he wouldn't tell anyone what he had dreamed. Perhaps he had forgotten the dream, or perhaps he was putting his counselors to the ultimate test. He simply threatened to tear "limb from limb" every one of his advisors unless someone could tell him both the dream and its meaning. Daniel was one of those counselors; how did he handle the situation?

> When Arioch, the commander of the king's guard, had gone out to put to death the wise men of Babylon, Daniel spoke to him *with wisdom and tact*. He asked the king's officer, "Why did the king issue such a harsh decree?" Arioch then explained the matter to Daniel. At this, Daniel went in to the king and asked for time, so that he might interpret the dream for him. (Dan. 2:14-16, italics added)

Daniel first calmed a tense moment, then bought himself some time. He could have made a smart remark to Arioch and hastened his own death. He could have confronted the king with a sermon on how corrupt the whole government system was, giving Nebuchadnezzar a piece of his mind before meeting his Maker. On the other extreme, Daniel could have simply accepted his sentence as the will of God and blessed his persecutors before losing his head. Instead, he used cunning.

The apostle Paul, too, got out of a tight spot on more than one occasion by the use of cunning. About to be flogged for allegedly starting a riot at the temple in Jerusalem, Paul averted punishment by asserting his rights as a Roman citizen (see Acts 21:27–22:29). There's nothing particularly noble about enduring a flogging you don't deserve, or unnecessarily hastening your own death. Love is not naive.

In a fallen world, the odds are on the carnivores. Reaching to find the best metaphor for how surprising heaven will be, Isaiah prophesied that the "wolf will live with the lamb" (11:6). In the meantime, the wolf will live *on* the lamb. It is pointless to live without love as our primary motive. But we are lovers in a dangerous time. We must be cunning lovers, yet lovers all the same.

Faith Versus Fear and Doubt

Wilberforce was so convinced of the rightness of his cause, he thought he would win fairly quickly. He introduced his first bill for abolition in 1789. Parliament buried it in committee. When it finally came to a vote two years later, he lost. For years, he reintroduced the bill, and each year he lost. In 1805, after losing for the sixteenth time by only seven votes, the clerk of the House pulled him aside. "Mr. Wilberforce," he said, "you ought not to expect to carry a measure of this kind . . . you and I have seen enough of life to know that people are not induced to act against their interests by abstract arguments." Wilberforce replied, "Mr. Hatsell, I do expect to carry it, and what is more, I feel assured I shall carry it speedily."[8] Two years later, he won. Wilberforce's remarkable perseverance was born of faith.

Do you recall the story of Daniel in the lions' den? As a result of being framed by jealous colleagues, Daniel is thrown into a pit with starving lions. It proved to be a sleepless night, not for Daniel but for Darius, the king at the time, because he liked Daniel and feared for his life. As the account goes:

> At the first light of dawn, the king got up and hurried to the
> lions' den. When he came near the den, he called to Daniel in an

"anguished" voice, "Daniel, servant of the living God, has your God, whom you serve continually, been able to rescue you from the lions?" Daniel answered, "O king, live forever!" (Dan. 6:19-21)

The king was a wreck; Daniel was composed. He essentially said, "I'm fine, king, don't worry about me. Everything's fine. We're all fine down here." What a dramatic difference in the attitudes of these two men. The power of steadfast faith to resist fear is also the theme of Psalm 11.

In the Lord I take refuge. *How then can you say to me*: "Flee like a bird to your mountain. For look, the wicked bend their bows; they set their arrows against the strings to shoot from the shadows at the upright in heart. When the foundations are being destroyed, what can the righteous do?" (vv. 1-3, emphasis added)

The question "When the foundations are being destroyed, what can the righteous do?" is often taken out of context. It is typically used as a righteous lament of our nation's moral decline. But in fact, it is a *temptation* that David refuses to entertain! He says, "How can you say that? It's godless." So David replies:

The Lord is in his holy temple; the Lord is on his heavenly throne. He observes the sons of men; his eyes examine them. The Lord examines the righteous, but the wicked and those who love violence his soul hates. On the wicked he will rain fiery coals and burning sulfur; a scorching wind will be their lot. For the Lord is righteous, he loves justice; upright men will see his face. (vv. 4-7)

In other words, you've forgotten one thing—God is still in charge and very interested in the affairs of men. As authors Dan Allender and Tremper Longman say:

It is possible to face injustice and suffering and work for its demise as a response to the gospel. . . . Or injustice can be fought as a screaming protest to God's silent inactivity. In fact the subtlety between the two options may be profound. Both may be involved in working with abused and battered women, protesting

against abortion clinics, nourishing children who have been sexually assaulted and boycotting stores that sell pornography. . . . One
will serve with humble, quiet grace and the other with angry,
demanding assertion. One fights for a General who has already
won, the other for a revolution that is in question. The latter
enters the fray with a frenetic, scrambling energy that is busily in
control, the former with a centeredness that is strong and
passionate.[9]

We see this centeredness in Daniel and in Wilberforce. There is none
of the desperate scraping, scratching, clawing, biting in them. They
fought for a revolution that was never, ultimately, in question—and so
do we.

Hope Versus Desperation and Despair
In 1 Peter 3:15, the apostle tells us to always be ready to reply when
someone asks us for "the reason for the hope" we have. What's striking
about the passage is the presumption that we will be asked. But this is not
a common experience for most Christians. Could it be that our hopes
are not much different than those of the non-Christian? We hope that
our kids will grow up to be healthy adults, we hope our marriages have
what it takes to go the distance, we hope the biopsy comes back negative,
we hope to have enough to make ends meet. We hope life will work out.
There's nothing wrong with these hopes; the problem is, if they are all we
have, we are pitiful.[10]
  In fact, this kind of limited hope leads to a kind of quiet desperation, a grasping for whatever we can get in this life. Could the angry,
desperate tone of some "activists" be a reflection of their commitment
to try to build heaven on earth? Ironically, it has been the men and women
of God most convinced of, and eager for, the coming of His kingdom
who have had the greatest social impact. J. I. Packer observes:

It is a paradox of the Christian life that the more profoundly one
is concerned about heaven, the more deeply one cares about
God's will being done on earth. The Christians who show most
passion to serve others in this world are regularly those with the
strongest hold on other-worldly realities. This has always been
true, whether we look at ministers, missionaries, statesmen,

reformers, industrialists, physicians, men of wealth and power or ordinary laypeople.[11]

IS THERE ANY HOPE?

First, we must hold fast to the fact that a day is coming when justice will be served once and for all. Our longings for a peaceful and prosperous community will be met beyond our wildest dreams. Swords will be beaten into plowshares. The victim will be vindicated. Every tear will be wiped from our eyes. We will begin the adventure for which this life has merely been the training. Hebrews 6:19 says, "We have this hope as an anchor for the soul." As a church, we have lost the hope of the fulfillment of God's kingdom. We have set our eyes almost entirely on the here and now. No wonder so few get asked about their hope.

> The expectation of the promised future of the kingdom of God which is coming to man and the world to set them right... makes us ready to expend ourselves unrestrainedly and unreservedly in love.[12]

Second, we need to remember that God is not finished with us yet. Who can tell what will happen in our times? But this we know: God loves to be a God of last-minute deliverance. Daniel spent the night in the lions' den; Shadrach, Meshach, and Abednego walked through the fiery furnace; Wilberforce heard of the final emancipation of the slaves only three days before he died—fifty years after he began his campaign. "It's always darkest before the dawn" is no empty platitude.

Finally, God delights to use the foolish things of the world to confound the wise. Who would have thought a Hebrew prisoner of war would become prime minister of Babylon? Who would have thought that a tiny Englishman of frail health would free the slaves? One of the reasons for our hope is the thousands of wonderful, God-fearing men and women across this country who may not seem much in their own eyes or in the eyes of the world, but they are saints in the eyes of God, the salt of the earth, the light of the world. These are the Wilberforces of our generation, the hometown heroes. Some of their stories are told in chapter 9.

His divine power has given us everything we need for life and godliness through our knowledge of him who called us by his own glory and goodness. Through these he has given us his very great and precious promises, so that through them you may participate in the divine nature and escape the corruption in the world caused by evil desires. For this very reason, make every effort to add to your faith goodness; and to goodness, knowledge; and to knowledge, self-control; and to self-control, perseverance; and to perseverance, godliness; and to godliness, brotherly kindness; and to brotherly kindness, love. For if you possess these qualities in increasing measure, they will keep you from being ineffective and unproductive in your knowledge of our Lord Jesus Christ. (2 Pet. 1:3-8)

DISCUSSION QUESTIONS

1. Why is character such an important issue for the social reformer?
2. Was there a particular quality to Daniel or Wilberforce that you feel is essential?
3. Eldredge argues that love must be cunning. Do you agree? Why or why not?
4. How has this chapter affected your thinking about faith, hope, and love as they apply to our social crisis?

CHAPTER 8

Uncommon Friends, A Common Enemy

by Alan R. Crippen II

THE BIG IDEA

"Is it all right to work with people and groups outside of my church?" This question is frequently asked by individuals considering social and political involvement. In this chapter, I anticipate the question and answer it with a hardy "Yes!"

"Co-belligerence" is the term I use to describe political alliances among members of various Christian traditions, as well as with non-Christians. Among evangelicals, the idea of working with other Christians in the arenas of politics and culture was sown by the late Francis A. Schaeffer more than a decade ago. Today, the seed has taken root. There is more and more organized cooperation among evangelical Protestants, traditional Roman Catholics, and Eastern Orthodox Christians in the public square.

I believe this is a good trend with biblical warrant. Finding historical precedent for evangelical and Catholic political cooperation in late-nineteenth-century Holland, I will offer an encouraging example of what can be done in the public square when Christians work together. Regarding the idea of a co-belligerency extending beyond Christians to include non-Christians, a discussion introducing the doctrine of common grace is offered as a theological rationale for finding common ground with non-believers in order to achieve the common good.

"When the world is on fire . . . we need each other."
—Francis A. Schaeffer

◆ ◆ ◆

In 1517, reformer Martin Luther nailed his 95 theses to the Castle Church door in Wittenberg, Germany, thus unintentionally initiating the Protestant Reformation. This small and seemingly insignificant event was catalytic to a religious and spiritual revival heretofore unseen in the history of Christianity. European religion, culture, and politics would be reformed, and the social impact of the Reformation would last for several hundred years. The Roman Catholic Church lost its hegemony over Europe, but it too would begin to reform itself. The tragedy, however, was that in the midst of this tremendous spiritual awakening, Christendom was severely and bitterly fractured.

Furthermore, in the heat of theological and political controversies surrounding the Reformation, there was also the threat of military invasion from the Ottoman Empire. From 1520 onward, Europe expected an attack from the Muslim Turks. At risk was European Christian civilization. In view of this threat, the defense of Christian civilization was to take priority over the deep theological differences between Catholics and Protestants. After all, in comparison to the differences between Islam and Christianity, Protestants and Catholics held much in agreement. A European Christian military alliance of co-belligerents was established to defend faith, fiefdoms, and families against the onslaught of the Ottoman Turks. Europe was saved.

HERE COME THE HUNS

In the late twentieth century, American religion is experiencing a new and fascinating theological realignment with political implications. Not all that long ago, evangelical Protestants often defined themselves as antipapists, and Catholics often described evangelicals as schismatics—the church people of the Yellow Pages. Just a few years ago, the idea of a passionate Protestant cheering for the "papists" of Notre Dame football would have been unheard of. Yet now three of evangelicalism's most distinguished scholars teach at the Catholic university.[1]

Times have changed, for today in the ideological trenches of America's "culture wars," an evangelical will soon discover that he has

Reprinted by permission of Tribune Media Services

a traditional Catholic comrade on his left and right as well as an Eastern Orthodox Christian in reserve. What has pacified these previously warring factions of Christendom to take up arms in the mutual defense of cultural conservatism? A common enemy, a new barbarian—the "cultural Hun." Intensely secular, liberal, and "progressive" in their thinking, the new Huns are unsympathetic, if not openly hostile to the cultural authority of tradition and transcendence. In other words, they have no regard for the roots of Western civilization and the authority of God, Bible, church, or history. Their notions of truth, right and wrong, good and bad, acceptable and unacceptable are as alien to Christians as is the Klingon Empire of Gene Roddenberry's *Star Trek*. What is most alarming is that the new Huns are no longer at the gates of city, but they are inside its very walls. American civilization has capitulated to their invasion.

In this drastic situation, therefore, whatever theological differences currently exist between Protestant, Roman Catholic, and Eastern Orthodox Christians pale in significance when compared to the vast cultural chasm that divides the Christians from the Huns. Those who affirm traditional values are separated by light years from the socially liberal and progressive. In view of this threat, the recapture of American civilization has taken priority over the doctrinal distinctives of evangelical Protestant, traditional Catholic, and Eastern Orthodox Christians. As a result, there is a developing Christian political alliance of co-belligerents. Christians of all denominations are contending together for truth, religious freedom, legal protection for the unborn, parental choice in education, a free society (including a vibrant market economy), family-friendly and religion-friendly governmental policies and programs.

The late Francis A. Schaeffer heralded an earlier call for co-belligerency among Christians in the struggle for truth and justice. Writing in 1984, he exhorted his readers:

> Finally, we must not forget that the world is on fire. We are not only losing the church, but our entire culture as well. We live in the post-Christian world which is under the judgment of God. . . . And if this is true in our moment of history, we need each other. Let us keep our denominational distinctives. And let us talk to each other about our distinctives as we keep them. But in a day like ours, let us recognize a proper hierarchy of things. Our distinctives are not to be the chasm. We hold our distinctives because we are convinced that they are biblical. But God's call is to love and be one with all those who are in Christ Jesus, and then to let God's truth speak into the whole spectrum of life and the whole spectrum of society. That is our calling. . . . In a day like ours, when the world is on fire, let us be careful to keep things in proper order. . . . Learning from the mistakes of the past, let us raise a testimony that may still turn both the churches and society around—for the salvation of souls, the building of God's people, and at least the slowing down of the slide toward a totally humanistic society and an authoritarian suppressive state.[2]

It seems that after several years, Schaeffer's message is taking root. We would do well to continue to heed his call.

A CALL FOR UNITY

The Bible commands us to "Make every effort to keep the unity of the Spirit through the bond of peace. There is one body and one Spirit—just as you were called to one hope when you were called—one Lord, one faith, one baptism; one God and Father of all, who is over all and through all and in all" (Eph. 4:3-6). A unified body is the kind of church that our Lord had in mind when He prayed "that all of them [believers] may be one, Father, just as you are in me and I am in you" (John 17:21). As may be inferred from these verses, the basis of true unity is belief in the one who is "the way and the truth and the life" (John 14:6). Our Lord submitted the essential question to the Pharisees when He asked them, "What do you think about the Christ?" (Matt. 22:42). It is the believer in Christ for whom Jesus prayed to be united. Therefore, true unity is a thing to be very much desired and sought after in the Body of Christ. On the other hand, disunity is a sin to be confessed and repented.

Given the present reality of our denominational distinctives, unity can be achieved by focusing on the "essentials" of our faith. By concentrating on those core beliefs we hold in common, we can attain unity. The essentials, or core beliefs, are the fundamentals of the faith expressed in the historic confessions and creeds of the church: the doctrines of the virgin birth, the deity of Christ, the atonement, the resurrection, the authority of Scripture, and the second coming of Christ. These essentials constitute what C.S. Lewis called "mere Christianity," and they are the basis for true unity. Within the boundaries of these tenets, we must stand together in witnessing of the saving power of Jesus Christ and proclaiming the Good News that "God was reconciling the world to himself in Christ, not counting men's sins against them" (2 Cor. 5:19). Christians *must* be united in words and deeds of love and mercy while seeking truth and justice in a fallen world because "[God] has committed to us the message of reconciliation" (2 Cor. 5:19). If we are not reconciled to one another, how can our message be credible? We are "Christ's ambassadors," and in this calling, the promise of Christ's ultimate victory is our hope. Satan's fortress shall not prevail (see Matt 16:18). Until then, love for God and our neighbors compels us to contend together against the spirit of the age, against secularism, relativism, radical individualism, hedonism, and their manifestations in church and society.

Unity can only be maintained if we allow for diversity in the "nonessentials" of our faith. This is not to say that the nonessentials are unimportant. To the contrary, many of them are very important. But the nonessentials are not crucial, though they are often the distinctives of our denominations—distinctives that each of us believes to be true to the teaching of Scripture. Our convictions about communion, baptism, church government, free will or predestination, the millennium, and so on, are important matters that often divide and preclude us from building churches and worshiping together. After 2,000 years of Christian history, only the naive could hope that these differences will be settled this side of heaven. It is by focusing on the essentials and allowing for diversity on the nonessentials that we will effectively witness for Christ and contend against all that opposes Him and His Kingdom.

Though the basis of unity is belief, the bond of unity is love. In his book *The Mark of the Christian*, Schaeffer said that love is "the mark that will arrest the attention of the world . . . love that true Christians show for each other and not just their own party."[3] This bond of love is what Schaeffer described as "the final apologetic" of the faith. After all, Jesus' prayer says: "I pray . . . that all of them may be one, Father, just as you are in me and I am in you. May they also be in us so that the world may believe that you have sent me" (John 17:20-21). The simple fact is that the world will know we are Christians by our love for one another.

The time has come for Protestants, Catholics, and Eastern Orthodox Christians to stand together in the public square for love, mercy, truth, and justice. Whether Calvinist or Arminian, high church or low church, liturgical or nonliturgical, all who agree on the essentials of the faith must work together amidst the prevailing storm of secularism, radical individualism, moral relativism, and self-gratification that has assailed our culture. Though Baptist and Catholic disagree on several points of theology, they can agree on the sanctity of human life and work together for the rights of the unborn to be protected by law. Though Episcopalian and Presbyterian disagree on church government, they can agree that atheistic secularism ought not to be the established religion of public schools. Though Protestant, Catholic, and Eastern Orthodox Christians disagree on the issue of papal authority, they can agree that Pope John Paul II's tenth encyclical, *Veritatis Splendor* (The Splendor of Truth), rightly reasons that objective truth and morality secure politics, law, and culture. Schaeffer was right, "When the world is on fire . . . we need each other."

THE PAST IS PROLOGUE

Political co-belligerency among Christians is not a new idea for the public square. In fact, it was effectively implemented by the Dutch statesman Abraham Kuyper at the turn of the last century. Kuyper is perhaps one of the greatest Reformed Protestant intellects of modern times. His life (1837-1920) chronicles a record of noteworthy achievements beyond the reach of even the ablest of people. Kuyper's career began as a country parish pastor. Later, he would become a successful newspaper editor, political organizer and party leader, member of parliament, university teacher-theologian, and administrator and founder of the Free University of Amsterdam. But Kuyper's accomplishments surpassed even these impressive achievements, for the former country parish pastor went on to become prime minister of the Netherlands. Of his life's goal, he said:

> One desire has been the ruling passion of my life. One high motive has acted like a spur upon my mind and soul. And sooner than that I should seek escape from the sacred necessity that is laid upon me, let the breadth of life fail me. It is this: That in spite of all worldly opposition, God's holy ordinances shall be established again in the home, in the school, and in the State for the good of the people; to carve as it were into the conscience of the nation the ordinances of the Lord, to which the Bible and Creation bear witness, until the nation pays homage again to God.[4]

In Kuyper's time, Holland was in some ways much like America today. Secularism was breaking out everywhere. Its inroads had reached the cultural elites, especially in government circles. Like in our own day, liberalism was entrenched and the intellectual fruits of the Enlightenment and the French Revolution were in a direction totally opposed to Christian faith. Public schools and the universities were in disarray. Modern socialism was on the rise with its totalitarian visions of a utopian welfare state. However, these alarming trends corresponded with a spiritual awakening among evangelicals, which led to a more organized Christian response. Kuyper was the monumental leading figure of this movement.

The central field of conflict in Holland's culture wars was the public school. The near century-old *Schoolstrijd* ("school struggle") came to a climax during this period, and it was Kuyper's spiritual and political leadership that rallied Christian parents to reclaim and eventually regain control of their children's education from a so-called religiously neutral and statist public education system. By 1917, Kuyper's school reform efforts resulted in a full-scale choice of schools (including religious confessional schools) for all Dutch families.

It is unfortunate that so few American evangelicals today know about Abraham Kuyper. His Christian vision for public life could be helpful for informing the pro-family movement. Nearly a century ago, Kuyper advocated political co-belligerency with Catholics against secularist political forces. In 1901, his political party found practical agreement with Catholics and formed a coalition government. As a result, Kuyper became the prime minister of the Netherlands and served in that capacity until 1905. The success of his election and succeeding administration was due, in large measure, to his ability to establish and maintain a governing coalition of Reformed Protestants and Roman Catholics. Kuyper's emphasis on unity in essentials not only increased Christian influence in the public square, but it ultimately secured some important political reforms in his country, such as school choice. His example can be our future, as William Shakespeare reminds us, "What's past is prologue."[5]

ALLIES AND AXIS POWERS

Franky Schaeffer writes that a unity of "orthodoxy in friendship [is] forged as alliances are forged in war. It is orthodoxy with a purpose—to win the war of ideas, culture, politics, and the life of the nation."[6] We must seek allies if we are going to win what Dr. James C. Dobson has called the "great civil war of values."[7] Potential allies exist in your community, and you may already have contact with them. If not, how do you establish contact? And how do you go about cultivating and forging an alliance?

First of all, you must actively seek out and build bridges to those of different denominations. Within evangelicalism, there are already several vehicles for doing this. Parachurch organizations such as Promise Keepers, Mothers of Preschoolers (MOPS), various home-schooling associations, local Christian schools, and so on provide ample opportunities to meet other Christians of various denominations. Within these circles of contacts, find out who shares your social concerns and make new friends. Visit their churches to learn and appreciate something of their tradition and to meet their friends. Invite them home for coffee, tea, or dessert. Meet them for lunch. Discuss your social concerns with one another. Talk about your vision and involvement. Ask them what their church is doing or would like to do in these matters. By doing these sorts of things you will be well on your way to forging an alliance.

Second, based on your new friendship and common goals, begin working together on specific projects to reach those goals. For example, you might coordinate a voter registration drive throughout churches in your community. Or perhaps you could mobilize a number of citizen Christians to appear at township, borough, or city meetings dealing with an issue such as a domestic partner ordinance or zoning for an adult bookstore. The active participation of several informed Christians may make the difference on issues like these. Or you could establish an interdenominational telephone alert chain to notify parents in your school district about important issues, such as sex education curriculum. Should the volunteer staffing for the local crisis pregnancy center be limited only to Baptists or Methodists? Why not recruit volunteers from Lutheran, Presbyterian, Episcopalian, Catholic, and Orthodox churches, too? The cause is so great, the fronts are so many, and the needs are so innumerable that an alliance of Christian co-belligerents is both necessary and appropriate.

BEYOND CHRISTIAN UNITY

Sometimes there are opportunities for working with groups outside the church to achieve specific public policy goals. An understanding of the Christian doctrine of God's common grace allows us to seek and make common cause even with non-Christians. According to the late theologian Louis Berkhof, common grace is "the light of God's revelation that shines in nature and lightens every man coming into the world."[8]

Since we believe that humankind (though fallen and marred by sin) bears the image of God and that the created order displays "God's invisible qualities—his eternal power and divine nature" (Rom. 1:20) and that "the heavens declare the glory of God" (Ps. 19:1), the non-believer can discover truth, if even imperfectly. Though the believer has the added advantage of knowing the propositional truth of the Scriptures, there is a large body of truth generally revealed in all that God has made, to which all of humankind has access. By God's common grace to humanity, the non-believer can know and understand the truth in creation, though not completely.

Concerning the importance of this doctrine to the area of public policy, Berkhof writes that government is a "fruit and means of common grace" and that:

[Common grace] results in the forming of a public opinion that is in eternal conformity with the law of God; and this has a tremendous influence on the conduct of men who are very sensitive to the judgment of public opinion. . . . It is due to common grace that man retains some sense of the truth, the good and the beautiful, often appreciates these to a rather surprising degree, and reveals a desire for truth, for external morality and even for certain forms of religion. . . . Common grace enables man to perform . . . that which is right in civil or natural affairs . . . natural good works that are outwardly and objectively in harmony with the law of God, though entirely destitute of any spiritual quality.[9]

It is by virtue of God's common grace that we can hope to persuade and work with non-believers to achieve our public policy goals. What's more, a proper understanding of God's common grace offers even greater possibilities for political alliances with organizations outside the Christian tradition. Focus on the Family's activities at the United Nations' Fourth Conference on Women held in Beijing, China, involved building alliances with Islamic pro-family organizations. Ironically, the "Turks," which I wrote of earlier in this chapter, have joined forces with the Christians. Muslim leaders led the charge in defense of the family in Beijing. Dr. A. Majid Katme, president of the Islamic Medical Association, assailed the conference's anti-family agenda as threatening to "Muslim women, women of the world and all humanity . . ." and as the "most dangerous Conference for mankind."[10] Faced with an overwhelming anti-family feminist agenda, a Judeo-Islamic-Christian defense of the traditional family emerged to challenge and check the radical agenda proposed.

Christians in the pro-life movement have cooperated with organizations such as "Feminists for Life." Though not a Christian organization, Feminists for Life is committed to the fundamental right to life for the unborn, a position "outwardly and objectively in harmony with the law of God," to use Berkhof's words. Therefore, to make common cause with them in the pro-life movement is completely appropriate.

As another example, most feminists oppose pornography, believing that it degrades and exploits women. And since Christians oppose pornography for the same reasons, as well as many others, we can make common cause with feminists on this issue as well.

Other socially conservative, non-Christian leaders, like radio talk-show host Dennis Prager, syndicated columnist Don Feder, media critic Michael Medved, religious leader Rabbi Daniel Lapin of Toward Tradition, and U.S. Senator Orrin Hatch of Utah, share many of the same social and public policy concerns with Christians. There are people in your community like them. They read *Reader's Digest* and teach traditional notions of right and wrong to their children. On the Little League field, these parents and grandparents instill traditional notions of justice and fair play in their children. Why not join forces with everyday people like these to achieve a common good?

It has been said that "politics makes strange bedfellows." Yet in the case of political co-belligerency on the moral and social issues that threaten the family and society, our "bedfellows" may not appear so strange when compared to our ideological opponents. Christians, after all, have far more in common with each other than they do with homosexual activist members of Act-Up or the Lesbian Avengers. Christians also have far more in common with traditional Jews and even Muslims than they do with Bella Abzug and her cohort of anti-family ideologues. Christians even have more in common with Mormons than they do with organizations such as the ACLU, People for the American Way, Americans United, and other secularists who would exclude religion from any significant role in American public life.

Political co-belligerency may initially have the uncomfortable feeling of a young Luke Skywalker walking into an alien barroom as in the movie *Star Wars*. You may even ask yourself, *What am I doing here with all these strangers?* Nevertheless, I invite you to consider the alternative. By refusing to work with others (even aliens), you would be conceding the fight to Darth Vader—the invading cultural Hun. Unless we learn to contend together on these crucial issues, we are sure to "hang separately" (to borrow an analogy from the American founders).

DISCUSSION QUESTIONS

1. What is co-belligerency?
2. What beliefs do Catholics and evangelicals hold in common? On what doctrines do they differ?
3. Why is there increasing political cooperation among Catholics and evangelicals?

4. What do you think Francis Schaeffer meant when he said, "The final apologetic is love"?
5. How does the life of Abraham Kuyper inform American Christians today?
6. Is there any biblical-theological rationale for Christians to work with non-Christians in the political arena?

CHAPTER 9

The Gospel in Action:
The Extraordinary Impact
of Ordinary People

by Diane Hesselberg

THE BIG IDEA

Diane Hesselberg's message is that you don't have to be a William Wilberforce, let alone the prophet Daniel, to make a difference in your community. You can just be you, because God uses the ordinary to accomplish the extraordinary.

From her experience as a staff writer for *Citizen* magazine's "Hometown Heroes" column, Hesselberg presents some inspiring accounts of how ordinary people are making a difference. She observes that "the stark line between activism and ministry" is "increasingly blurred."

Are Christian activists the "snarling, harsh, narrow-minded, intolerant rabble-rousers" so often portrayed by Hollywood and the news media? In a word, no. Hesselberg tells the stories of regular moms and dads, children and grandmothers, who have taken seriously Jesus' great commandment to love their neighbors. These modern-day Samaritans are an inspiration to us all.

*"Whoever finds his life will lose it,
and whoever loses his life for
my sake will find it."*

—Jesus Christ

◆ ◆ ◆

Sandi was desperate. She needed to escape the lifestyle that held her captive but saw no way out. Nevertheless, God was at work, preparing Carolyn McKenzie to provide a lifeline to Sandi.

Two years before, Sandi had earnestly searched for a job. Things hadn't been going well at home with her mother, and she wanted to be on her own with her young daughter.

"A minimum-wage job wouldn't take care of it," Sandi said. "I saw an ad in the paper for a waitressing job that promised more money, so I went down and picked up an application."

The club hired Sandi on the spot. She purchased her uniform at the lingerie shop that carried them, and she was shocked. "I couldn't believe I paid $95 for a lot of lace and some stockings," Sandi said. "When I first put them on, I asked, 'Am I supposed to walk out there like this?' I wanted to hide behind my serving tray."

When Sandi made $225 her first night as a waitress, however—while average waitresses earn $50-75—she decided she could tolerate the uniform. After all, she was wearing so much more than the topless dancers in the club.

"But I swore I would never dance," she said.

Dancers make as much as $150 per hour when the customers are tipping well. At the time, "exotic" dancers in Tennessee evaded indecency prosecution by wearing G-strings and latex "panties" that gave the appearance of nudity.

However, after co-workers introduced Sandi to crystal methane, her resolve not to dance crumbled: "The work wasn't half as hard as waitressing, and the pay was three times as good."

Sandi's new "career" boosted her income but deflated her self-esteem. "I couldn't go to work sober," she said. "I dreaded going to work. Every night, I would stay in the shower until it ran out of hot water."

But Sandi saw no way out. She cut back her living expenses as much as possible, hoping to resume waitressing. "It's a trap," she said. "You can't go back. I was too used to the money I made, and I couldn't live on less."

If waitressing at the club wouldn't provide enough money, no "legitimate" job would either. After two years in the club, at 21 years of age, Sandi was desperate.

Sandi's mother knew about her daughter's dancing. She also knew how badly her daughter wanted out of it. In fact, she still had the phone number of a woman she had heard on the radio several months before, expressing her concern for victims of pornography—especially the girls who worked in Memphis's topless clubs.

"Mom told me, 'If you really want out, call this number,'" Sandi said. "I was afraid this woman would put me down, but I was ready to take any chance."

In April 1994, Sandi called Carolyn McKenzie and found her way out. Carolyn agreed to talk with Sandi in person.

Carolyn said, "I asked her, 'If I guaranteed you that your expenses would be taken care of for six or eight weeks—long enough for you to find a job—would you promise never to go back to the club?'"

Sandi promised. And she kept her promise. Today, she has a legitimate full-time job in Memphis. And she is thrilled to see her friends from the club, one by one, coming to Carolyn, too.

◆ ◆ ◆

Carolyn McKenzie was one of *Citizen* magazine's Hometown Heroes in December 1994.[1] Each month, that column features four stories of successful pro-family activism. Since the column's inception, I have been honored to help select the heroes, interview them, and write their stories. But why does *Citizen*—Focus on the Family's public policy magazine—consider Carolyn McKenzie a hero? Can her action really be classified as "activism"? After all, she didn't push for legislation to prohibit topless clubs. Her efforts didn't result in the prosecution of the owners of any of the clubs that have shipwrecked so many young women. In fact, her effort sounds more like a ministry than activism.

Our original idea for the Hometown Heroes column was to include stories of intense activism only; "softer" ministry, we reasoned, should be covered in a different publication. But as the months passed, I encountered many powerful pro-family successes that, though lacking the hard edge we sought, still had undeniable impact.

As I interviewed dozens of activists in nearly every state, the stark line between activism and ministry began to appear increasingly blurred.

The truth soon became clear: For all practical purposes, no significant difference exists between activism and ministry. Activists and ministers alike are motivated, after all, by issues that affect humankind—flesh and blood *people*. The issues they address touch humanity in the most profound way. Thus, Christ's mandate to "love your neighbor as yourself" (Matt. 22:39), while finding immediate expression in the provision of food, shelter, and encouragement to those in need, also applies directly to every political and social issue.

ONE PERSON CAN MAKE A DIFFERENCE

Many times, upon concluding an interview with a Hometown Heroes candidate, I would ask, "Is there anything you'd like to add—anything you'd like to tell our readers?"

With uncanny consistency, the response I received was, "Tell them that one person *can* make a difference."

From the most humble, reticent "minister" to the most outspoken, confident "activist," this, invariably, was their counsel: "Do what you can, within your sphere of influence, regardless of how small it may seem." Each person, after having come through the fire of social action, possessed a deep realization that God had placed him or her in that particular situation "for such a time as this"—just as He placed Esther in a position of influence in Persia at the precise moment when the Jews needed a spokesperson before the king.[2] No one else could substitute for the individual who was called to accomplish the task; therefore, to wait for someone else to do it—even if the task was something as routine as prayer—would be futile.

When Kitty England of Bellevue, Washington, learned at a Washington Family Council meeting about various anti-family legislation her state's Assembly was considering, she knew she was called to act.[3] As the leader of Westminster Chapel's Community Impact Committee, Kitty recruited church members to pray for their state legislators. She wasn't an assemblyperson, nor was she a professional lobbyist. But she found a way to lobby heaven on behalf of truth and justice, and the legislators said they felt the difference.

One legislator, an openly homosexual man, told the woman who was praying for him that he welcomed her prayers. Kitty wrote, "He and other legislators commented that things in Olympia seemed to be different that session, and they attributed the difference to the prayers."

Had Kitty not operated in her own way—within her sphere of influence—the situation would have been politics as usual in Olympia that session. Community impact groups across the nation followed Kitty's lead, and legislative prayer projects were conducted in 30 states during the 1995 session.

In Grand Rapids, Michigan, 84-year-old stroke victim "Grandma" Margaret Koster reaches into people's lives in the only way she is physically able.[4] She rises before dawn each day to pray for more than 1,200 missionaries, community leaders, and families on her correspondence and prayer list.

Grandma began sending birthday and anniversary cards 50 years ago, but a few years back, a stroke rendered her unable to write. "I couldn't even read my own handwriting," Grandma said. "I thought I was going to have to quit writing cards, but my children said, 'Oh, no. You can't stop writing,' and they bought me a typewriter."

Now Grandma spends several hours at the beginning of each day on her knees and the rest of her waking hours at her typewriter, using her one functional finger to infuse encouragement and strength into the lives of others.

Grandma's friend Dawn Gelder said of Grandma's impact, "I know that pornography and these other issues are important, but Grandma's prayers and cards touch people personally. She equips hearts to confront those issues."

ON-THE-JOB TRAINING

Most of the people featured as Hometown Heroes are not experienced political activists. When they took on their projects, few knew how to maneuver within the political system or work with the media. In fact, they fit perfectly Paul's description of the Corinthian church:

> Brothers, think of what you were when you were called. Not many of you were wise by human standards; not many were influential; not many were of noble birth. But God chose the foolish things of the world to shame the wise; God chose the weak things of the world to shame the strong. (1 Cor. 1:26-27)

But the Hometown Heroes I have written about didn't let lack of knowledge or experience stop them; they learned as they worked. In fact, most found it easy to learn about an issue when they cared so passionately about it.

Ben and Margaret Go of Cypress, California, heard rumors that their city council was considering a proposal to open a card casino at the local race track—a move that would directly subject their community to the debasement of gambling. But they had no idea how to begin to fight the proposal.[5]

The issue was important, however, so they got involved. They attended community meetings and soon found themselves to be leaders in the crusade against the casino. Four months later, the referendum was defeated, and the Gos were encouraged by their success. Ben admits he now enjoys political involvement—in fact, he's "hooked." Prior to the 1994 elections, Ben helped lead campaign efforts for two conservative city-council members. Both campaigns were successful.

Paul and Susan Madore of Lewiston, Maine, were also inexperienced in political action, but they made their campaign against a homosexual-rights initiative a "family affair."[6]

"We got involved because the proposal was a violation of family values," Paul Madore said. "The political climate here is not family-friendly, and it took families like ours who were offended by the proposal to get the attention of officials who were out of touch with the wishes of the people."

The family's nine children helped in neighborhood literature distribution, and they all learned along the way. Voters certified the Madores' on-the-job training by soundly defeating the initiative.

Cathy Enz and her husband, Kurt, own a small print shop in the St. Louis area and invest their time in their children at home. But after Cathy attended a Community Impact Seminar in Kansas City in November 1993, she decided to run for the Missouri House of Representatives in 1994 against a liberal, pro-choice incumbent. Cathy and Kurt put together a grass-roots campaign based on a family-values theme, and, despite modest funding and no political renown, Cathy was elected.

HEED THE CALL

As these stories illustrate, many activists don't plan to become so involved. They don't *look* for an issue to promote; rather, issues tend to find *them*. Undoubtedly, at some time in the past, an issue has sought each of us as well. Such prodding, such annoyance, may well be God's attempt to prompt us into action on a particular issue that touches us personally and deeply. Those opportunities, if not heeded, will continually twinge our consciences with a regret that can be allayed only by an obedient response to future calls.

A few years ago, when April Hanson was a fourth-grader in Puyallup, Washington, she heeded such a call.[7] April noticed increasing amounts of obscene graffiti in the girls' rest rooms at Sunrise Elementary School, the public school she attended. She was a student-council representative, so she had a natural outlet for her grievance. But the council was reluctant at first to address April's concern. The group was working on another big project and probably didn't feel they had time to worry about a few scratches on a few inconsequential metal surfaces. But April persisted, and eventually she convinced the group to send a letter to the principal about the problem.

The principal received the letter well: He agreed to have the rest room walls sanded and repainted. April made it her job to continue to monitor the graffiti situation and was pleased to note throughout the school year that, almost as soon as new writing appeared, it was removed. The student council initiated a full-scale campaign against the graffiti, complete with a slogan ("It's not cool to write on the school"), student assemblies, and a play encouraging students to take pride in their school facilities.

At the outset, April probably didn't expect that she—just one person, and one of the youngest student-council representatives, at that—could bring about such a major shift in her fellow students' attitude. She put it simply: "I felt kind of pleased that I had brought the issue up and initiated it."

DISPROVE THE MISCONCEPTIONS

The news media often portray Christian activists as snarling, harsh, narrow-minded, intolerant rabble-rousers who care only about themselves and their ideologies and have no time for compassion. Sadly, a few who work in the name of Christ *do* embody that stereotype, which is then carelessly cast on the rest of us. Thus, when we take on a social or political issue, we work not only *for* truth and justice, but also *against* the misconceptions the culture has about us and the hostility they generate.

Dick Wright reprinted by permission of United Feature Syndicate, Inc.

The challenge, then, is to counter public opinion while staying on task. Such a challenge faced William Devlin when he approached the homosexual issue in the "city of brotherly love."[8] In June 1993, Philadelphia's city council was considering an ordinance that would grant special rights to homosexuals. As an elder at New Life Presbyterian Church and director of Philadelphia Christian Action Council (now Philadelphia Family Policy Council), Devlin used his influence to orchestrate a campaign against the proposal. When city hall received a record-breaking 250,000 postcards from citizens who opposed the ordinance, the council dropped the issue. But the homosexual population didn't. They took personal offense at Devlin's efforts and started what they called a "phone zap" campaign against him.

Within days, seven obscene phone calls—including three death threats—were recorded on the answering machine at the Devlin household. The calls terrified his wife and children, but he acted on Christ's command to "love your enemies" and hastily added a message to his answering machine. In it, he extended an invitation to any homosexuals who wished to join him for dinner at his home.

Devlin's thinking, in a nutshell: "I believe that although homosexuals are engaged in a destructive lifestyle, they are human beings created in the image of God. I'm not afraid of homosexuals, and I wanted to convince them of my concern for them by offering to have a meal with them."

His attitude certainly contradicts society's view of a Christian activist. He is not a cookie-cutter Christian, pressed into the mold of public opinion and half-baked into some self-righteous quasi-evil entity. He opened his home, made himself and his family vulnerable, and took an emotional and—based on the phone messages—physical risk in making this offer. Several members of the homosexual community accepted his invitation. On many occasions, Devlin has entertained homosexual guests, and he has also dined with them in their homes and "on their turf."

But in his outreach to homosexuals, Devlin doesn't compromise his convictions. He gently, lovingly builds a bridge of communication from his shore to theirs without neglecting his responsibility to point out to them the destructiveness of their lifestyle.

"The most compassionate thing I can do is tell them the truth," Devlin said. "I tell them, 'If you continue, there is a strong possibility that you will die.' As an elder in the Presbyterian church, I tell heterosexuals the same thing: In this day and age, having sex outside of marriage is like holding a gun to your head and pulling the trigger."

In December 1994, the homosexual magazine *Au Courant* "honored" Devlin with its "Ass of the Year" award and published a disparaging four-page article about him. Devlin says, "I consented to the interview in order to share the gospel with the reporter, and now the gospel is going out via the article to the homosexual movement here in Philadelphia. It reinforces my idea of loving the unlovable even when they are in the process of ridiculing you." And in response to the "award," he sent the staff a Christmas gift basket with his best wishes—undoubtedly *not* the reaction they anticipated.

A community impact group in Melbourne, Florida, used a similar approach.[9] The group planned a Back-to-School Send-Off for area public- and home-school students, educators, school officials, and county commissioners. Nolan and Jill Head organized the event. Nolan wrote, "We wanted everyone to know what the students' constitutional privileges were before school started, instead of entering school unarmed with the truth."

The event's positive approach surprised critics and brought revolutionary results. A Bible club, a Fellowship of Christian Athletes huddle, a student worship service, and a monthly prayer breakfast were initiated, and attendance at See You at the Pole (in which students meet at the flagpole to pray for their school) increased tenfold. A county commissioner who attended made the comment, "This is so much more effective than waving signs in protest and being against something."

NOT ALWAYS HERE, NOT ALWAYS NOW

Success in social and political action can't always be measured in temporal terms. Nor can it always be measured quantitatively. It can be as intangible as the personal satisfaction and confidence born of simply having done the right thing. The personal triumph of taking a difficult stand for your deeply held beliefs or undertaking your first "public" project is not to be taken lightly. On the other hand, success is sometimes as concrete as newspaper headlines declaring you to have been the driving force behind new legislation that restricts obscenity in your community.

Either way, success is success. Tim and Rosalie Blount of Salem, Oregon, haven't allowed circumstances to steal their victory.[10] The Blounts worked for 10 years to build their company, New Phase Home Improvements, but the construction field is sometimes a hard taskmaster. Early in 1993, New Phase was in financial trouble, and the Blounts prayed fervently for recovery. They submitted a bid for a relatively large project—the remodeling of a medical clinic—and were ecstatic when they got the contract. Imagine their grief when they learned that the clinic belonged to Planned Parenthood, and that, when the remodel was completed, abortions would be performed there.

The Blounts returned the advance check they had received in partial payment for the job, knowing full well that their principled decision doomed their business and bankrupted them personally. The emotional and financial stress took its toll on Rosalie, who has suffered from multiple sclerosis for years. She is now confined to a wheelchair, and, without her help, Tim is unable to reopen his business. For Planned Parenthood, on the other hand, business is booming. The organization found another contractor to complete its clinic, which opened without much delay.

The Blounts have an exceptional attitude about their decision and its consequences, though. Nearly two years after canceling the contract, Tim said, "It took its toll, and I grieve still. But when you stop and think about it, how many people in a lifetime get a chance to take a stand for the Lord like we did? We did what we could, and that's where the rubber meets the road."

A group of public school students in Kansas City, Missouri, is claiming victory, too, despite how the situation looks from the outside. The students decided to take a stand against MTV's infamous antiheroes Beavis and Butt-Head.[11] The fourth-grade class of Center Elementary School led a petition drive at its school, and several neighboring schools adopted the project as well. Center Elementary sent nearly 2,000 petition signatures to MTV, requesting that the company either remove the violent content from the program or cancel it altogether.

Not surprisingly, MTV took little notice. Around that time, the program was bumped a couple of hours later nationwide, but the repulsive content remains, and no acknowledgment was made by MTV to the students that their petitions played any part in the decision.

The students, however, are forever changed by the experience. One girl said she learned that "you can do something as a kid, instead of waiting until you're a grown-up." In this case, the biggest victory may be yet to come: If those kids stay on track, they will surely be a credit to their communities when they reach adulthood—even if Beavis and his friend still spout obscenities and carry on foul debates about the female anatomy.

TOGETHER AGAIN

Benjamin Franklin said it so well at the signing of the Declaration of Independence in 1776: "We must all hang together, or assuredly we shall all hang separately." The Christian community has been fragmented far too long; we have squandered precious time concentrating on the splinters in our brothers' eyes while we overlooked the wooded overgrowth that threatens to obscure our society's vision altogether.

Eleven ministers who represent all eight denominations in Long Prairie, Minnesota, found a way to "hang together." When The Main Event, a restaurant/bar that featured erotic dancing, opened just outside of town, the ministers rallied together in support of a county ordinance that restricts erotic dancing. After reviewing the group's documentation of damage suffered by other communities after they introduced "adult" establishments, the county commissioners passed the ordinance.[12]

David Sorensen, pastor of Long Prairie's American Lutheran Church, explained why such a level of cooperation was possible: "The coalition of people who oppose [erotic dancing] is very broad. Our base of support includes conservatives, liberals, feminists—and why not?

They're all concerned about the community."

Less than a year after the ordinance took effect, The Main Event closed its doors.

In Sacramento, California, several churches' community impact committees worked together to fight pornographic programming on public cable television.[13] Janet Gross, a mother who was mobilized against obscene programming when she saw homosexual acts blatantly portrayed during prime time, was asked to speak to the county board of supervisors about the issue. The community impact groups gathered more than a thousand signatures to add the needed weight to her argument.

PERSONAL TOUCH

The business of community standards, county ordinances, and state statutes can seem dry and uninviting at first glance. How can interminably monotonous meetings run by parliamentary procedure accomplish anything toward advancing the kingdom of God? Can culture—or any part of it—be reformed in this way? Paperwork, petitions, placards—are these the vehicles by which families are protected and righteousness restored? In the heat of the debate, it can be easy to forget that at the heart of every issue are real, flesh-and-blood people who are God's creation, and their pain greatly grieves their Father in heaven. Some of those people are unborn; others have been so exploited by life that they see no escape from their circumstances.

Carolyn McKenzie's social action has a tangible effect on the lives of the young women she rescues from Memphis's topless clubs. Her impact is something she can reach out and touch—and, indeed, it has touched her deeply as well. The poignant truth is that, at any time, almost *anyone* could have intervened in any number of ways and dramatically altered the course of those young women's lives.

Cathy left the topless scene more than 12 years ago. Occasionally, because of the unpleasant memories, she catches herself turning her head away from topless clubs as she drives past them. She urges Christians to stop "turning their heads away" and ignoring the truth of what's in their communities: "People need to realize that it *is* touching lives. It's closer than they think—it's at their back doors." Cathy added that if she had known of *one* person who cared who she was—what she was—she would have left the clubs much sooner.

BEYOND THE COMFORT ZONE

Many forms of social and political action, however, do not so tangibly affect lives. Nor do they all come so naturally as taking several young women under your wing and giving them a chance to start over. Some kinds of action require superhuman patience and fortitude, and the work can be more grueling than digging ditches under a hot sun. Stephen Fellows, a grandfather in Irving, Texas, found this to be true when he proposed a traditional-values resolution to the school board in his district.[14] The local media called his resolution "a joke," writers to the local newspaper called it "a hoax," and angry citizens "took personal shots" at him during school board meetings.

"It got to a point where I wondered whether it was worth it all," Fellows said. "I don't see myself as someone standing up in the limelight in the first place. I'm just not comfortable in that realm." But his strong conviction that God was involved in his endeavor carried him through. The school board adopted the resolution, and teachers in the Irving Independent School District are now encouraged by the board to teach traditional moral values—including sexual abstinence. In addition, nearly 500 school districts across the nation have requested copies of the resolution. Several have adopted similar resolutions; many more are considering them. Because Fellows pushed hard for truth and justice, teachers are now free to present to multiplied thousands of students—most of whom Fellows will never meet—truth that could prevent inestimable pain in their lives. But it wasn't accomplished without pain and sacrifice on Fellows's part.

Others describe their experience as something they didn't want to do; as a time of frightening responsibility; as a valley of depression; as a trial that brought them to their knees more often than ever before; as a time when they felt desperately alone as community support melted away; as a time when they were "dying inside."

NO REGRETS

Of all the Hometown Heroes I've interviewed, however, not one regrets the experience. No one told me, "I'll never do anything like that again." Each individual, through his experience, grew in confidence in himself and God. One woman said she hated the experience but wouldn't have missed it for the world. Hence, person by person, cooperation and involvement spread.

The Hometown Heroes are correct. Through love and conviction, any one average "Joe or Joyce Citizen" *can* make a difference. The system can still be made to work. When compassionate people realize this, they get involved—regardless of whether their involvement more closely resembles activism or ministry.

This is a great time to be alive, because opportunities to demonstrate truth and justice are everywhere. God's people must act out their deeply held convictions in every area of their lives. That won't always be comfortable. Social action will stretch us beyond the familiar, the usual, the secure. But Jesus has called us to be risk-takers. He said, "Whoever finds his life will lose it, and whoever loses his life for my sake will find it" (Matt. 10: 39). When we put our personal comfort on the line for Jesus' sake—and for society's sake—Jesus said we will "find" our lives. Herein lies one of God's great mysteries: By laying down our lives, we discover who we really are and what makes life worth living.

God asks none of us to change the world; that's beyond any individual's reach. He asks us only to work to improve our own corner of the world, however large or small that may be. It's far better to do something small than to sit, paralyzed by fear or apathy, and attempt nothing. Getting started takes just one small step: one phone call, one letter, one meeting, one prayer. Throw just one pebble into the pond. Who knows how far the ripples will reach?

DISCUSSION QUESTIONS

1. Do you agree with the author's conclusion that "no significant difference exists between activism and ministry"? Why or why not?
2. Has a lack of knowledge or experience ever stopped you from becoming involved with an issue? Describe the situation.
3. What is your impression of William Devlin's brand of activism? Would it work for you?
4. How can Christians encourage their children to take on issues, as April Hanson and the fourth-graders in Kansas City did?
5. What should be the Christian activist's response to name-calling and prejudice?

6. The Planned Parenthood clinic that Tim and Rosalie Blount refused to remodel opened with little delay in spite of their stand. Was their decision to cancel their contract wise? Why or why not?
7. Conservatives have been elected to office at all levels of government across the nation. What should be the Christian's plan of action now?

CHAPTER 10

A Call to Action

by Alan R. Crippen II

THE BIG IDEA

Discipleship is more than memorizing Scripture, attending church, and raising a strong family. Though these things are important aspects of being a good disciple, discipleship involves much more. To follow Christ is to appropriate the vast spiritual resources that are life-transforming. Spiritual disciplines such as prayer, sacrament, Bible study, meditation, fasting, and so on are crucial for contending against the spirit of the age in America's culture wars. For it is Christ in us, "the mystery that has been kept hidden for ages and generations" (Col. 1:26), that will ultimately transform our being, thinking, and acting. Likewise, it is Christ in us who will reform American politics and culture. Without Christ, we can do nothing. With Christ, however, we can do all things.

In this chapter, I will relate a modern story of human compassion and social vision in the life of a youngster who has touched thousands of lives in an American city. Readers will then be challenged with a call to personal action. Readers will further be challenged to consider what an organized cadre of citizen Christians can do through concerted action within a congregation.

Community impact committees in local parishes are presented as a model for "getting on with the social and political tasks that we are called to as the people of God." This chapter offers practical ideas and specific steps as to how to go about organizing for social and political service within the local church.

"Christ has no body now on earth but ours,
no hands but ours, no feet but ours:
ours are the eyes through which Christ's compassion
looks out on the world,
ours are the feet with which He is to go about doing good,
and ours are the hands with which He is to bless us now."

—Saint Theresa of Avila

◆ ◆ ◆

Our Lord wept over Jerusalem.[1] Today, He weeps over a world that, like the people of Jerusalem, fails to recognize the time of His coming. For such a time as this Jesus' call to us is clear. We are to make disciples.[2] But *being* a disciple precedes *making* disciples. In the opening chapter of the books of Acts, Luke records Jesus' last words to His disciples prior to His ascension into heaven: "You will be my witnesses in Jerusalem, and in all Judea and Samaria, and to the ends of the earth" (1:8). What is important to notice is that Jesus did not tell His disciples "to witness," but rather to "be witnesses." This distinction between doing and being is important for our understanding of discipleship. Discipleship focuses first on the development of personal character rather than on activity and achievement. John Eldredge reminds us in chapter 7 that the social and political reforms achieved by William Wilberforce in England and the prophet Daniel in ancient Babylon originated in a deep spirituality of their personal character. This was also true of Abraham Kuyper and his political work in Holland. Therefore, the Christian's call to social and political action involves putting first things first.

PUTTING FIRST THINGS FIRST

A Christian is often tempted to put second things first in the arenas of politics and culture. Those of us who are called to work in these arenas tend to have a bias toward action, which many times comes at the neglect of spiritual contemplation and reflection. Yet it is the spiritual disciplines that will transform, energize, and sustain us for the long haul amidst the political, cultural ,and even spiritual conflicts that we face. The culture wars are only the temporal manifestations of the deeper spiritual conflicts that the apostle Paul writes about in Ephesians: "For our struggle is not against flesh and blood, but against the rulers, against the authorities, against the powers of this dark world and against the spiritual forces of evil in the heavenly realms" (6:12). How can we hopefully engage these powers without appropriating the resources of the spiritual disciplines? Prayer, sacrament, Bible study, meditation, fasting, and other disciplines are the tools for both being a disciple, as well as making disciples. They are the weapons for contending against the spirit of this age.

In 1940, the civilized world was horrified at the advance of the Nazis across Europe. Czechoslovakia, Austria, Poland, and France had fallen to the Swastika of Adolf Hitler's Third Reich. The British army had been driven back across the English Channel to their island country by Herman Goering's Luftwaffe and Heinz Guderian's panzers. In that desperate hour, the people of Great Britain feared a German invasion that could have initiated a new dark ages for Western civilization. Amidst a cloud of uncertainty, C.S. Lewis wrote to his fellow Britons:

> It will be replied that our concern for civilization is very natural and very necessary at a time when civilization is so imperilled. But how if the shoe is on the other foot? How if civilization has been imperilled by the fact that we have all made civilization our *summum bonum* [greatest good]? Perhaps it can't be preserved in that way. Perhaps civilization will never be safe until we care for something else more than we care for it.... Our ancestors were cruel, lecherous, greedy, and stupid, like ourselves. But while they cared for other things more than for civilization—and they cared at times for all sorts of things, for the will of God, for glory, for personal honour, for doctrinal purity, for justice—was civilization often in serious danger of disappearing?[3]

The point that Lewis was making to his countrymen was this: "You can't get second things by putting them first; you get second things only by putting first things first."[4] Civilization and a flourishing culture are the fruits of the gospel. In this respect, they are "second things," by-products of faith in God, love for our neighbors, and the Golden Rule. If we are to reclaim the culture and reform its politics and civic life, our lives must be defined by a passion and demand for the first things of the gospel. In other words, in order to bring a holy influence to society, we must first become a holy people. Therefore, our model of social engagement must be in following Jesus Christ as His disciples, and this entails putting first things first.

TRANSFORMED TO REFORM

The emphasis on *being* before *doing* is an incarnational and character-centered approach to political and social involvement. This approach is modeled after the life of Christ. God Himself became fully human in His Son in order to encounter humanity with the message of reconciliation and redemption. The message of the Immanuel is "God with us." And that is why Christians celebrate the birth of Christ, a veiling of deity with human flesh. According to the late theologian H. Richard Niebuhr, this approach to the Christian's calling and culture is based upon an understanding that:

> [Christ's] work is concerned not with specious, external aspects of human behavior in the first place, but that he tries the hearts and judges the subconscious life; that he deals with what is deepest and most fundamental in man. . . . And this he does not simply by offering ideas, counsel, and laws; but by living with men in great humility, enduring death for their sakes, and rising again from the grave in a demonstration of God's grace rather than argument about it.[5]

The incarnation of God in Christ is the archetype for the incarnation of Christ in us. And Christ in us is "the mystery that has been kept hidden for ages and generations," our "hope of glory" (Col. 1:26-27). So then, our personal character, cognition, and conduct—especially as it relates to our political being, thinking, and acting—should reflect the life of Christ in us. Our lives, including our political life, are to be brought into conformity with Christ. This is the transformational principle. As Christ transforms us, so we transform our culture, even its politics, through Christ.

The reformation of American politics and culture will be an impossible undertaking apart from the rich spiritual resources that are available to us in life with Christ. It is only by appropriating these vital resources that we can be transformed for reforming our neighborhoods, communities, and nation.

WHAT CAN ONE PERSON DO?

After school one cold winter afternoon in 1983, an 11-year-old boy turned on the television news in the comfort of his parents' home in a well-to-do suburb of Philadelphia. That day, young Trevor Ferrell would begin a transition from the idealistic world of *Mary Poppins* and *Peter Pan* to the real world of humanity's heartbreaks and hard knocks. For on that particular evening, the feature news story was about Philadelphia's homeless people. During the broadcast, Trevor's tender eyes remained glued to the television set as the shocking images of people living inside cardboard boxes atop city sidewalk grates introduced him to a world previously unknown.

Later that night over supper, Trevor expressed his dismay and disbelief that there were people in the city who actually lived on the streets. He pleaded with his parents, Frank and Janet, to take him downtown so he could see for himself. They reluctantly agreed to their son's request, deciding that it was time to broaden Trevor's worldview.

After supper, the family loaded up in their station wagon for a new adventure, leaving their 16-room house with a swimming pool, two acres of woods, and a Rolls Royce in the garage. Trevor took a pillow and his old, yellow blanket to give away to the first homeless person he would meet.

As the family neared city hall in center of downtown, Trevor spotted an emaciated man crumpled up on a sidewalk grate trying to keep warm. Frank stopped the car, and Trevor got out and handed the man his yellow blanket and pillow.

This compassionate encounter altered the Ferrells' lives from that day forward. The family began making nightly trips downtown to help street people in small ways. Blankets and clothes were collected from family, classmates, and neighbors. Peanut butter sandwiches, and later hot meals, were distributed. Within weeks, the local television media carried the story, and the Ferrells were soon able to raise enough money to open a shelter called Trevor's Place.

To the 24,000 homeless on the streets of Philadelphia, Trevor became known as the "little Jesus." Media coverage made him a local celebrity, a sort of twentieth-century Good Samaritan. Eventually, his efforts were brought to the attention of the nation and the world. President Ronald Reagan saluted Trevor in his 1986 State of the Union address. Mother

Teresa invited him to India twice, and he went. He addressed the United Nations General Assembly and attended an international conference on the homeless in Africa. And a made-for-TV movie about Trevor has aired three times on network television, most recently on CBS. A docudrama has also premiered on HBO.

Though Trevor is grown now and doing other things, his vision continues as Trevor's Campaign for the Homeless. This nonprofit humanitarian organization coordinates street outreach with an army of 1,500 volunteers; offers transitional housing and services for homeless families and adults; operates a distribution center with donations of furniture, household goods, and clothing; and conducts public education and advocacy work for the homeless across the United States and in France.

Granted, this story may seem to be a larger-than-life example of what one person can do, but it's not really. It is a true-life account of what compassion coupled with a social vision can do for love of our neighbors. What makes this story so remarkable is that a child's compassion and vision were the impetus behind all of these efforts. In Scripture, we read that "a little child will lead them" (Isa. 11:6). Trevor Ferrell, the "little Jesus" to Philadelphia's homeless, challenges and leads us to consider the possibilities of what we can do in our own communities.

WHAT CAN YOU DO?

Your opportunities for community involvement are limited only by your imagination. As you become informed about the issues and aware of the human needs in your community, you will soon discover no shortage of things to do. Rather, your challenge will be to focus on the "one significant something, rather than the all-embracing nothing."[6] In determining what to do, you should seek the Lord's direction, and this will involve understanding His will, assessing your own talents and abilities, and evaluating the desires of your heart. With so many important moral issues and human needs confronting us, there are no simple formulas for deciding what to do and what not to do.

The sections that follow provide ideas for personal involvement in your community. This listing is not exhaustive; to be sure, there are many other ideas for social action that I have not mentioned. Hopefully, as you read these ideas, even more opportunities for involvement will come to mind.

On Elections

Voting is one of the most direct ways to influence government. Certainly, the bare minimum responsibility of good citizenship is to vote. But in the interest of getting more qualified pro-family candidates in public office, there is much more you can do as an individual. You may want to consider the following:

- Conduct a voter-registration drive at your church.
- Help to distribute voter guides.
- Join a local party committee; become a delegate or precinct chair.
- Volunteer to serve on a campaign.
- Run for office.

On Grassroots Lobbying

Lobbying is another direct way to influence government. By directly contacting your elected representatives regarding a specific issue, you can have a significant influence in the policy-making process. In state government, it has been said that five personal visits and 10 written letters from constituents are often enough to change a legislator's mind on any issue. And since most family policy battles are fought and decided at the state government level, just think of the impact that a small cadre of Christians could have on an elected official. Here are some grassroots lobbying ideas:

- Write a letter to your city, county, state, or federal representatives about legislation or issues affecting the family.
- Host a monthly "letter-writing night" to encourage and equip others to do the same.
- Establish a telephone alert chain for mobilizing grassroots influence.
- Visit your elected officials to establish good relations with them and communicate your concerns.
- Send a "thank you" to them when they vote as you hoped they would, even if you expected them to.

On Public Schools

Service is the principle for effective involvement in public education. You will be far more persuasive among the school community if you are

Reprinted with special permission of King Features Syndicate

recognized as a servant-leader. Do not let your first contact with teachers, administrators, school-board members, and other parents be surrounded by political controversy and confrontation, if possible. Become involved as a responsible volunteer first. Then you will have earned the right to be heard when controversial issues surface. Here are some ideas for involvement in your local school:

- ♦ Volunteer to tutor, serve as a teacher's aide, coordinate a fundraiser for the school, become a part of a parents' advisory or curriculum review committee.
- ♦ Join the Parent Teacher Association (PTA).
- ♦ Start a Moms in Touch group to pray for your children.
- ♦ Attend school board meetings.
- ♦ Run for the local school board or become involved in a pro-family candidate's campaign.
- ♦ Introduce the local school board to alternative sex education curricula that emphasizes abstinence.
- ♦ Donate pro-family books and magazine subscriptions to the school library.

On the Media

Here are some ways to influence the news media and entertainment industry:

♦ Write letters to the editor of your local newspaper on social issues affecting the family.
♦ Volunteer to serve on a citizen's committee that governs cable TV in your community.
♦ Write the television networks and their local affiliates to support good programs and oppose bad ones. Write to their sponsors as well.
♦ Help to promote boycotts of offending sponsors' products.
♦ Write the Federal Communications Commission (FCC) to alert them to inappropriate radio or television programming. Make sure you have accurate information regarding the incident (date, time, station, title of the program, and specific examples of the content).
♦ Encourage your local telephone company to drop its dial-a-porn services. If they refuse, organize public pressure for them to do so.
♦ Call in to local talk radio programs to contend for traditional values in an articulate, informed, and responsible manner.
♦ Support alternative media, such as Christian radio, newspapers, and magazines.

On Community Service

Compassionate voluntarism is probably the best way to make our communities a better place to live. Before the emergence of the twentieth-century welfare state, it was primarily Christian philanthropy that weaved together and suspended America's social safety net. Voluntary associations such as the Salvation Army, the Young Men's Christian Association (YMCA), and the Womens Christian Temperance Union (WTCU) were active in obeying our Lord's commandment to "Love thy neighbor." Here are some community service ideas for you to consider:

♦ Become a Big Brother or Big Sister.
♦ Help a local shelter for the homeless. Volunteer your time and talent. Donate money, clothing, furniture, and food.
♦ Volunteer at a local hospice.
♦ Provide transportation to the elderly, shut-ins, and the handicapped.

- Lend your help to the local prison ministry.
- Become a foster parent.
- Support your local crisis pregnancy center. Volunteer time. Donate baby clothes and supplies.
- Do sidewalk counseling in front of an abortion clinic to lovingly persuade young women to let their babies live.
- Open your home to an unwed mother until she can provide for her child.
- Participate in a Life Chain.
- Become a hospital volunteer.
- Join a community action group to fight pornography in your community.
- Ask local video stores to remove pornographic videos from their inventories.
- Visit or write your local district attorney and ask if obscenity laws are being enforced in your county.
- Donate pro-family books and magazine subscriptions to your local library.
- Run for your local library board.
- Volunteer at a local AIDS hospice. Join an AIDS support group.
- Inquire about joining a hospital's ethics committee.
- Speak on moral, ethical, and social issues threatening the family at your local Rotary, Lions, Kiwanis, or Jaycees meetings.
- Help with a literacy campaign.
- Join a support group for single parents.

As you can see, the needs are great, and no one person can do it all. That is why in addition to encouraging individual Christians to social and political action, Focus on the Family has been actively promoting the idea that churches should act corporately on these issues and needs. By appropriately responding to the moral and social crises facing the community, the local church can have an effective outreach for evangelism.

CALLING, COMMUNITY, AND CONCERTED ACTION

The biblical concept of being "called" to a certain endeavor or mission affirms that our labors are best accomplished by organized groups and associations. In other words, calling implies that work should be done in community for the community. And since the church is not an aggregate of individuals but rather a community of faith, members fulfill their individual callings for the benefit of the whole in accomplishing God's purposes. Each of us has a special calling of God for the edification of the entire Body. We are dependent upon God and mutually interdependent upon each other. Simply put, we need to work together.

People called to do business form or seek partnerships and corporations. Those who are called to the medical field set up or join practices and hospitals. Individuals who are called to humanitarian service establish or join nonprofit organizations. Scholars found or enter universities. Christians called to the foreign field form or affiliate with mission agencies, and those called to support them organize or become members of missions committees in their churches. All of these associations constitute people working together to serve society in their respective callings.

In order to get on with the social and political tasks that we are called to as the people of God, Focus on the Family encourages Christians to organize for this activity within their churches. We have found that the most influential churches in their communities have an organized activity devoted to social and political concerns. These activities are called by different names—social concerns committees, current issues councils, or Christian citizenship committees—but their function is the same: to provide spiritual and organizational leadership on social and political issues facing their congregation and community. They have responsibility for educating and equipping the membership toward responsible and effective social action. We call these organized activities "community impact committees."

STARTING A COMMUNITY IMPACT COMMITTEE

There are five steps necessary to start a community impact ministry in your church. They are as follows: (1) Pray; (2) Seek the affirmation and approval of church leadership; (3) Recruit others for involvement; (4) Develop a mission statement and organize for action; and (5) Begin the flow of information. Let's briefly look at each of these steps.

1. Pray
Personal prayer is the first step in the development of your social vision and the establishment of a community impact committee in your church.

Because of the importance of prayer, it seems almost trite to devote only a few sentences to it here. Prayer is a central priority to the Christian life and one that has no substitute. E.M. Bounds, a nineteenth-century authority on prayer, wrote on this idea in his spiritual classics on prayer:

> There can be no substitute, no rival for prayer; it stands alone as the great spiritual force, and this force must be imminent and acting. . . . It must be continuous and particular, always, everywhere, and in everything. . . . Many persons believe in the efficacy of prayer, but not many pray. Prayer is the easiest and hardest of all things; the simplest and the sublimest; the weakest and the most powerful; its results lie outside of human possibilities—they are limited only by the omnipotence of God.[7]

Therefore, personal prayer must be the first priority as you work toward establishing a community impact committee in your church. Put first things first by taking this spiritual discipline seriously. There can be no substitute for prayer.

Many people have a fundamental misunderstanding or misconception about the purpose of prayer. They believe that by petitioning God to "change things," God's will can, in effect, be brought into conformity with human desires. However, the true purpose of prayer is just the opposite. It is to bring our will into conformity with God's will, not vice-versa. When Jesus said, "If you remain in me and my words remain in you, ask whatever you wish, and it will be given you" (John 15:7), He was not supplying a prescription for the manipulation of God. Instead, He was saying that by remaining in fellowship and being of one mind in Christ, our will would be brought into conformity with Christ's. In this relationship, our asking would be in accordance with God's desire.

Likewise, when Jesus exhorted the disciples to "ask in my name" (John 15:16), He was not providing a kind of alchemist's formula for getting prayers answered. The act of asking in Jesus' name implies unanimity of purpose, or intent, with God. When we ask in the name of Jesus, we are asking in accordance with His will and for His sake. Therefore, asking in Jesus' name is more than tacking a postscript on the end of our petition; it involves the process of discerning and then conforming to God's will. In teaching the disciples how to pray, Jesus did not say, "My will be done." He said, "Thy will be done." In this manner, prayer brings us in conformity with God's will for our lives.

It must be said that in order to pray in this way, you should prepare yourself through Bible study. Many people do not pray because they do not know how to pray. They think that prayer is a monologue that is uttered before God. Prayer is more correctly understood as a dialogue between God and the intercessor. If prayer is a dialogue, then God has something to say to you that He normally communicates through His written Word, the Bible. Therefore, we encourage you to prayerfully read the Bible, especially where it speaks to issues of social concern. In this way, you prepare yourself not only to speak to God but to listen to Him as well on these matters.

Start with some of the biblical material presented by John Eldredge in chapter 4 for prayerful reflection. The Old Testament book of Amos is also a great study of public justice and could well enhance you prayer life in this area. James W. Skillen, executive director of the Center for Public Justice, recommends the following topical studies.[8] These passages would also be beneficial for prayerful reflection in the honing of your social vision and preparation for community ministry:

> *On God's lordship, kingship, justice, and righteousness:* Isaiah 9:2-7; 30:18; 40:13-31; Daniel 4:34-37; Matthew 28:16-20.

> *On God's will for justice for all people:* Psalm 33:5; Isaiah 1:17,27; 3:14-15; 5:2; 61:8; Jeremiah 9:23-24; 22:15-16; Micah 6:1-8.

> *On government institutions, the use of force, punishment, and retribution:* Genesis 9:1-7; Exodus 18:13-26; Deuteronomy 1:9-17; 16:18-20; 17:14-20; 19:1-21; 20:1-20; 21:18-23; 24:16; 1 Samuel 7:15–8:22; Proverbs 8:15-16; Isaiah 45:1-13; John 19:10-11; Romans 13:1-7; Titus 3:1; 1 Peter 2:13-17.

> *On economic justice, equality, and social harmony:* Leviticus 25:1-55; Deuteronomy 15:1-18; 22:1-4; 24:10-15, 17-22; James 5:1-6.

Personal Bible study equips you with things to pray about. It provides you with a knowledge of God's revealed will so that you can talk with God about your relationship with Him in reference to His Word. We encourage you to converse with the Father and let your prayers arise out of what you have read. Andrew Murray said that prayer is to make a person "a partner with God."[9] Consider that idea for a moment. We are to be God's partners as He extends His rule over the nations of the earth. This fact only underscores the importance of discerning and conforming to His will for our lives. Regarding prayer and your efforts to begin a community impact committee, Dr. Albert E. Day summarizes my thoughts on the matter:

> This can be said without presumption—that one who truly prays will have keener insight, will form sounder judgment, will evolve more intelligent plans, will achieve a greater mastery of situations, and will sustain more creative relationships with people than he ever would without prayer.[10]

2. Seek the affirmation and approval of church leadership

This is the second step in starting a community impact committee in your church. Personal vision and commitment are not enough. As previously stated, the church is not an aggregate of individuals but a community of faith under the authority of Christ, administered through ordained and appointed leaders. As the writer of Hebrews reminds us, "Obey your leaders and submit to their authority. They keep watch over you as men who must give an account. Obey them so that their work will be a joy, not a burden, for that would be of no advantage to you" (Heb. 13:17). The church must affirm and approve your vision and plans to establish a community impact committee, and you must submit to their examination. Without these two elements, most community impact committees fail.

Near the end of the apostle Paul's letter to the Romans, he extends personal greetings to several friends by name. One of those persons is Apelles, of whom the apostle says, "Greet Apelles, tested and approved in Christ" (Rom. 16:10). Of Apelles we know next to nothing. However, his description of being "tested and approved" is relevant to our discussion. What exactly does this phrase mean? Who did the testing and approving? Part of the process no doubt involves being tested and approved in Christ.

How can this happen? The process is a function of the church leadership. If your calling is to social and political service and God has equipped you with the appropriate gifts, then the community of God's people should recognize and affirm you in this calling. Insight into this procedure can be gleaned from the apostle Paul's letter to Timothy. The apostle exhorts Timothy, "Do not neglect your gift, which was given you through a prophetic message when the body of elders laid their hands on you" (1 Tim. 4:14; compare with 2 Tim. 1:6). Though this passage refers specifically to Timothy's ordination to the gospel ministry, there is a principle here that applies to all callings within the Kingdom: Your spiritual overseers should recognize and affirm your calling and gift.

I encourage you to seek the counsel of your pastor or priest, elders, deacons, vestry, or the persons who are responsible for your spiritual oversight in determining your calling to social and political service. These leaders see you in a different way than you see yourself, and this brings more objective spiritual knowledge and discernment into the process. The book of Proverbs is replete with exhortations to seek the advice of counselors. One particular proverb affirms the idea that the church is not an aggregate of individuals when it says, "The way of a fool seems right to him, but a wise man listens to advice" (12:15).[11]

Seek the affirmation of fellow believers and those charged with your spiritual oversight. With the affirmation of your gifts and calling, and the official approval to organize a community impact committee in your church, you are now ready to begin recruiting others.

3. Recruit others who share your vision and calling

Let me emphasize that in one sense *everyone* has a calling to the basic responsibilities of citizenship (e.g., abiding by law, paying taxes, voting intelligently, and so on). In another sense, however, social and political service is not for everyone. In fact, it probably will not be of interest to the majority of people in your church. If it were, who would be left to serve on the missions, evangelism, or worship committees? In forming a community impact committee, you should look for "a few good men and women"—just like the Marine Corps. You should seek to find those people in your church who share a similar calling and desire to be part of a group that will help other church members be better citizens.

To get started, you need to identify those persons in your church who have a social vision and invite them to pray and study together as a fellowship group. You may already know who these people are, or you may have to go about finding them in your church. One idea is to place an announcement in the church bulletin inviting any interested parties to meet for prayer and study concerning social issues. Another idea may be to network within your Sunday school classes to identify others of like mind. After you have gotten people interested in meeting, then set a time and place to meet and get started. The net effects of meeting together will be mutual encouragement, shared vision, and increased guidance and direction.

The biblical concept of encouragement has been rediscovered in the modern business world. The idea is contained in the word *synergy*. Stephen Covey, one of today's most respected authorities on leadership and management, has popularized this word in his best-selling book *The Seven Habits of Highly Effective People*. The brilliance of Covey is demonstrated in his ability to take biblical concepts and popularize them in today's management lingo. Covey has masterfully accomplished this in his discussion of synergy.

What is synergy? "Simply defined, it means that the whole is greater than the sum of its parts. It means that the relationship which the parts have to each other is a part in and of itself. It is not only a part, but the most catalytic, the most empowering, the most unifying, and the most exciting part.... The essence of synergy is to value differences—to respect them, to build on strengths, to compensate for weaknesses."[12]

Synergy is nothing more than the biblical concept of encouragement repackaged for the modern mind. As helpful as Covey may be on this topic, a far more profound discussion of the idea is found in 1 Corinthians 12. You may want to take a few moments to read this passage. The New Testament writer of Hebrews also fully understood and communicated this idea of synergy when he said, "And let us consider how we may spur one another on toward love and good deeds. Let us not give up meeting together, as some are in the habit of doing, but let us encourage one another—and all the more as you see the Day approaching" (10:24,25). An understanding of synergy can even be found in the wisdom literature of the Old Testament: "As iron sharpens iron, so one man sharpens another" (Prov. 27:17).

In meeting together with those who share your calling and vision, the synergy will "spur" all of you "on toward love and good deeds." At your first meeting, let those in attendance share their burdens and interests relating to moral and social issues. In this way, you will get to know something of the personal and common concerns of the group. Pray together about these matters, for each other, and for specific discernment, guidance, and direction about what to do. Then begin a study on biblical principles for social involvement. Spend time together in prayer and study to groom and ground one another in these principles of social involvement. For this kind of study, John Stott's book *Decisive Issues Facing Christians Today* (Revell, 1984,1990) has my highest recommendation. (Other resources are identified in Appendices A and B.) Another group study idea is to read Christian political biographies for discussion. Biographies about the British parliamentarian William Wilberforce, British prime minister William Gladstone, Dutch prime minister Abraham Kuyper, and the American statesman William Jennings Bryan are inspiring accounts of Christian people who were guided by evangelical principles in their public policy efforts.

These times together will provide opportunity for a leader (or leaders) to surface. As the organization of your community impact committee evolves, the leadership requirements may be different from what characterizes the stereotypical "activist" in your church. Be sensitive to the need for servant-leaders who demonstrate a depth of spiritual maturity and respect within the church body. As you seek to determine who your leader shall be, the qualifications for leadership found in 1 Timothy 3:2-12 and Titus 1:6-9 provide an ideal as well as a valuable rubric for candidate screening and selection. Persons of this character and maturity will have the wisdom, respect, and credibility to help make your committee a success.

4. Develop a mission statement and organize for action
The organization of your community impact committee will be determined by three factors: mission, tasks to be accomplished, and available human resources. Mission is like a charter because it sets the committee's future direction and establishes a basis for organizational decision-making. All planning, goals, and objectives should be tested in relation to the mission statement, because a mission statement is your committee's reason for existence. Organizational tasks and structure should be examined to determine how they serve the committee's mission.

The formulation of your mission statement involves a clear understanding of your purpose within the church and surrounding community. You must determine exactly in what kind of "business" it is that you plan to be. As a church committee, your mission statement should be more focused than that of the church, but it should also be derived from the church's mission. In formulating this statement, four primary questions should be answered. First, what function or functions will the committee perform? They may include any or all of the following: (a) prayer concerts for government leaders and officials, policies, international peace initiatives, and so on; (b) citizenship education and the dissemination of information relevant to moral and social issues; and (c) effective political activism and social advocacy on our neighbor's behalf in the interests of love, mercy, truth, and justice. Second, for whom will the committee function? The church membership, its leadership, or someone else? Third, what actions or activities will the committee conduct to fulfill its functions? And finally, why will the committee exist, for what purpose or end?[13]

The process of working through these questions can be difficult and time consuming, but the process will be as valuable to your group as the final product itself. By wrestling with the "what," "who," "how," and "why" questions, the committee will be able to assess personal, group, and church values relative to social and political involvement. This exercise will provide even more insight on the tasks that you initially will need to undertake. Additionally, each member of your group will develop a sense of ownership in the committee's vision.

Here is a draft of a sample community impact committee mission statement for your consideration:

> The community impact committee exists to serve this church by helping disciple its membership toward a fuller expression of Christian faith in the public square. In this effort, the committee endeavors to foster the biblical virtues of love, mercy, truth, and justice on our neighbor's behalf through prayer, citizenship education, and organized social action within local, state, national, and international communities.

This draft is not provided for you to "shortcut" the process, because the process of developing a mission statement is as important to your committee as the end result. Instead, the sample committee mission statement is only an example. You are welcome to use it, in full, in part, or not at all.

Once you have formulated the mission statement, you will need to determine the tasks necessary to accomplish your stated mission. You will want to spell out in some detail the paths by which you intend to accomplish your mission. What are the future "impacts" that you would like to make in your community, and what are the sequential steps necessary to achieve these goals? Who will be responsible for these steps?

Your committee's organization will finally be determined by both the number of people available to serve and the talents and abilities that they bring to the group. In a small church, the committee may only be a handful of people; in a larger church, a committee could number in the dozens. If your committee is small, it is probably unrealistic for you to effectively engage 15 pressing social issues in your community. It is possible that one or two issues will strain your committee's human resources. In this situation, you will need to prioritize between what is important and what is crucial for your church and community. What can you do effectively with the resources God has given you? Once you have determined these things, organize accordingly.

On the other hand, if you are part of a 50-member community impact committee in a church of 3,000 members, then several opportunities can be addressed. Parents and teachers could work on education issues, attorneys on religious liberty and church-state issues, and medical professionals on human life and health care issues. The possibilities are endless, depending upon the composition of your committee. The availability of someone with desktop publishing skills may help you develop a newsletter, bulletin inserts, information sheets, and more. Someone with the talent for persuasive writing may open an avenue for influencing public opinion in the editorial section of your newspaper. People who like to bake or make crafts could be involved in coordinating a bake sale or bazaar as a fundraiser for the local crisis pregnancy center, soup kitchen, or prison ministry.

A final consideration in the organization of your committee is the government of your church. What are the local requirements for leadership and organization of standing committees in your church? Some churches constitutionally stipulate that a pastor, elder, deacon, vestry member, or other leaders serve as a member of all standing committees. Be sure to investigate your church polity requirements in such cases to ensure that your committee complies with church order.

5. Begin the flow of information

Solid education should undergird the actions of every community impact committee and must be an important function of your mission. Effective education is crucial toward building a consensus in your church regarding social and political involvement. Furthermore, the dissemination of timely, accurate, and pertinent information on moral and social issues is a prerequisite to informed and responsible activism. Addressing the "why," "what," and "how" questions of social and political involvement must be a priority.

Busyness is pandemic in our culture. Most people just cannot find the time to stay informed. Pastors are often overworked and far too busy to keep up with every social issue. In this regard, your community impact committee can be extremely valuable. By supplying leadership with the information to direct the congregation in matters of social and political involvement, you provide a much-needed service. Reliable information will win both gratitude and confidence of leadership and better equip your church for action. This increased confidence can only enhance the efforts of your committee. You would do well to consider the church leadership your primary constituency. The best service you can render the church is to serve them.

Church members may not be socially and politically involved simply because they don't have the time. Save them time by providing accurate information and analysis. For example, a handy-sized voter's guide on the local school-board candidates would be a valuable digest of information that the average voter may not otherwise be able to get without great effort. In simple ways like this, you can serve the church membership, too.

Your church probably has a standing committee devoted to missions or evangelism. Most likely, the mission of this committee is to help church members fulfill their responsibilities to the Great Commission. A community impact committee shares a similar role by helping church members to fulfill their responsibilities as disciples and citizens in the public square. Your committee's mission augments and supports the ministry of your church and pastor by helping to teach the congregation about the Christian's role in society. In this manner, you contribute to the overall effort of making disciples.

Your committee will need to read and study the issues. Continue your own education by subscribing to some informative periodicals. You may also want to tune in to "Family News in Focus," a public policy broadcast of Focus on the Family that features up-to-the-minute reports on moral and social issues relating to the family. A number of excellent resources are listed in Appendix B at the end of this book.

Maintain a reading schedule of good books pertinent to social and political involvement, and encourage "issue expertise" within your group.

Each of you will have special interests. Cultivate these interests by reading and studying books, articles, and background papers in the areas of concern. Someone in your group may be concerned about educational reform. Another may be interested in the abortion issue. Yet another may have a burden for AIDS victims. Still another may be concerned about homelessness, poverty, and welfare policy issues. Fan these sparks of interest to become arenas of social engagement and involvement. You need neither a large budget nor a staff of researchers to stay informed, since there are many organizations that can help. Contact these organizations and build on their publications and networks. Local libraries may also carry books and periodicals helpful to your work.

Effective action on social and political issues is predicated upon knowledge coupled with insight and understanding. By staying informed and meeting with others who share your concerns, you will gain a deeper commitment to the cause and develop keener insight and understanding. All of these qualities will enhance your efforts at principled persuasion in the public square.

THE FIVE I'S OF COMMUNITY IMPACT

Now that we have established the five steps to beginning a community impact committee, I would like to provide a five-phased model strategy for cultivating social and political involvement in your church. These principles, if properly applied, will help you foster and develop increased consciousness, involvement, and vision for the culture in which we live. Specifically, this is a model strategy for motivating people in your church who have little or no interest in the moral and social issues, and encouraging them to become more responsible citizens. If we are serious about reclaiming the culture from the prevailing ideas of secularism, relativism, and individualism, greater numbers of Christian people will need to be involved in a principled and persuasive way. One of the greatest challenges of a community impact committee will be to move Christians from no action to pro-action. The social involvement continuum is a strategy to accomplish this.

The social involvement continuum can be summarized as the "Five I's of Community Impact"—identification, information, interest, involvement, and investment. Think of these "Five I's" as a cycle for motivating people to increased participation in social issues and public affairs.

The Five I's of Community Impact

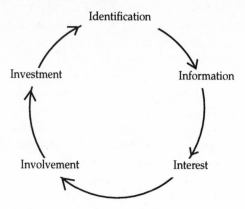

Identification

This phase concerns the process of identifying those you want to be more socially and politically involved. Who and where are they in your church? What worship services and programs do they attend? Are they young people, baby busters, baby boomers, empty-nesters, or seniors? What are their social concerns relating to family, community, national, and international life? These types of questions will help you better inform them about the issues and concerns they care about and reach them with the appropriate media.

Information

Once you have identified your target audience, you must provide them with information. Disseminate facts about the social and moral issues of concern to them, then broaden that information to the spectrum of issues relating to justice in the public square. Where the people are will help to determine the media you use. Are they in the morning worship service? Use bulletin inserts. Are they in the fellowship hall between Sunday school and worship hours? Set up an information table with a newsletter and issue briefs. Do they use the church library? Stock it with books and periodicals that highlight social and political involvement. Do you have their mailing address? Create a newsletter or "piggyback" on the church newsletter as a supplement. Do they attend adult Christian education classes? Seek to offer a course on Christian involvement in public issues. Find every creative and tasteful way to get the information out.

Interest

If you are providing relevant, accurate, and reliable information in a format of professional quality, people's interest will be piqued. When you reach people with information that affects their lives, you will have a window of opportunity to move them to some level of action or involvement.

Involvement

This step is critical because it moves people from passivity to active participation. Involvement needs to be recruited on the basis of information disseminated and interest created. At this point, involvement is best solicited personally—face to face:

- ◆ "Bob, I'm going to the school board meeting on Tuesday night, and your presence would be an encouragement to me and the other parents concerned about the new curriculum. Would you be available to join us?"
- ◆ "Sue and Bill, we'd love to have you come over for dinner next Sunday after worship services. Following dinner, our family will be participating in the Life Chain on Main Street, and we thought it would be enjoyable for our families to do this together. Will you join us?"
- ◆ "Cliff, three or four of us are meeting with the police commissioner to address our concerns about teen violence and to brainstorm about what we can do as a church to help keep kids off the streets. I'd like you to be a part of this meeting. Would you be willing to join us?"
- ◆ "Sally, a number of us are attending the town council meeting next Thursday to express our opposition to the proposed domestic partnership ordinance. Would you be willing to come with us?"
- ◆ "George, we're organizing a work day to clean up and repair the city mission two weeks from Saturday. We could greatly use your help. In fact, the whole family is welcome to pitch in. Are you available to join us?"

After recruiting the involvement of the people you have identified, informed, and interested, they may not be ready to make long-term commitments. Begin by soliciting simple one-time action commitments that they will find satisfying. Make them as positive and enjoyable as you can. You can do this by organizing the involvement around other group activities. Follow up the social-political activity with a pizza party, coffee and dessert, or family get-together. Remember the previous discussion about synergy? No one likes to do things alone. Look for things to do together that will provide meaning and significance. These involvement experiences will then lead to longer and deeper commitments, or what I call "investments."

Investment

This reflects the highest degree of commitment to the cause, because at this phase, there is a willingness to contribute one's time, talents, and treasure. At this point, people are asking to be involved, joining the community impact committee, leading a march for life, organizing a voter registration drive, contributing financially to the cause that they so deeply care about, and asking others to do the same. This level of commitment, however, is cultivated. It doesn't happen overnight. A common mistake of many community impact committees is to move from the identification phase to the investment phase by skipping all the important cultivation processes in between. This shortcut leads to frustration and discouragement. Cultivating social involvement takes a long time, and our encouragement to you is to be patient. Gear up for the "long haul." If you follow the social involvement continuum, I am confident you will see increased social and political consciousness, vision, and involvement in your church.

This chapter has been a call to action. Hopefully, it has provided some general ideas, specific action steps, and a model for getting involved in your church and community.

DISCUSSION QUESTIONS

1. Why do you think Christian activists are tempted to neglect the spiritual disciplines? How can they be encouraged to put "first things first"?
2. Explain what is meant by the incarnational and character-centered approach to social and political involvement.

3. Does the biblical concept of calling correspond to the formation of community impact committees? If so, how?

4. What are the five steps for starting a community impact committee? Outline ideas for implementing each step in your church.

5. Why is the development of a mission statement important for community impact committees?

6. How can the "Five I's of Community Impact" be applied to raising the social consciousness of your church?

Can Revival Save America?

by Charles W. Colson

THE BIG IDEA

Charles W. Colson, a former political insider with the Nixon White House, believes American culture will only be profoundly improved when the church appropriates a "holy power" to do it. Our country does not need a revival; the church does. But Colson wonders if we know what revival is. According to him, revival is not the salvation of society or the saving of ourselves and our comfortable lifestyles. Rather, revival is the saving of our souls.

We need revival because sin is in all of us. What good there is in us "comes only through the righteousness of Jesus Christ."

And sin is why we need repentance. Colson argues that biblical repentance is a changing of mind, intellect, and values that occurs when one is confronted by one's own sinfulness in the face of God's holiness. He cites the biblical model of Nehemiah's repenting before rebuilding Jerusalem's walls as an example of the relational order of repentance, spiritual revival, and social reform.

Colson maintains that prayer and Bible study are the "fruits of repentance" and the "life-blood of true spiritual movements." According to Colson, "The most convincing evidence of spiritual awakenings has been their impact on society; a revived church inevitably changes the morality and values of a culture."

◆ ◆ ◆

"Mr. Colson, what's wrong in our country? Why can't we get a revival going that will save America?"

The questioner—a distinguished-looking man in his early 60s—fit comfortably into the opulent surroundings of the downtown city club where I was speaking to 25 community leaders. My topic that morning had been the need for genuine spiritual awakening.

I've been asked the same question hundreds of times, most often by people—like this businessman—who fear runaway inflation and the creeping encroachment of big government. To many of them, *revival* is a magic word. It means having the sort of close relationship with God that just might offer side benefits as well. With traditional values and authority caving in, they hope God can be cajoled by the "revived" into saving our well-heeled lifestyles, protecting our positions and possessions.

The anxieties reflected by this question are epidemic in our nation today. It's understandable—and very human—that amid such uncertain times, we want to cling to what we have, yearning nostalgically for the "good old days." But while millions of Americans, myself included, pray fervently for revival, we must ask ourselves whether we're asking God to save our society, ourselves, or our souls; whether we actually know what God demands of us; whether we really know what revival is.

Normally, I avoid a direct answer to this revival question when I think, as I did that morning, that the questioner is more concerned about his pocketbook than about genuine spiritual awakening. But that morning, tired from tours of several prisons and a hard night on a lumpy hotel mattress, I responded forthrightly. "The real trouble is that we Christians are not willing to accept the gospel for what it is," I said. "It doesn't tell us how to save anything but our souls.

"You see," I continued, "it's a two-edged sword. Jesus came not only to comfort the afflicted, but also to afflict the comfortable. Any hope for revival must begin with genuine repentance, our willingness to give up what we have, and our desire to change."

As I studied the expressions around the table, I realized that idea of giving up what we have—losing our lives for His sake, as Christ tells His disciples to do—is not any more popular today, in our obsessively materialistic society, than it was with the rich young ruler.

Revival is more than salvation from economic troubles, more than protection for our cozy lifestyles. Far from being linked with prosperity or the righting of precarious economies, the great revivals in the history of the church have begun when people have had to submit totally, in ways that seem antithetical (by human and cultural standards) to everything they should have done to survive.

A prime example is England at the time of the Second Great Wesley Awakening. The Christian revival there was evidenced by Parliament's vote to support the crusading Christian parliamentarian Wilberforce and put a stop to the slave trade. That decision of conscience went directly against their own economic interests as a nation.

Recent awakenings in nations such as Romania, Argentina, and the Soviet Union have come about under conditions of great human oppression. The key seems to be that only when individuals, whether by will or by force, subordinate their own interests and desires for self-preservation will God begin to move in a powerful way.

The message for American Christians is the same one Aleksandr Solzhenitsyn learned amid unspeakable human suffering in a Soviet prison: "The meaning of earthly existence is not, as we have grown used to thinking, in prosperity, but in the development of the soul."

Before any awakening can begin, I am convinced that we Christians must come to terms with some hard spiritual truths, just as Solzhenitsyn did in prison. Instead of "using" the gospel to protect what we have, we need to come before our sovereign Master in repentance and surrender.

Revival is God's work; man cannot engineer it. But if we, in good conscience, ask our sovereign Creator to favor us with a mighty moving of His Spirit, we must obey His clear commands and never distort His gospel for our own self-seeking purposes.

The gospel is good news. But Jesus never said it was easy news. The central truth about the cross is death before life, repentance before reward. Before His gospel can be the good news of redemption, before we can experience revival, we must accept the bad news that we are, each and every one, the worst of sinners.

THE TERRIFYING TRUTH: WE ARE ALL NORMAL

In the course of research for my book *Loving God*, I discovered a dearth of contemporary writing on sin. After a long search, however, an unlikely source—Mike Wallace of "60 Minutes"—furnished just what I was looking for. Since Christians are not accustomed to gleaning theological insights from network TV, I'd better explain.

Introducing a recent story about Nazi Adolf Eichmann, a principal architect of the Holocaust, Wallace posed a central question at the program's outset: "How is it possible . . . for a man to act as Eichmann acted? . . . Was he a monster? A madman? Or was he perhaps something even more terrifying: Was he normal?"

Normal? The executioner of millions of Jews *normal?* Most self-respecting viewers would be outraged at the very thought.

The most startling answer to Wallace's shocking question, however, came in an interview with Yehiel Dinur, a concentration camp survivor who testified against Eichmann at his trial in 1961. A film clip of the proceedings showed Dinur walking into the courtroom, stopping short, and seeing Eichmann for the first time since the Nazi had sent him to Auschwitz 18 years earlier. Dinur began to sob uncontrollably, then fainted, collapsing in a heap on the floor as the presiding judicial officer pounded his gavel for order in the crowded courtroom.

Was Dinur overcome by hatred? Fear? Horrid memories?

No; it was none of those. Rather, as Dinur explained to Wallace, all at once he realized Eichmann was not the godlike army officer who had sent so many to their deaths. This Eichmann was an ordinary man. "I was afraid about myself," said Dinur. "I saw that I am capable to do this. *I am . . . exactly like he.*"

Because we must never forget the evil that lurks in man...

Reprinted with permission of Copley News Service and Mike Ramirez

Wallace's subsequent summation of Dinur's terrible discovery—"Eichmann is in all of us"—is a horrifying statement, but it indeed captures the central truth about man's nature. For as a result of the Fall, *sin is in each of us*—not just the susceptibility to sin, but sin itself.

The 3,500 years of recorded history confirm this truth. Science, evolution, and education—which Socrates argued would eliminate sin—have done nothing to alter man's moral nature. Only the gospel of Jesus Christ can change our hearts. But we can't see that truth unless we first see our hearts as they really are.

Why, then, is sin so seldom written or preached about? Dinur's dramatic collapse in the courtroom gives us the clue. For to truly confront evil—the sin within us—is a devastating experience.

If the reality of man's sin was forthrightly preached, it would have the same shattering effect on blissful churchgoers that it had on Dinur. Many would flee their pews, never to return. And since church growth is today's supreme standard of spirituality, many pastors steer away from such confrontational subjects; so do authors who want their books bought and read. So do television preachers whose success depends on audience ratings.

The result is that the message is often watered down to a palatable gospel of positive thinking that will "hold the audience." That's what Nazi victim Dietrich Bonhoeffer called "cheap grace"—that in which "no contrition is required, still less any real desire to be delivered from sin."

But the very heart of a Christian conversion is to confront one's own sin and to desperately desire deliverance from it. Once we've seen our sin, we can only live in gratitude for God's amazing grace. I know this most intimately from personal experience.

During the throes of Watergate, I went to talk with my friend Tom Phillips. I was curious, maybe even a little envious, about the changes in his life. His explanation—that he had "accepted Jesus Christ"—baffled me. I was tired, empty inside, sick of scandal and accusations, but not once did I see myself as having really sinned. Politics was a dirty business, and I was good at it. And what I had done, I rationalized, was no different from the usual political maneuvering. What's more, right and wrong were relative, and my motives were for the good of the country—or so I believed.

But that night, when I left Tom's home and sat alone in my car, my own sin—not just dirty politics, but also the hatred and pride and evil so deep within me—was thrust before my eyes, forcefully and painfully. For the first time in my life, I felt unclean. And worst of all, I could not escape. In those moments of clarity, I found myself driven irresistibly into the arms of the living God.

In the years since that night, I've grown increasingly aware of my own sinful nature; what is good in me I know beyond all doubt comes only through the righteousness of Jesus Christ. And for that *fact*, my gratitude to God deepens with each passing day, a gratitude that can only be expressed in His service.

Dinur, the Auschwitz survivor, is right—Eichmann is in us, each of us. But until we can face that truth, dreadful as it may be, cheap grace and lukewarm faith—the hallmarks of ungrateful hearts—will continue to abound, and we will never experience true revival.

SORRY ENOUGH TO HURT

Many remember Mickey Cohen, infamous gangster of the post-war era. One night Cohen attended an evangelistic meeting and seemed interested. Realizing what a dramatic impact his conversion could have on the world, many Christian leaders began visiting him. After one long night session, he was urged to open the door and let Christ in, based on Revelation 3:20. Cohen responded.

But as the months passed, people saw no change in his life of crime. When confronted, he responded that no one had told him he would have to give up his work or his friends! After all, there were Christian football players, Christian cowboys, Christian politicians; why not a Christian gangster?

It was only then that he was told about repentance. And from that point, he wanted nothing to do with Christianity. What happened to Mickey Cohen is an unhappy illustration of what happens when, in our zeal to win people to Christ, we try to make the gospel more "appealing."

Repentance is one of the prerequisites for revival that we often ignore. Contemporary sermons and books on the subject are rare. Because it can be an offense, as I discovered the morning I confronted 25 affluent business leaders with the need to repent, Christians often don't want to talk about it.

Jesus' evangelistic message, on the other hand, was plain and pointed: "Repent and believe the good news!" (Mark 1:15). Like John the Baptist before Him, Jesus consistently preached repentance. It is, in fact, the keynote of His message, the cornerstone upon which faith must rest.

To many, repentance conjures up images of breast beating, self-flagellation, or a monastic life of self-denial in sackcloth and ashes. The biblical meaning, however, is far less theatrical. Paul described it as "sorrow over sin." He wrote to the Corinthians, "Now I am happy ... because your sorrow led to repentance. ... Godly sorrow brings repentance that leads to salvation and leaves no regret, but worldly sorrow brings death" (2 Cor. 7:9-10).

Repentance is, as a prisoner in South Carolina said, "when you are so sorry that it hurts." When we truly understand the condition in us that causes us to lie, cheat, and hate, we are inescapably made sorrowful. And that sorrow leads to a desire to change, to want the righteousness of God in place of our own sinful selves.

The Greek word for "repentance" found in the New Testament is *metanoia: meta*, meaning "change," and *noia*, meaning "mind." Repentance, as Christ preached it, is a changing of the mind, the intellect, the values. That inevitably produces a profound change of the heart and emotions, a total, radical transformation from seeking to please self to seeking to please God. Repentance leads to nothing less than a human revolution. And *that* is revival.

The majority in prison with whom we work understand repentance; they can identify with the poignant moments of Jesus' death on the cross, with two thieves hanging on either side. The first thief saw Jesus as a way out. "Aren't you the Christ?" he taunted. "Save yourself and us!" It's the way all of us instinctively react in tight spots. We call upon God to save our skins.

But the second thief understood the deeper spiritual reality. "We are getting what our deeds deserve," he rebuked the first. "But this man has done nothing wrong." *That is repentance*—seeing one's sin and recognizing the holiness of God.

"Remember me," he then asked Jesus. And our Lord replied, "I tell you the truth, today you will be with me in paradise" (see Luke 23:39-43). *That is the result of repentance.*

Repentance is demanded not only for our individual sins, but for the sins for which we inescapably share responsibility as well. We are part and parcel of the society in which we live and the church to which we belong. One of my favorite Old Testament figures is Nehemiah. He clearly understood the need to repent for himself and for the sins of his people. Before undertaking the seemingly impossible task of bringing the exiled Jews back to Jerusalem and rebuilding its walls, Nehemiah confessed "the sins we Israelites, including myself and my father's house, have committed against you" (1:6). A repentant Nehemiah was greatly used by God; revival followed in the land.

The issue today is whether we are to be a church of Mickey Cohens or a church of Nehemiahs. Just as there is no individual salvation without repentance, so there can be no spiritual power in an unrepentant church. Southern Baptist scholar Foy Valentine sums it up in his magnificent book *What Do You Do After You Say Amen?* "Without a fundamental change of mind about all sin, a stuttering, stumbling, stalling church can never act redemptively in a sinful world."

And the church acting redemptively in a fallen, sick world is the only key to survival and the hope of mankind.

LIFE-BLOOD FOR REPENTANT HEARTS

Pollster George Gallup has reported that one in three American adults is born again, 84 percent believe the Ten Commandments are valid today, and church attendance and missions giving are at record levels. Yet, despite these signs of religious resurgence, pornography is rampant, more children are aborted than born, violent crime is epidemic, and the family is disintegrating.

Historically, the most convincing evidence of spiritual awakenings has been their impact on society; a revived church inevitably changes the morality and values of a culture. Why is it not happening today?

One reason is our failure to heed the biblical call to prayer. Repentance produces total dependence on God, which leads to reliance on prayer. Indeed, the significant Christian awakenings of past centuries have been marked by intense, fervent prayer.

I was reminded of the centrality of prayer to spiritual vitality when, during a trip to the Orient, I preached at the Full Gospel Church of Seoul, Korea, reportedly the largest church in the world. When I stood in the pulpit, I was awed not by size—15,000 people crammed in the sanctuary and 10,000 in overflow halls for just one of the six Sunday services—but by the sense of God's Spirit moving powerfully.

Later, as the pastor explained the workings of the church, the source of that power became clear. The church membership is divided into thousands of cell groups that meet every morning for two hours of Bible study and prayer. The real church is in the homes; Sunday morning is simply the culmination of a week of intense worship.

Prayer and Bible study are fruits of repentance, the life-blood of true spiritual movements.

Paul wrote in 1 Corinthians 15:31, "I die every day," meaning that repentance is more than a one-time confession. Only as we continue our desire to change—the very essence of repentance—can we grow in grace and a continuing, deepening appreciation of God's grace and mercy. This is the key, I believe, to Christian impact on society, the answer to the great paradox of our time.

I've talked with hundreds of Prison Fellowship volunteers, often trying to determine why they selflessly toil in prisons. There is no glory, no fame for them there. Though their words may vary, their answer is always the same. They see their service as the only possible response to God's grace. For it is out of gratitude to God for His grace and mercy that the Christian is moved to serve Christ in this sick world.

We share the Good News, feed the hungry, visit the imprisoned, seek justice for the oppressed, and care for the widows and orphans, not because we are do-gooders or taken in by a social gospel, but out of appreciation for what God has done in our lives. When Christians by the millions practice this kind of obedience in all walks of life, we will see the culture profoundly affected; for the strongholds of Satan cannot stand against that kind of holy power.

Only God can bring revival. And when it comes, we may be surprised: It may not make life easier but harder. Still, if we have any expectation or hope that He will so favor us, we'd best get down to serious and sacred business. And the place to begin, as Jesus commanded, is with repentant hearts.

◆ ◆ ◆

DISCUSSION QUESTIONS

1. According to Colson, what is revival?
2. Explain the meaning of the idea that "Eichmann is in all of us."
3. What is repentance, and how does it relate to revival?
4. Colson maintains that "the most convincing evidence of spiritual awakenings has been their impact on society." What spiritual awakenings in the past support or challenge this idea?
5. In Colson's view, what are the "fruits of repentance" and the "lifeblood of true spiritual movements"?
6. Are revivals worked up or prayed down? Explain your answer.

Reclaiming the Culture:
An Annotated Bibliography

by Alan R. Crippen II

On the genealogy of an idea:

> Abraham Kuyper begat H.R. Rookmaaker; H.R. Rookmaaker begat
> Francis Schaeffer; Francis Schaeffer begat Beverly LaHaye and everyone
> else who speaks about "secular humanism."
> —Professor D. Clair Davis, Westminster Theological Seminary

In 1990, Dr. James C. Dobson and Gary L. Bauer co-authored *Children at Risk:
Winning the Battle for the Hearts and Minds of Your Children*. Their book offers an
insightful analysis of America's "Second Civil War," in which the fields of battle
are public school classrooms, television, pop culture, church, and family. This conflict is, according to Dr. Dobson, "a great civil war of values" where "two sides
with vastly different and incompatible world-views are locked in a bitter conflict
that permeates every level of society . . . the struggle now is for the hearts and
minds of the people. It is a war of ideas."

In this conflict, if the family is to be defended, it must be defended on the
battlefield of ideas. There can be no question that the unraveling of the social
order testifies to the truth that ideas have consequences—that bad ideas have
bad consequences, as Greg Jesson has demonstrated in chapter 3. Like a cavalry
troop's guidon, our rallying flag in this ideological struggle is that good ideas
have good consequences. Christianity has the most positively powerful ideas
in the world. The ideas of love, compassion, truth, righteousness, justice, mercy,
forgiveness, and so on are revolutionary concepts on both the personal and
social level. That bad ideas have overrun good ideas of late is not due to the
inherent weakness of the good ideas but to the inability of Christians to propose
and defend them. In short, we have failed to "be prepared to give an answer to

everyone who asks ... the reason for the hope"[1] that we have.

Christian ideas and values began to lose their influence in Europe and America centuries ago. Christians lost the intellectual battle on the field of ideas, and ever since, we have become increasingly marginalized in the culture, so much so that in many places the culture is even against us. Today, we are witnessing the destructive social effects of materialism, radical individualism, moral relativism, subjectivism, militant feminism, homosexual activism, and barnyard morality. Our nation and our communities need good ideas to supplant these bad ones. Indeed, our culture is crying out for new ideas, new approaches, new answers, and new solutions to stem the unraveling of the social order. As Irving Kristol has observed, "The beginning of political wisdom in the 1990s is the recognition that liberalism today is at the end of its intellectual tether."[2]

Dr. James Dobson shares a similar observation: "The stranglehold that the 'cultural elites' have held on America is coming to an end."[3] In other words, because of the bankruptcy of these bad ideas, their assumptions are giving way. The crises in family life, education, media, law, government, and business provide an opportunity for Christians to let their light shine. People, such as your neighbors, are beginning to ask questions. This means that you now have a new opportunity to give an answer to everyone who asks the reason for the hope that you have.

Where can you go to find the reasons? Books. Books contain the great ideas that will help us and our neighbors pick up the shattered pieces of our culture and rebuild it with the Christian ideals, values, and virtues that produced Western civilization. In chapter 9, Diane Hesselberg conveys the insight of Christian activist Stephen Fellows: "If people would just read and become knowledgeable ... they could make a real difference." In the spirit of this counsel, I have compiled the following list of books to point you in the direction of further study so that you can make "a real difference" in your community.

The bibliography is divided into the following interest categories: The Quick-Study Essential Reading List; On the Unraveling of the Social Order; Understanding Our Culture; Church-State Relations; Making the Case; Histories of Christian Social and Political Involvement; Christian Political Biographies; and Religion and Society. In each section, I have tried to rank the books in an order of priority for reading.

THE QUICK-STUDY ESSENTIAL READING LIST

If you are interested in girding yourself in the foundational principles of Christian social and political involvement, or are seeking a short survivor's course on Christian activism, the following books have my highest recommendation:

Decisive Issues Facing Christians Today by John R.W. Stott (Revell, 1984,1990)
> This book is perhaps the best case for Christian social and political involvement in print. Stott presents a compelling call to integrate evangelism with social action. This book is unequalled for equipping you for your unique role and purpose at work, at home, in the classroom, in our nation, and as a member of our global community.

A Christian Manifesto by Francis A. Schaeffer (Crossway, 1981)
> A practical discussion about the Christian's relationship to government, law, and civil disobedience. Demonstrating how adherence to either of two competing worldviews—relativism versus Judeo-Christian thought—determines one's position on virtually every critical social issue, Schaeffer illustrates the undesirable results of secularism in law and government. His exhortation to view all of culture as being under Christ's lordship is especially pervasive and noteworthy.

Against the Night: Living in the New Dark Ages by Charles W. Colson (Servant Books, 1989)
> A highly readable critique of American culture and an absorbing challenge for Christians to stand firm by regaining a vision of what it truly means to live as members of the Kingdom of God. Colson's discussion of relativism is especially valuable and accessible.

Culture Wars: The Struggle to Define America by James Davison Hunter (Basic Books, 1991)
> Is probably the best mapping of our socio-political battlefields. Hunter, an evangelical and professor of sociology and religion at the University of Virginia, says the "fault-lines" are not economic, ethnic, nor racial, but competing worldviews or different visions of human origin and end.

The Naked Public Square: Religion and Democracy in America by Richard John Neuhaus (Eerdmans, 1984,1986)
> Neuhaus is one of today's foremost authorities on religion and society, and this book is must-reading for anyone interested in advancing the church-state debate.

ON THE UNRAVELING OF THE SOCIAL ORDER

For those interested in reading more about the social dynamics of the moral crises facing our nation and local communities, the following books should prove interesting:

The Index of Leading Cultural Indicators: Facts and Figures on the State of American Society by William J. Bennett (Touchstone, 1994)
> A moral, social, and cultural report card on America. Bennett monitors social data on issues relating to crime, family and children, youth pathologies, education, pop culture, and religion since 1960. What he finds are sweeping and alarming trends about American society.

The De-Valuing of America: The Fight for Our Culture and Our Children
by William J. Bennett (Focus on the Family, 1992,1994)

> A personal account of Bennett's years in government service as chairman of the National Endowment for the Humanities, secretary of education, and director of the Office of National Drug Control Policy. Calling for a return to morality and discipline while condemning bureaucratic waste and shifting standards, Bennett provides an insightful analysis of what's wrong with our culture, who's at fault, and how it can be reclaimed for our children's future.

Before the Shooting Begins: Searching for Democracy in America's Culture War by James Davison Hunter (The Free Press, 1994)

> A sequel to *Culture Wars* (as cited above) and continues the analysis begun in his earlier work. His insight concerning the use of rhetoric and the effects of multiculturalism are especially helpful.

Virtual America by George Barna (Regal, 1994)

> Evaluates social data that is helpful to understanding America's "reshaped reality." This book explores the most current research on changes in American life, including thought, word, and action.

The American Hour: A Time of Reckoning and the Once and Future Role of Faith by Os Guinness (The Free Press, 1993)

> As a sociologist and former associate of Francis Schaeffer, Guinness provides a penetrating analysis of America's crisis of cultural authority in this book.

UNDERSTANDING OUR CULTURE

In addition to Colson's *Against the Night* (cited above), for those interested in reading more about the ideas that have brought our culture to its present crisis, I recommend the following:

Post-Modern Times: A Christian Guide to Contemporary Thought and Culture by Gene Edward Veith Jr. (Crossway, 1994)

> A valuable examination of post-modernism and its creed that truth, meaning, and individual identity do not exist (except as social constructs); that human life has no special significance above plant and animal life; and that all social relationships, institutions, and values are no more than expressions of will to power. Veith helps the reader to understand how a Christian can counter this prevailing culture and proclaim the sufficiency of Christ to our society's most pressing needs.

Escape from Reason by Francis A. Schaeffer (InterVarsity, 1968)

> In the spirit of communicating the gospel on the eve of the twenty-first century, Schaeffer explains how Western thought has been characterized by a dualism of fact and value, faith and reason. This situation has lead modern humanity into a "leap in the dark," non-rational world. Schaeffer helps the reader understand

the thinking patterns of today for more effectively communicating the unchanging truth of God's Word.

How Should We Then Live? by Francis A. Schaeffer (Crossway, 1983)

This popular classic provocatively provides "an analysis of the key moments in history which have formed our present culture, and the thinking of the people who brought those moments to pass." Furthermore, the book offers some solutions to the many problems we face today.

Twilight of a Great Civilization: The Drift Toward Neo-Paganism by Carl F.H. Henry (Crossway, 1988)

A prophetic clarion call to Christians concerning the culture's rejection of God and the Judeo-Christian foundation of Western civilization. It is helpful for understanding the tragic drift of American culture and what can be done about it. This book influenced Charles W. Colson to write *Against the Night*.

When Tolerance is No Virtue: Political Correctness, Multiculturalism and the Future of Truth and Justice by S.D. Gaede (InterVarsity, 1993)

An excellent primer on the ideology of multiculturalism and political correctness that has beleaguered our educational system and heralded the death of ideas. Gaede affirms the virtue of tolerance, but not at the expense of truth. Rather, tolerance should be viewed as a means to an end (the truth), rather than the end itself.

Christian Reflections by C.S. Lewis (Eerdmans, 1967,1992)

This book offers some insightful essays on our culture. Especially helpful are the essays "On Ethics," "The Poison of Subjectivism," and "De Futilitate."

The Abolition of Man: How Education Develops Man's Sense of Morality by C.S. Lewis (MacMillan, 1947,1978)

A masterful defense of objective moral absolutes and a warning of the danger of ignoring their existence in the education of our children.

Idols for Destruction: Christian Faith and Its Confrontation with American Society by Herbert Schlossberg (Crossway, 1993)

A provocative critique of contemporary culture from a Christian perspective. Schlossberg utilizes the biblical motif of idolatry as a framework for understanding our times.

What's Wrong with the World by G.K. Chesterton (Sugden, Sherwood & Company, 1992)

A classic work reminding us that "culture wars" are not new: In many ways, we are replaying yesterday's debate. Chesterton's timeless work is a reminder that our clash is one of strategic moral vision.

The Closing of the American Mind: How Higher Education Has Failed Democracy and Impoverished the Souls of Today's Students by Allan Bloom (Simon and Schuster, 1987)

> A powerful critique by a distinguished political philosopher of the intellectual and moral confusions of our age. In his view, America's current political and social crisis is really an intellectual crisis precipitated by the universities that no longer provide the knowledge of the classics that makes students aware of the order of nature and mankind's place within it.

The Crisis of Our Age by Pitirim A. Sorokin (Oneworld, 1941,1992)

> A profound, lucid, and challenging critique of the crisis of modern society as it affects art and science, philosophy and religion, ethics and law—our entire culture. According to Sorokin, the whole advancement of human history is caught in a titanic cycle of materialistic and spiritual cultures, each collapsing and being replaced by the other. As early as 1941, Sorokin observed that the current materialistic order was near collapse. With this anticipation, he offered a positive vision of the transformation of values and lifestyles to a more spiritual understanding of humanity.

The Culture of Narcissism: American Life in an Age of Diminishing Expectations by Christopher Lasch (W.W. Norton, 1979)

> A superb and penetrating analysis of America's social and moral condition from an unlikely source—a Freudian, neomarxist historian. Though not written from a Christian perspective, Lasch's critique is helpful.

Modern Times: The World from the Twenties to the Eighties by Paul Johnson (Harper & Row, 1983)

> A brilliant history of our modern culture beginning with the first chapter, "A Relativistic World."

Civilisation by Kenneth Clark (Harper & Row, 1969)

> This book distills the essence of all that is precious in our heritage. In his view, our civilization is in jeopardy by a new upsurge of barbarism.

Modern Art and the Death of a Culture by H.R. Rookmaaker (Crossway, 1970,1973,1994)

> A uniquely Christian assessment of modern culture through an evaluation of its art. Rookmaaker was a close friend and associate of the late Francis Schaeffer.

The Dust of Death: The Sixties Counterculture and How It Changed America Forever by Os Guinness (Crossway, 1994)

> This book charts the journey of the '60s generation—out from the technological wasteland and into the "Promised Land" of radical politics, Eastern religion, psychedelic drugs, and the occult. Guinness rejects both technological society and the '60s' counterculture, calling for a "Third Way."

CHURCH-STATE RELATIONS

In addition to Neuhaus's *The Naked Public Square* (cited above), I recommend the following books for those interested in the church-state debate:

The Culture of Disbelief: How American Law and Politics Trivialize Religious Devotion by Stephen L. Carter (Basic Books, 1993)

> Carter is a Yale University School of Law professor who has received much attention in the news media. President Clinton has read the book and endorsed its thesis that religion should be taken more seriously in American public life, especially in the courts and legislatures.

Religious Liberty in the Supreme Court: The Cases that Define the Debate Over Church and State, Terry Eastland, editor (Ethics and Public Policy Center, 1993)

> This volume contains 25 of the most important Supreme Court opinions on church-state questions with various contemporary reactions to those decisions, as well as three essays by well-known legal scholars on First Amendment jurisprudence.

Religion and Politics: The Intentions of the Authors of the First Amendment by Michael J. Malbin (American Enterprise Institute, 1978)

> Malbin argues that the modern Supreme Court has almost reversed the original understanding of the two religion clauses of the First Amendment. This booklet is a brief and well-researched primer on the subject.

Articles of Faith, Articles of Peace: The Religious Liberty Clauses and the American Public Philosophy, James Davison Hunter and Os Guinness, editors (Brookings Institution, 1990)

> This book examines the contemporary challenges to religious liberty and explores ways to answer the vital question: How do we, in an age of expanding pluralism, live with our deepest differences? Several distinguished contributors offer thought-provoking discussions on this question.

Religion, Public Life and the American Polity, Luis E. Lugo, editor (University of Tennessee, 1994)

> The essayists offer valuable historical interpretations, as well as contemporary insights on the church-state dilemma.

Faith and Order: The Reconciliation of Law and Religion by Harold J. Berman (Scholars Press, 1993)

> Berman argues for the mutually supporting roles of religious faith and legal order in society, because, "At the highest level, surely the just and holy are one." Showing how religious beliefs have shaped constitutional law, criminal law, and contract law, he exposes the fallacies of current law theories that fail to account for religious dimensions.

Positive Neutrality: Letting Religious Freedom Ring by Stephen V. Monsma
(Greenwood, 1993)
>The author argues for the recognition of pluralism and for government to
>act with "positive neutrality" toward all religious and nonreligious groups in
>our society. Monsma says the Supreme Court should stop thinking in terms
>of sacred/secular in trying to keep government free of entanglement in reli-
>gion. Rather, the Court should look to see if any group is being favored by
>law and whether state aid is supporting programs with "direct, this-world
>benefits."

Neither King Nor Prelate: Religion and the New Nation 1776-1826 by Edwin
S. Gaustad (Eerdmans, 1987,1993)
>An excellent book on the history of church-state relations with respect to the
>founders. Gaustad portrays the religious life of the nation from the time of the
>Revolution to the deaths of Thomas Jefferson and John Adams, while consider-
>ing the developing relationship between church and state in America.

The First Liberty: Religion and the American Republic by William Lee Miller
(Alfred A. Knopf, 1986)
>Another helpful history that re-creates the fierce debates among the founding
>fathers over the means of establishing public virtue in the absence of an estab-
>lished religion.

*A Government of Laws: Political Theory, Religion, and the American
Founding* by Ellis Sandoz (Louisiana State University Press, 1990)
>A searching analysis of the sources of political and constitutional theory of the
>American founders. Much attention is given to the distinctively Christian and
>spiritual aspects in the political thinking of the founders.

*Founding Fathers: Brief Lives of the Framers of the United States
Constitution* by M.E. Bradford (University of Kansas, 1981,1982,1994)
>Bradford offers perhaps the only concise compilation of short biographies on
>the founders available. The founders included a shoemaker, surveyor, lawyer,
>jurist, lay theologian, and statesman.

Undermined Establishment: Church State Relations in America 1880–1920
by Robert T. Handy (Princeton, 1991)
>This book chronicles a pivotal period in American history marking the passage
>of a Christian and largely Protestant America to a more pluralistic nation
>comprised of greater religious diversity. The result was increasing conflicts
>between public and private school systems, excitement over imperialism, the
>growth of progressive politics, the rise of the social gospel, and the impact of
>World War I. Handy shows how these developments affected church-state
>relations.

MAKING THE CASE

Books that should be helpful for making your case in the public square are as follows:

Roaring Lambs: A Gentle Plan to Radically Change Your World by Bob Briner (Zondervan, 1993)
> Briner offers a practical strategy for re-entering the world for God and His Kingdom by believing that the Christian faith and its teaching belong in every arena of public discourse.

Uncommon Decency: Christian Civility in an Uncivil World by Richard J. Mouw (InterVarsity, 1992)
> This book is helpful for learning how to communicate with people who disagree with you on the issues that matter most.

Evangelism: Doing Justice and Preaching Grace by Harvie M. Conn (Presbyterian and Reformed, 1982)
> Conn offers a practical model for integrating evangelism and social action.

The Samaritan Strategy: A New Agenda for Christian Activism by Colonel V. Donor (Wolgemuth & Hyatt, 1988)
> The author provides a compassionate and comprehensive vision of hope for the future through social and political action.

Life-Style Evangelism: Crossing Traditional Boundaries to Reach the Unbelieving World and *Gentle Persuasion: Creative Ways to Introduce Your Friends to Christ* by Joseph C. Aldrich (Multnomah, 1981 and 1988)
> These volumes speak directly to issues of personal evangelism. However, the principles contained in these books can be applied to social and political involvement.

God in the Dock: Essays on Theology and Ethics by C.S. Lewis (Eerdmans, 1970)
> Lewis offers several helpful essays, including: "Christian Apologetics" and "Before We Can Communicate."

HISTORIES OF CHRISTIAN SOCIAL AND POLITICAL INVOLVEMENT

One of the best-kept secrets is that Christians were socially and politically active long before the formation of the Moral Majority in 1979. A case can be made that this involvement began nearly two millennia ago. The books that follow specifically focus on Christian social and political involvement in American history:

Discovering an Evangelical Heritage by Donald W. Dayton (Hendrickson, 1976,1992)
> An informative study of the nineteenth century reform movements led by evangelical Christians. Chapters on Jonathan Blanchard, Wheaton College founder and abolitionist; Charles G. Finney, father of modern revivalism; and Catherine Booth, cofounder of the Salvation Army make fascinating reading.

One Nation Under God? Christian Faith and Political Action in America by Mark A. Noll (Harper & Row, 1988)
> Addresses the style, strategies, and influence of Christian political action in America's history. Furthermore, Noll offers principles to guide Christian political action in our own times.

Religion and American Politics: From the Colonial Period to the 1980s, Mark A. Noll, editor (Oxford, 1990)
> In this work, several scholars examine how religion and politics have interacted in American history.

Religion and American Culture by George M. Marsden (Harcourt Brace Jovanovich, 1990)
> This book offers an interpretive account of religion and culture exploring the intriguing issues of how American religion fits into American civilization.

Fundamentalism and American Culture: The Shaping of Twentieth-Century Evangelicalism 1870-1925 by George M. Marsden (Oxford, 1980) and its sequel *Understanding Fundamentalism and Evangelicalism* (Eerdmans, 1991)
> Both are excellent histories that pay special attention to social, political, intellectual, and distinctly American aspects of Protestant fundamentalism and evangelicalism.

The Search for Christian America, Mark A. Noll, Nathan O. Hatch, and George M. Marsden, editors (Helmers & Howard, 1983,1989)
> This book takes on the "Christian America" debate in a scholarly fashion by examining America's religious past and the influence of Christian ideas in society. It is a valuable discussion on how history should inform our response to the challenges we face today.

A Christian America: Protestant Hopes and Historical Realities by Robert T. Handy (Oxford, 1971,1984)
> Handy explores the efforts of Protestant denominations to Christianize the United States in the nineteenth and twentieth centuries.

Religion in American Public Life by A. James Reichley (Brookings, 1985)
> A scholarly historical study of the actual impact of religion and religious groups on American public life. The book also offers a valuable discussion of how the involvement of religious groups can be carried on within the constitutional context of the separation of church and state.

Spiritual Politics: Religion and America Since World War II by Mark Silk (Touchstone, 1988)

> A helpful modern history of religion and public life. Silk traces intriguing connections between religion and politics in the Cold War, the civil rights and antiwar movements, and the religious right's link with conservative populism.

Under God: Religion and American Politics by Garry Wills (Simon & Schuster, 1990)

> This book moves back to show the continuity of present controversies with past religious struggles. Wills demonstrates how religion has been a progressive force in American politics. (The first abolitionists, women's suffrage groups, and civil rights groups were associated with churches.) Though Wills is politically liberal, his historical interpretation is valuable. The influence of evangelicals William Jennings Bryan and Francis Schaeffer in American politics receives favorable treatment in this book.

No Longer Exiles: The Religious New Right in American Politics, Michael Cromartie, editor (Ethics and Public Policy Center, 1993) and ***Disciples and Democracy***, Michael Cromartie, editor (Ethics and Public Policy Center/Eerdmans, 1994)

> Excellent discussions on the impact of the religious right in the politics of the 1990s. For those interested in the current political landscape, Cromartie's books will prove helpful.

CHRISTIAN POLITICAL BIOGRAPHIES

To get a closer look at some of the people whose faith dramatically influenced public policy and social issues, the following books are recommended:

Saints in Politics: The 'Clapham Sect' and the Growth of Freedom by Ernest Marshall Howse (George, Allen & Unwin, 1953,1976)

> This book brings to life the people, personalities, and convictions of the religious reform group led by William Wilberforce in England during the late eighteenth and early nineteenth centuries. Despite staunch opposition from the British ruling classes, this committed "brotherhood of Christian politicians" set in motion the moral, philanthropic, and religious ideas that later transformed England and her colonies.

God's Politician: William Wilberforce's Struggle to Abolish the Slave Trade and Reform the Morals of a Nation by Garth Lean (Helmers & Howard, 1987)

> An insightful and stirring account of how Wilberforce and his colleagues in the "Clapham Sect" put their faith into action and changed the course of history.

The Practice of Political Spirituality: Episodes from the Public Career of Abraham Kuyper, 1879-1918 by McKendree R. Langley (Paideia Press, 1984)
> A stirring account of a pastor, educator, and journalist who eventually became prime minister of the Netherlands, leading his nation's social and moral reform. This book evaluates his Christian vision and tireless efforts to apply the Christian faith to political life.

William Ewart Gladstone: Faith and Politics in Victorian England by David W. Bebbington (Eerdmans, 1993)
> The story of a nineteenth century British politician and prime minister of Great Britain who was regarded as the greatest Christian statesman of his day. Gladstone operated from a thoroughly Christian worldview, incorporating his faith into every sphere of life.

Liberty of Conscience: Roger Williams in America by Edwin S. Gaustad (Eerdmans, 1991)
> A moving biography of the founder of Rhode Island and champion of religious liberty. Gaustad discusses Williams's significance in his own day as well as his legacy in American constitutional history.

William Jennings Bryan: Champion of Democracy by LeRoy Ashby (Twayne, 1987)
> A probing examination of one of America's most important evangelical politicians. Bryan was not only Woodrow Wilson's secretary of state, three times a democratic candidate for president, and champion of the common people, but he was also the prosecuting attorney in the infamous Scopes Monkey Trial. Ashby helps the reader understand this fascinating leader.

RELIGION AND SOCIETY

The following books are included for persons interested in studying the relationship between religion and society:

Christ and Culture by H. Richard Niebuhr (Harper & Row, 1951,1975)
> A classic survey of various Christian approaches to culture. Some major categories he includes are "Christ Against Culture," "Christ Above Culture," and "Christ Transforming Culture." This book will be immensely helpful for your own thinking on social involvement and for understanding why other Christians think and act as they do.

Creation Regained: Biblical Basics for a Reformational Worldview by Albert M. Wolters (Eerdmans, 1985,1994)
> An excellent and concise statement on the essentials of a Christian worldview. The book contains several helpful family and public policy analogies and illustrations. As a blueprint for thinking "Christianly" about issues, it is highly recommended.

Lectures on Calvinism by Abraham Kuyper (Eerdmans, 1931,1987)
    Probably the best manifesto on cultural engagement from a "Christ-transforming-culture" perspective. Do not let the title scare you. "Calvinism" as used in this book refers to a distinctly Protestant Christian worldview. The writings of Abraham Kuyper, a pastor, theologian, and former prime minister of the Netherlands, were influential in Francis A. Schaeffer's understanding of how the Christian faith engages culture.

God and Politics: Four Views on the Reformation of Civil Government, Gary Scott Smith, editor (Presbyterian and Reformed, 1989)
    This book discusses four approaches to politics within the "Christ-transforming-culture" perspective. Sixteen contributors representing theonomy, principled pluralism, Christian America, and national confessionalism engage each other in a lively exchange of ideas on how Christians should work more effectively in the public square.

Citizen Christians: The Rights and Responsibilities of Dual Citizenship, Richard D. Land and Louis A. Moore, editors, (Broadman & Holman, 1994)
    This book will be of special interest to Southern Baptist readers. This book contains a collection of essays on current issues by prominent national figures.

Politically Incorrect: The Emerging Faith Factor in American Politics by Ralph Reed (Word, 1994)
    A defense of the political participation rights of religious people that also offers a constructive critique of Christian involvement and noninvolvement.

No God But God: Breaking with the Idols of Our Age, Os Guinness and John Seel, editors (Moody, 1992)
    Chapters two, three, and four are especially relevant to Christian political involvement and provide practical insights on the dangers of politicizing the gospel.

Kingdoms in Conflict by Charles W. Colson (Morrow/Zondervan, 1987)
    A helpful work for navigating the respective religious and political spheres by a former Washington political insider.

Piety and Politics: Evangelicals and Fundamentalists Confront the World, Richard John Neuhaus and Michael Cromartie, editors (Ethics and Public Policy Center, 1987)
    This provocative book on evangelical social and political involvement is an anthology of 26 essays by notable participants and observers of evangelical politics in America.

Being Christian Today: An American Conversation, Richard John Neuhaus and George Weigel, editors (Ethics and Public Policy Center, 1992)
    This is an interdenominational discussion that explores the social-ethical crisis from evangelical Protestant, ecumenical Protestant, and Roman Catholic points

of view. Among the various distinguished contributors, Mark A. Noll's essay "The Scandal of Evangelical Political Reflection" and Carl E. Braaten's essay "Protestants and Natural Law" will be of special interest to evangelicals concerned about political theory.

"William B. Eerdmans Publishing Company's Encounter Series," Richard John Neuhaus, general editor

A helpful "dialogue" about religion and politics in America. Diverse experts from the fields of theology, ethics, philosophy, and public policy encounter one another in a forum on issues. Among this series *The Bible, Politics, and Democracy* (Eerdmans, 1987) and *Unsecular America* (Eerdmans, 1986) are especially helpful for understanding the Christian's role in society.

A Christian Perspective on Political Thought by Stephen Mott (Oxford, 1993)

The author develops the Christian foundation for politics and political evaluations. Mott, an evangelical, evaluates political ideologies and offers a valuable introduction to Christian political thought.

Pluralisms and Horizons by Richard J. Mouw and Sander Griffioen (Eerdmans, 1993)

The authors explore the compatibility of Christianity and modern democratic theory. Mouw and Griffioen specifically address the issue of Christians contributing in a meaningful way to public life in a modern pluralistic society.

Political Order and the Plural Structure of Society, James W. Skillen and Rockne McCarthy, editors (Scholars, 1991)

This anthology examines and compares three varieties of pluralist social theory: (1) historical doctrines of custom and tradition; (2) Catholic doctrines natural law and subsidiarity; and (3) Protestant/Reformed doctrines of common grace and sphere sovereignty. Essays from leading proponents of each view are included.

Recharging the American Experiment: Principled Pluralism for Genuine Civic Community by James W. Skillen (Baker, 1994)

As a Christian political theorist, Skillen offers a solid theoretical framework from which to resolve current disputes in America's culture wars. His chapters on religious freedom and schooling are especially helpful.

The Scattered Voice: Christians at Odds in the Public Square by James W. Skillen (Zondervan, 1990)

A survey of Christian involvement that is helpful for understanding why Christians disagree on social and political issues.

To Empower People: The Role of Mediating Structures in Public Policy by Peter Berger and Richard John Neuhaus (American Enterprise Institute, 1977)

Berger and Neuhaus argue for a more effective role of "mediating structures" such as the family, church, neighborhood, and other voluntary organizations in society. They recommend that government policy ought to strengthen these institutions rather than weaken them.

Building the Free Society: Democracy, Capitalism, and Catholic Social Teaching, George Weigel and Robert Royal, editors (Eerdmans, 1993)

This is a compilation of writing from 10 distinguished Catholics, who examine modern Catholic social doctrine through a review of key Catholic documents written within the last 100 years.

We Hold These Truths: Catholic Reflections on the American Proposition by John Courtney Murray, S.J. (Image, 1960, 1964)

A classic, lucid, and intellectually stimulating overview of the position of Catholicism in American society. Murray asserts that Catholic faith and tradition can coexist, even thrive, in America's pluralistic society. The book explores a number of issues relating to the First Amendment, such as state aid to parochial schools, religion in universities, censorship, morality and war, and the relevance of natural law theory to the political challenges facing America. This book is not only a challenge to Catholics, but to all Americans of religious conviction.

In Search of a National Morality: A Manifesto for Evangelicals and Catholics, William Bentley Ball, editor (Baker/Ingnatius, 1992)

A call for the co-belligerency of evangelicals and Catholics on common public interests such as secularization, moral relativism, the sanctity of human life, the family, education, and human rights.

A Topical Index of Community Issue Resources

This appendix contains numerous resources (periodicals, books, and organizations) for community involvement. Not all of the resources contained in the pages that follow are explicitly Christian, nor does their inclusion here constitute an endorsement by Focus on the Family. Immediately listed below are periodicals that would be helpful in keeping you apprised of current issues. Following these resources, you will find a directory of national policy and activist organizations that are involved on the many fronts of America's culture wars. Last of all, several issue-oriented organizations and resources are topically arranged in alphabetical order.

PERIODICALS

Citizen—is available for a suggested donation of $20 per year ($24 in Canada) from Focus on the Family, Colorado Springs, CO 80995; magazine memberships may also be requested by calling 1-800-A-FAMILY. This 16-page monthly periodical covers a broad range of social issues with an emphasis on practical ways to become involved. Stories highlight successful efforts by citizens striving to incorporate pro-family values in their schools, neighborhoods, cities, and states. Editions in many states include a four-page insert from that state's family policy council, providing timely updates regarding legislation and other activities of state and local interest.

Washington Watch—is complimentary upon request from the Family Research Council, 700 13th St., N.W., Suite 500, Washington DC 20005; (202) 393-2100. This four-page monthly newsletter provides late-breaking news from our nation's capital and practical insights for making your voice heard.

First Things—is published by the Institute on Religion and Public Life and is available for $29 per year by writing Department FT, P.O. Box 3000, Denville, NJ 07834-9847, or by calling 1-800-875-2997. Each issue provides thought-provoking and insightful commentary regarding issues of Christianity and our culture.

World—is available for $39.95 for a one-year subscription (40 issues). To order, write to God's World Publications, Inc., at Box 2330, Asheville, NC 28802, or call 1-800-951-NEWS. A 24-page magazine that covers national and international news from a biblical worldview, *World* is an excellent alternative to the major news weeklies.

The Family in America—is available for $24 per year from the Rockford Institute, 934 N. Main St., Rockford, IL 61103-7061; (815) 964-5053. This monthly publication provides in-depth analysis backed by solid research on a broad array of family policy subjects. A "new research" supplement included with each issue makes an excellent library resource.

NATIONAL ORGANIZATIONS
(Think and Do Tanks)

The following organizations provide information and/or resources on a wide array of public policy issues relating to the family. These groups are divided into two categories: (1) oganizations primarily concerned with public policy research and education; and (2) organizations whose primary aim is to initiate political change by informing, equipping, and motivating grassroots efforts.

National Policy Research and Education Organizations

ACTON INSTITUTE
161 Ottawa Street Northwest, Suite 405 K, Grand Rapids, MI 49503; (616) 454-9454.
   The Institute is a nonprofit, nondenominational education and research organization whose mission is to educate the religious community on the moral foundations of free markets, limited government, and individual responsibility.

AMERICAN ENTERPRISE INSTITUTE
1150 Seventeenth Street, N.W., Washington, DC 20036; (202) 862-5800.
   AEI is a policy research and education organization committed to the principles
   of limited government, free enterprise, and individual liberty.

AMERICAN STUDIES PROGRAM
327 Eighth Street, N.E., Washington, DC 20002; (202) 546-3086.
   This is a Washington, D.C.-based undergraduate semester studies program of
   the Coalition of Christian Colleges and Universities. Students explore political
   issues in light of biblical truth through seminars and internship experience on
   Capitol Hill and in various government agencies.

CENTER FOR PUBLIC JUSTICE
P.O. Box 48368, Washington, DC 20002-0368; (410) 263-5909.
> Through policy research and civic education, this organization strives to integrate biblical principles in the public policy debate to promote a more just society.

CROSSROADS
10 East Lancaster Avenue, Wynnewood, PA 19096; (610) 645-9399.
> Crossroads is a network of Christian scholars and policy practitioners, which promotes evangelical reflection on public affairs. Published monographs on a variety of issues are available.

ETHICS AND PUBLIC POLICY CENTER
1015 Fifteenth St., N.W., Suite 900, Washington DC 20005; (202) 682-1200.
> Founded in 1976, EPPC strives to ensure that the Judeo-Christian moral tradition is an essential component in the public policy debate. Its programs include research, writing, and conferences. An extensive list of publications is offered.

HERITAGE FOUNDATION
214 Massachusetts Ave., N.E., Washington, DC 20002; (202) 546-4400.
> The Heritage Foundation is a research and education institute dedicated to formulating and promoting conservative public policies based on principles of free enterprise, limited government, individual freedom, traditional American values, and a strong national defense. Its flagship publication, *Policy Review: The Journal of American Citizenship*, is a bimonthly periodical for advancing the conservative vision of civil society and is available for $22 a year.

INSTITUTE FOR FAMILY STUDIES
8605 Explorer Drive, Colorado Springs, CO, 80920; (719) 548-4560.
> IFS is a division of Focus on the Family that offers an undergraduate semester studies program in which students explore family issues in light of current philosophical, cultural, political, and economic trends through seminars and a practicum experience. Areas of study include philosophy and culture, social policy, psychology, and leadership. The program is endorsed by the Coalition of Christian Colleges and Universities.

INSTITUTE ON RELIGION AND DEMOCRACY
1521 16th Street, N.W., Suite 300, Washington, DC 20036; (202) 986-1440.
> IRD works to advance and strengthen democracy and religious liberty around the world through the church. Founded in 1981 by both Protestants and Catholics, IRD also strives to affect a more constructive Christian involvement in social and political issues through education and resources.

INSTITUTE ON RELIGION AND PUBLIC LIFE
156 Fifth Ave., Suite 400, New York, NY 10010; (212) 627-2288.
> The Institute is an interreligious, nonpartisan research and education organization whose purpose is to promote a religiously informed public philosophy as a

basis for public life. IRPL publishes *First Things: A Monthly Journal of Religion and Public Life*, which is available for $29 per year.

THE ROCKFORD INSTITUTE
934 N. Main St., Rockford, IL 61103; (815) 964-5053.
>The Institute publishes a variety of literature designed to buttress the position of the family and traditional values in society. A monthly journal, *Chronicles* (subtitled "A Magazine of American Culture"), is available for $39 per year.

National Pro-Family Activist Organizations

AMERICAN FAMILY ASSOCIATION
P.O. Drawer 2440, Tupelo, MS 38803; (601) 844-5036.
>AFA is a grassroots organization pressing for the restoration of traditional family values.

CHRISTIAN COALITION
P.O. Box 1990, Chesapeake, VA 23327; (804) 424-2630.
>This organization works to promote pro-family legislation and family-friendly public policy at the local, state, and national levels. Founded by Pat Robertson, the Coalition also distributes a national nonpartisan voter guide.

CHRISTIAN LIFE COMMISSION
Southern Baptist Convention, 901 Commerce St., Suite 550, Nashville, TN 37203; (615) 244-2495.
>The CLC works to educate Christians about critical moral, religious liberty, and public policy issues.

CONCERNED WOMEN FOR AMERICA
370 L'Enfant Promenade, S.W., Suite 800, Washington, DC 20024; (202) 488-7000.
>CWA provides information regarding the status of political, family-oriented issues. This organization also makes federal voting records available during the fall of election years.

EAGLE FORUM
P.O. Box 618, Alton, IL 62002; (618) 462-5415.
>Headed by Phyllis Schlafly, Eagle Forum supports conservative, pro-family policies at every level of government. The organization also publishes the *Phyllis Schlafly Report*, available for $20 per year.

FAMILY RESEARCH COUNCIL
700 13th St., N.W., Suite 500, Washington, DC 20005; (202) 393-2100.
>FRC serves as an advocate for the family in our nation's capital. Under the leadership of former White House adviser Gary Bauer, FRC helps equip citizens at the grassroots level to address family issues and to influence the public policy process.

FREE CONGRESS FOUNDATION
717 Second St., N.E., Washington, DC 20002; (202) 546-3000.
> FCF seeks to restore traditional values to public policy through a multifaceted program of research and education, targeting the grassroots level, opinion leaders and policy makers. National Empowerment Television, a product of FCF, is an innovative effort to link local conservatives with government officials and others in positions of political influence.

NATIONAL ASSOCIATION OF EVANGELICALS
Office of Public Affairs, 1023 15th Street, N.W., Suite 500, Washington, DC 20005; (202) 789-1011.
> The Office of Public Affairs is the public policy arm of the NAE, which seeks to serve the evangelical community as a representative voice in national affairs.

TOWARD TRADITION
P.O. Box 58, Mercer Island, WA 98040; (206) 236-3046.
> Toward Tradition is a national organization that fosters the cooperation of Christians and Jews for an American agenda that injects Judeo-Christian values into our society to help restore a more traditional and conservative vision to culture, economics, and politics.

TRADITIONAL VALUES COALITION
139 C Street, S.E., Washington, DC 20003; (202) 547-8570.
> TVC is a grassroots political action organization that seeks to restore traditional values in public policy discourse and debate.

ABORTION
Organizations
AMERICAN LIFE LEAGUE, INC.
179 Courthouse Road, Stafford, VA 22554; (540) 659-4171.
> ALL is committed to defending the unborn child. Available is a news magazine entitled *Celebrate Life!* which features news of interest regarding the pro-life movement from across the nation (annual subscription is $12.95 for 6 issues).

AMERICANS UNITED FOR LIFE
343 S. Dearborn Street, Suite 100, Chicago, IL 60604; (312) 786-9494.
> This legal arm of the pro-life movement defends life through judicial, legislative, and educational efforts.

CHRISTIAN ACTION COUNCIL
109 Carpenter Drive, Suite 100, Sterling VA 20164; (703) 478-5661.
> The nation's largest Protestant pro-life organization tracks legislation and other political developments regarding the pro-life movement. The Council's CARE NET ministry offers resources and support for nearly 500 crisis pregnancy centers across the United States and Canada and helps develop new CPCs. CARE NET also has a post-abortion ministry.

LIFE ISSUES INSTITUTE
1721 W. Galbraith Road, Cincinnati, OH 45239; (513) 729-3600.
> LII is a pro-life research and education organization. They offer educational materials and products emphasizing the "Love them both" theme.

NATIONAL RIGHT TO LIFE COMMITTEE, INC.
419 Seventh St., N.W., Suite 500, Washington, DC 20004; (202) 626-8800.
> NRLC provides national leadership in the right-to-life movement and seeks passage of pro-life legislation. The *National Right to Life News*, a biweekly newspaper, provides in-depth coverage of pro-life news, including important developments in Congress.

PLEASE LET ME LIVE ("THE LIFE CHAIN PEOPLE")
3209 Colusa Hwy., Yuba City, CA 95993; (916) 671-5500.
> This coalition-building ministry sponsors the National Life Chain in the United States and Canada one afternoon each October. Also available is pro-life literature for door-to-door distribution.

Books—Abortion, General
Politically Correct Death by Francis Beckwith (Baker Book House, 1993).
> Dr. Beckwith has written a compelling book explaining the pro-life position in a logically consistent and reasonable manner. He shows how to argue persuasively for the pro-life perspective.

Abortion: A Rational Look at an Emotional Issue by R.C. Sproul (NavPress, 1990).
> Dr. Sproul removes emotionalism from the abortion debate and rationally answers central questions surrounding this critical issue.

Abortion Rites by Marvin Olasky (Crossway, 1992).

Pro-Life Answers to Pro-Choice Arguments by Randy Alcorn (Multnomah Press, 1992).

Sanctity of Life by Charles Swindoll (Word, 1990).

Whatever Happened to the Human Race? by Francis Schaeffer and C. Everett Koop (Crossway, 1983).

Books—Overpopulation
The Nine Lives of Population Control edited by Michael Cromartie (Ethics and Public Policy Center/Eerdmans, 1995).

Prospects for Growth: A Biblical View of Population, Resources and the Future by E. Calvin Beisner (Crossway, 1989).

The War Against Population: The Economics and Ideology of Population Control by Jacqueline Kasun (Ignatius, 1988).

Books—Helping Women Exploited by Abortion

Ministering to Abortion's Aftermath by Bill Banks and Sue Banks (Impact, 1982).

Abortion's Second Victim by Pam Koerbel (Victor, 1986).

Aborted Women: Silent No More by David C. Reardon (Crossway, 1987).

ADOPTION

Organizations

BETHANY CHRISTIAN SERVICES
901 Eastern Ave., N.E., Grand Rapids, MI 49503; (616) 459-6273.
   Bethany is a private, licensed Christian child-welfare and adoption agency.

NATIONAL COUNCIL FOR ADOPTION
1930 17th St., N.W., Washington, DC 20009; (202) 328-1200.
   The NCFA acts as an advocate for parents and children involved in adoption. It works to define ethical adoption practices at adoption agencies, consults with legislators on adoption-related legislation and issues, and advises overseas authorities on establishing effective international adoption networks.

Books

Adoption Beginning to End: A Guide for Christian Parents by Donald W. Felker and Evelyn H. Felker (Baker, 1987).

The Complete Adoption Handbook by Douglas Donnelly and Kay Strom (Zondervan, 1992).

Open Adoption: A Caring Option by Jeanne Warren Lindsay (Morning Glory, 1987).

The Whole Life Adoption Book by Jayne E. Schooler (Piñon Press, 1993).

AIDS

Organizations

AMERICANS FOR A SOUND AIDS/HIV POLICY
P.O. Box 17433, Washington, DC 20041; (703) 471-7350.
   ASAP's purpose is to educate the public as well as medical, religious, business and political communities about the impact of the AIDS/HIV epidemic. The organization's five basic tenets are the value of early diagnosis; limiting the spread of the epidemic through such measures as voluntary partner notification programs; a compassionate response to victims; the development of treatments, vaccines, and a cure; and access to health care.

(Information about AIDS may also be obtained from your family physician, Red Cross chapter, or local or state health department.)

Books

AIDS and Young People by Robert Redfield and Wanda Kay Franz (Regnery Gateway, 1987).

Gays, AIDS, and You by Enrique T. Reuda & Michael Schwartz (Devin Adair, 1987).

The AIDS Epidemic: Balancing Compassion and Justice by Glenn G. Wood and John E. Dietrich (Multnomah, 1990).

Christians in the Age of AIDS by Anita Moreland Smith and W. Shepherd Smith (Victor Books, 1990).

Rethinking AIDS by Robert Root-Bernstein (Free Press, 1993).

CREATIONISM vs. EVOLUTION

Organizations

ACCESS RESEARCH NETWORK

P.O. Box 38069, Colorado Springs, CO 80937-8069; (719) 633-1772.
> Formerly Students for Origins Research, this group provides a forum for discussing the creationism versus evolution controversy from a scientific, rather than religious, basis. Access publishes a bi-annual journal, *Origins Research*, and offers videos on the subject.

BIBLE SCIENCE ASSOCIATION

P.O. Box 260, Zimmerman, MN 55398; 1-800-422-4253.
> The Bible Science Association informs and educates people about the literal biblical account of creation from a philosophical and theological perspective. This organization offers a book catalog as well as a magazine, *Bible Science News*, published nine times a year and available for $25 per annual subscription.

INSTITUTE FOR CREATION RESEARCH

P.O. Box 2667, El Cajon, CA 92021; (619) 448-0900.
> ICR offers a wide variety of publications and audio- and videocassettes regarding science and creation.

REASONS TO BELIEVE

P.O. Box 5978, Pasadena, CA 91117; (818) 335-1480.
> Reasons to Believe exists to communicate a factual basis for belief in the Bible by integrating Scripture with science. Also available is *Facts and Faith*, a monthly newsletter that critiques recent scientific developments. Books, audio- and videocassettes are also available.

Books

Creation and Time: A Biblical and Scientific Perspective on the Creation-Date Controversy by Dr. Hugh Ross (NavPress, 1994).

Darwin On Trial by Phillip E. Johnson (Regnery Gateway, 1991).

Evolution: A Theory in Crisis by Michael Denton (Burnett Books, 1985).

The Origin of Species Revisited (Volumes I & II) by W.R. Byrd (Philosophical Library, Inc., 1989).

Of Pandas and People: The Central Questions of Biological Origins by Dean Kenyon and Percival Davis (Foundation for Thought and Ethics, 1989).

Reason in the Balance: The Case Against Naturalism in Science, Law, and Education by Phillip E. Johnson (InterVarsity Press, 1995).

The Soul of Science: Christian Faith and Natural Philosophy by Nancy R. Pearcey and Charles B. Thaxton (Crossway, 1994).

CRIMINAL JUSTICE

Organizations—Prison Ministry
INTERNATIONAL PRISON MINISTRY
P.O. Box 63, Dallas, TX 75221; (214) 494-2302.
> This ministry provides inmates with complimentary Bibles and other Christian literature.

PRISON FELLOWSHIP MINISTRIES
P.O. Box 17500, Washington, DC 20041; (703) 478-0100.
> Founded by Chuck Colson, Prison Fellowship ministers to prisoners, ex-prisoners, and their families through evangelism, instruction, and visitation. The ministry's monthly newsletter, *Jubilee*, is complimentary upon request.

Organizations—Prison Reform
JUSTICE FELLOWSHIP
P.O. Box 16069, Washington, DC 20041-6069; (703) 478-0100.
> Justice Fellowship is a subsidiary of Prison Fellowship Ministries, which works to promote biblical standards of justice in America's criminal justice system through victim and offender restitution and reconciliation, community-based sentencing, and so on.

Books—Prison Reform
Convicted: New Hope for Ending America's Crime Crisis by Charles Colson and Daniel Van Ness (Crossway, 1989).

Crime and Its Victims: What We Can Do by Daniel Van Ness (InterVarsity Press, 1986).

Crime and Punishment in Modern America edited by Patrick McGuigan and Jon Pascale (Free Congress, 1986).

Crime and the Responsible Community edited by John Stott and Nicholas Miller (Eerdmans, 1980).

CRISIS PREGNANCY

Organizations

CARE NET
109 Carpenter Street, Suite 100, Sterling, VA 22046; (703) 478-5661.
> A ministry of the Christian Action Council, CARE NET offers resources and support for nearly 500 crisis pregnancy centers across the United States and Canada, and helps develop new CPCs. CARE NET also has a post-abortion ministry.

CRISIS PREGNANCY CENTER MINISTRY OF FOCUS ON THE FAMILY
Colorado Springs, CO 80995, (719) 531-3400.
> This ministry provides limited referrals to CPCs around the country and supports the work of crisis pregnancy centers through the provision of resources and materials. A bimonthly newsletter designed for CPCs, *Heartlink*, is available for a suggested donation of $10 per year.

Books

More Than Kindness: A Compassionate Approach to Crisis Childbearing by Susan Olasky and Marvin Olasky (Crossway, 1990).

Handbook for Pregnant Teenagers by Linda Roggow and Carolyn Owens (Zondervan, 1984).

Should I Keep My Baby? by Martha Zimmerman (Bethany House, 1983).

DEFENSE AND FOREIGN POLICY

Organizations

AMERICAN ENTERPRISE INSTITUTE
1150 Seventeenth Street, N.W., Washington, DC 20036; (202) 862-5800.
> AEI offers policy research and education resources on issues relating to international affairs and national security.

ETHICS AND PUBLIC POLICY CENTER
1015 Fifteenth St., N.W., Suite 900, Washington, DC 20005; (202) 682-1200.
> From a Judeo-Christian perspective, EPPC addresses issues across the full range of U.S. political, economic, military, and human rights reponsibilities in the world.

HERITAGE FOUNDATION
214 Massachusetts Ave., N.E., Washington, DC 20002; (202) 546-4400.
> Heritage is a source for studies and information on foreign and defense policy issues.

INSTITUTE ON RELIGION AND DEMOCRACY
1521 16th Street, N.W., Suite 300, Washington, DC 20036; (202) 986-1440.
> The IRD investigates the state of religious freedom around the world and assists
> Christians who are working to enlarge these freedoms.

Books

The Christian Attitude Toward War by Loraine Boettner (Presbyterian and
Reformed Publishing Co., 1940, 1985).

Idealism Without Illusions: U.S. Foreign Policy in the 1990s by George Weigel
(Eerdmans, 1994).

Just War and the Gulf War by James Turner Johnson and George Weigel (Ethics
and Public Policy Center, 1991).

Might and Right After the Cold War, Michael Cromartie, editor (Ethics and
Public Policy Center, 1992).

Moral Clarity in the Nuclear Age by Michael Novak (Thomas Nelson, 1983).

Who Is For Peace? by Francis Schaeffer, Vladimir Bukovsky, and James
Hitchcock (Thomas Nelson, 1983).

Why Does God Allow War? by D. Martyn Lloyd-Jones (Evangelical Press of
Wales, 1939, 1986).

A World Without Tyranny: Christian Faith and International Politics by Dean C.
Curry (Crossway, 1990).

DIVORCE

Organizations

CHRISTIAN MARRIAGE ENRICHMENT
17821 17th Street, Suite 190, Tustin, CA 92680; (714) 544-7560.
> Founded by Dr. H. Norman Wright, this organization holds marriage seminars
> across the country. A referral system for marital and pre-marital counseling is
> also available.

INSTITUTE FOR AMERICAN VALUES
1841 Broadway, Suite 211, New York, NY 10023; (212) 246-3942.
> The Institute is a private nonpartisan organization devoted to research, publica-
> tion, and public education on family issues.

MARRIAGE SAVERS INSTITUTE
9500 Michaels Court, Bethesda, MD 20817; (301) 469-5870.
> For Christians concerned about the growing divorce rate and its damaging
> effects on families and society, Mike McManus, a syndicated newspaper

columnist and former *Time* correspondent, has developed creative church and community strategies for preparing people for marriage, strengthening existing marriages, and saving troubled marriages. His "Community Marriage Policy," which has been successfully implemented in Peoria, Illinois, has resulted in a dramatic drop in the divorce rate.

MICHIGAN FAMILY FORUM
611 South Walnut, Lansing, MI 48933; (417) 374-1171.
MFF is a state-based family policy research and education organization affiliated with Focus on the Family that has initiated divorce law reform in the state of Michigan.

NATIONAL FATHERHOOD INITIATIVE
600 Eden Road, Building E, Lancaster, PA 17601; (717) 581-8860.
NFI is a national civic organization whose mission is to reinstate fatherhood as a national priority. Working to deploy a national workforce for the purpose of restoring the meaning of, and personal committment to fatherhood, NFI offers a wealth of resources for local action.

Books

The Case Against Divorce by Diane Medved (Donald I. Fine, 1989).

The Divorce Revolution: The Unexpected Social and Economic Consequences for Women and Children in America (Free Press, 1985).

Fatherless America by David Blankenhorn (Basic Books, 1995).

Marriage Savers: Helping Your Friends and Family Avoid Divorce by Mike McManus (Zondervan, 1995).

Second Chances: Men, Women & Children a Decade After Divorce by Judith S. Wallerstein and Sandra Blakeslee (Ticknor & Fields, 1990).

ECONOMICS AND TAXATION

Organizations

AMERICAN ENTERPRISE INSTITUTE
1150 Seventeenth Street, N.W., Washington, DC 20036; (202) 862-5800.
AEI offers policy research and education resources on economic and taxation issues.

AMERICANS FOR TAX REFORM
1320 18th Street, N.W., Suite 200, Washington, DC 20036; (202) 785-0266.
ATR works to inform Americans of the full costs of taxation while advocating a tax system that is simpler, fairer, flatter, and more visable.

FAMILY RESEARCH COUNCIL

700 Thirteenth Street, N.W., Suite 500, Washington, DC 20005; (202) 393-2100.
FRC has published several informative papers on tax freedom and fairness for American families.

HERITAGE FOUNDATION

214 Massachusetts Ave., N.E., Washington, DC 20002; (202) 546-4400.
Heritage's Roe Institute specializes in budget and tax issues, the effects of regulation on the economy, environmental policy, competitiveness, and trade.

Books

Christianity and Economics in the Post Cold-War Era: The Oxford Declaration and Beyond Herbert Schlossberg, et al, editors (Eerdmans, 1994).
Several notable evangelical and Catholic scholars offer a discussion on the ways people can order their economic affairs with the insights and mandates of the Bible.

With Liberty and Justice for Whom? The Recent Evangelical Debate over Capitalism by Craig M. Gay (Eerdmans, 1991).
The author provides an insightful and balanced analysis of the debate among evangelicals over the pros and cons of modern capitalism.

The Spirit of Democratic Capitalism by Michael Novak (Simon & Schuster, 1982).
This book offers an intriguing look at the theological underpinnings that make the political economy of democratic capitalism possible. Divided into three sections, the book tackles these issues: the ideal of democratic capitalism; the twilight of socialism; and a theology of economics.

The Family Wage: Work, Gender, and Children in the Modern Economy, Bryce J. Christensen, editor (The Rockford Institute, 1988).

Poverty and Wealth: The Christian Debate over Capitalism by Ronald H. Nash (Crossway Books, 1986).

EDUCATION

Organizations—Christian Schools/Colleges

ASSOCIATION OF CHRISTIAN SCHOOLS INTERNATIONAL

P.O. Box 35097, Colorado Springs, CO 80935; (719) 528-6906.
ACSI exists to serve Christian schools in the United States and Canada to help improve the quality of Christian education. As a 3,411-member school organization, ACSI networks Christian primary and seconday schools with a total enrollment of 732,436 students.

COALITION OF CHRISTIAN COLLEGES AND UNIVERSITIES

329 Eighth St., N.E., Washington, DC 20002; (202) 546-8713.
The coalition is an association of 91-member Christ-centered colleges and universities representing more than 30 denominations.

Organizations—Higher Education
ACCURACY IN ACADEMIA

4455 Connecticut Ave., N.W., Suite 330, Washington, DC 20008; (202) 364-3085.
AIA defends academic freedom for both professors and students. The organization also publicizes cases of political discrimination and indoctrination of students on campus.

Books—Higher Education
The Closing of the American Mind by Allan Bloom (Simon & Schuster, 1987).
Bloom makes the assertion that the social and political crisis in our nation is really an intellectual crisis. He traces this dilemma to our institutes of higher education and their inability to adequately prepare students with either the intellectual knowledge or moral fortitude to meet society's challenges.

Illiberal Education by Dinesh D'Souza (Free Press, 1991).

Inside American Education: The Decline, the Deception, the Dogma by Thomas Sowell (Free Press, 1993).

The Soul of the American University by George Marsden (Oxford University Press, 1994).

Tenured Radicals: How Politics Has Corrupted Our Higher Education by Roger Kimball (Harper & Row, 1990).

Organizations—Educational Choice
CENTER FOR EDUCATION REFORM

1001 Connecticut Ave., N.W., Washington, DC 20036; (202) 822-9000.
The Center is a nonprofit, national clearinghouse working to make schools better for all children.

CITIZENS FOR EDUCATIONAL FREEDOM

927 S. Walter Reed Dr., Suite 1, Arlington, VA 22204; (703) 486-8311.
Founded in 1959, this organization addresses two primary issues: providing greater freedom of educational choice to parents and greater freedom of initiative to teachers. CEF is a membership organization with local chapters across the country.

Books—Educational Choice
School Choice: Why You Need It—How You Get It by David J. Harmer (Cato Institute, 1994).
This is a great primer on choice in education by the author of Proposition 174, California's 1993 school-choice initiative.

Democracy and the Renewal of Public Education, Richard John Neuhaus, editor (Eerdmans, 1987).

> The book's various contributors, including such leading Christian educators and educational analysts as Richard Baer (Cornell University), Charles Glenn (Boston University), Rockne McCarthy (Dordt College), and James Skillen (Center for Public Justice) contend that school choice must be a fundamental ingredient in the renewal of America's educational system.

The School Choice Controversy: What Is Constitutional? James W. Skillen, editor (Baker Book House and the Center for Public Justice, 1993).

> Experts in constitutional law and religious freedom provide grounding in constitutional law regarding the First Amendment and questions of education. The authors explain pertinent legal precedents and address such issues as whether secular education is religiously neutral and whether educational choice is legally defensible.

Politics, Markets and America's Schools by John E. Chubb and Terry M. Moe (Brookings Institution, 1990).

Privatization and Educational Choice by Myron Lieberman (St. Martin's Press, 1989).

Organizations—Home Schooling
HOME-SCHOOL LEGAL DEFENSE ASSOCIATION
P.O. Box 159, Paeonian Springs, VA 22129; (703) 882-3838.

> HSLDA provides low-cost legal advice for families that home-school. Parents pay $100 per year for membership and are defended free of charge should the necessity arise.

Books—Home Schooling
The Christian Home School by Gregg Harris (Wolgemuth & Hyatt, 1989).

Home Education: Rights and Reasons by John W. Whitehead and Alexis Irene Crow (Crossway Books, 1993).

The Successful Homeschool Family Handbook by Dr. Raymond and Dorothy Moore (Thomas Nelson, 1994).

Organizations—Public Schools
ASSOCIATION OF AMERICAN EDUCATORS
26012 Marguerite Parkway, Suite 333, Mission Viejo, CA 92692; 1-800-704-7799.

> AAE is a professional trade association that encourages and supports teachers who believe educating young people is about character as well as intellect. It offers a national non-union alternative with member benefits for teachers who share traditional values.

CENTER FOR EDUCATION REFORM
1001 Connecticut Ave., N.W., Suite 920, Washington, DC 20036; (202) 822-9000.
    The Center is a nonprofit, national clearinghouse that is working to make schools better for all children.

CHRISTIAN EDUCATORS ASSOCIATION INTERNATIONAL
P.O. Box 50025, Pasadena, CA 91115.
    CEAI exists to encourage and equip Christian teachers so they will be more effective in communicating Judeo-Christian values to children in public schools.

EAGLE FORUM (PHYLLIS SCHLAFLY)
P.O. Box 618, Alton, IL 62002; (618) 462-5415.
    Eagle Forum monitors legislation and trends that have a direct bearing on education. The organization publishes the *Education Reporter*, which is available for $25 per year.

GATEWAYS TO BETTER EDUCATION
P.O. Box 514, Lake Forest, CA 92630; (714) 586-5437.

Books—Public Schools
The Blackboard Fumble edited by Ken Sidey (Victor Books, 1989).
    Ten of today's brightest thinkers on the subject of public education tackle the question of promoting positive moral values in our nation's classrooms. They offer sound, practical advice for parents, educators, and concerned Christians desiring to initiate such reform.

The Closing of the American Heart by Ronald H. Nash (Probe Ministries International, 1990).
    Building on the insights in Allan Bloom's *The Closing of the American Mind*, Nash posits a prescription to the relativism that has damaged our public education system. He argues that a school-choice approach to education is essential for real reform.

Battleground: The Religious Right, Its Opponents, and the Struggle for Our Schools by Stephen Bates (Poseidon Press, 1993).

Cultural Literacy: What Every American Needs to Know by E.D. Hirsch, Jr. (Houghton Mifflin, 1987).

Dumbing Us Down: The Hidden Curriculum of Compulsory Schooling, by John Taylor Gatto (New Society Publishers, 1992).

Inside American Education: The Decline, the Deception, the Dogma by Thomas Sowell (Free Press, 1993).

The Myth of the Common School by Charles L. Glenn Jr. (University of Massachusetts Press, 1988).

The NEA and AFT: Teacher Unions in Power and Politics by Charlene Haar, Myron Lieberman, and Leo Troy (Pro-Active Publications, 1994).

A Parent's Guide to the Public Schools by Sally D. Reed (National Council for Better Education, 1991).

Public Education: An Autopsy by Myron Lieberman (Harvard University Press, 1993).

The Public Orphanage: How Public Schools Are Making Parents Irrelevant by Eric Buehrer (Word, 1995).

The Rights of Religious Persons in Public Education by John W. Whitehead (Crossway, 1991).

School Based Clinics and Other Critical Issues in Public Education, Barrett Mosbacker, editor (Crossway, 1987).

Why Johnny Can't Tell Right from Wrong: Moral Illiteracy and the Case for Character Education by William Kilpatrick (Simon & Schuster, 1992).

ENVIRONMENT

Organizations
AU SABLE INSTITUTE
Outreach Office, 731 State St., Madison, WI 53703; (608) 255-0950.
> This educational organization provides information on environmental issues from a Christian perspective to schools, churches, and others.

CHRISTIAN ENVIRONMENTAL ASSOCIATION
1650 Zanker Road, Suite 150, San Jose, CA 95112; (408) 441-1571.
> CEA is an evangelical organization that believes Christians should take the lead in environmental stewardship. The association publishes a monthly newsletter, *Christian Environmental News,* and offers academic programs, Bibles studies, and a short-term missions program.

EVANGELICAL ENVIRONMENTAL NETWORK
10 Lancaster Ave., Wynnewood, PA 19096; (610) 645-9390.
> EEN helps Christians to think biblically in their stewardship of creation. The network provides information to churches and training to clergy.

Books
Prospects for Growth: A Biblical View of Population, Resources, and the Future by E. Calvin Beisner (Crossway, 1990).

Pollution and the Death of Man by Francis A. Schaeffer and Udo Middleman (Crossway, 1992).

Trashing the Planet: How Science Can Help Us Deal with Acid Rain, Depletion of the Ozone, and Nuclear Waste (Among Other Things) by Dixy Lee Ray (Regnery Gateway, 1990).

The War Against Population: The Economics and Ideology of Population Control by Jacqueline Kasun (Ignatius, 1988).

EUTHANASIA

Organizations

NATIONAL RIGHT TO LIFE COMMITTEE, INC.

419 Seventh St., N.W., Suite 500, Washington, DC 20004; (202) 626-8800.
> NRLC provides national leadership in the right-to-life movement and seeks passage of pro-life legislation. A biweekly newspaper, *National Right to Life News*, provides in-depth coverage of pro-life news, including important developments in Congress.

THE CENTER FOR BIO-ETHICS AND HUMAN DIGNITY

2065 Half Day Road, Bannockburn, IL 60015; (708) 945-8800.
> The Center's offerings in the area of bio-ethics, which includes the issue of euthanasia, encompass conferences, degree programs, and individual courses in association with Trinity International University, as well as the journal *Ethics and Medicine*. Notable faculty specialists in the field of bio-ethics include Nigel Cameron, Harold O.J. Brown, and John Kilner.

THE INTERNATIONAL ANTI-EUTHANASIA TASK FORCE

P.O. Box 760, Steubenville, OH 43953; (614) 282-3810 or (510) 689-0170.
> This is the nation's primary source of information opposing euthanasia.

Books

Deadly Compassion: The Death of Ann Humphry and the Truth About Euthanasia by Rita Marker (William Morrow & Co., 1993).
> Rita Marker, director of the International Anti-Euthanasia Task Force, details the tragic and inhumane suicide of Ann Humphry, wife of Hemlock Society co-founder Derek Humphry. Marker exposes the darker side of the euthanasia movement.

Final Exit by Derek Humphry (Dell Publishing, 1991).
> This "how-to" suicide best-seller provides unique and disturbing insights into the euthanasia movements from one of its leading advocates.

Life on the Line: Ethics, Aging, Ending Patients' Lives, and Allocating Vital Resources by John F. Kilner (Eerdmans, 1992).
> The author presents solid biblical, theological, and ethic insight coupled with firsthand experience of the hospital setting to the euthanasia issue.

The New Medicine by Nigel M. de S. Cameron (Crossway, 1991).
> Dr. Cameron details how contemporary medicine has abandoned the Hippocratic Oath, which historically has upheld the sanctity of life for both young and old.

Prescription Death: Compassionate Killers in the Medical Profession by Reed Bell with Frank York (Huntington House Publishers, 1993).
> Some in the medical profession have incorporated death as part of their practice of "healing." Dr. Bell, former medical adviser for Focus on the Family, draws alarming parallels with this modern movement and doctors who served in Hitler's Reich.

Regulating Death: Euthanasia and the Case of the Netherlands by Carlos F. Gomez, M.D. (Free Press, 1991).

Whatever Happened to the Human Race? by Francis Schaeffer and C. Everett Koop (Crossway, 1983).

GAMBLING

Organizations

GAMBLERS ANONYMOUS
P.O. Box 17173, Los Angeles, CA 90017; (213) 386-8789.
> GA has more than 1,000 chapters nationwide to assist people struggling with gambling addictions.

MINIRTH-MEIER NEW LIFE CLINICS
2100 North Collins, Richardson, TX 75080; (800) NEW-LIFE.
> Located across the United States, these clinics provide outpatient counseling for gambling problems from a Christian perspective.

NATIONAL COALITION AGAINST LEGALIZED GAMBLING
2376 Lakeside Drive, Birmingham, AL 35244; (800) 664-2680.
> NCALG is an action-oriented grassroots organization dedicated to stopping the spread of legalized gambling in the United States. The coalition operates an information clearinghouse and conducts regional conferences.

Books
The Luck Business by Robert Goodman (Free Press, 1995).

HOMOSEXUALITY

Organizations
BCM INTERNATIONAL, DR. ELIZABETH MOBERLY
237 Fairfield Ave., Upper Darby, PA 19083; (610) 352-7177.
> Dr. Moberly is the director of psychosexual education and therapy for BCM International, a Christian organization. The author of three books on homosexuality

and originator of gender-affirmative therapy, Dr. Moberly presents seminars across North America, instructing Christians as to how to minister effectively, compassionately, and biblically to homosexuals.

DESERT STREAM A.R.M.
P.O. Box 17635, Anaheim, CA 92817; (714) 779-6899.
Desert Stream offers a wide range of support groups, conferences, seminars, and counseling for those struggling with homosexuality, as well as an AIDS ministry.

EXODUS INTERNATIONAL
P.O. Box 2121, San Rafael, CA 94912; (415) 454-1017.
Founded in 1976, Exodus is the premier resource and referral ministry for those seeking information or help with the issue of homosexuality. Exodus provides extensive literature and recommendations of ministries to homosexuals, both nationally and internationally. In Canada, contact: New Direction for Life Ministries, Box 1078, Station F, Toronto, Ontario M4Y 2T7; (416) 921-6557.

HOMOSEXUALS ANONYMOUS
P.O. Box 7881, Reading, PA 19603; (610) 376-1146.
Homosexuals Anonymous is a ministry designed to help those struggling with homosexual feelings or behavior. The ministry has support groups around the nation.

LOVE IN ACTION
P.O. Box 753307, Memphis, TN 38175, (901) 542-0250.
Love in Action is a ministry outreach to former homosexuals.

MINIRTH MEIER NEW LIFE TREATMENT CENTERS
1-800-NEW-LIFE.
Nationwide clinics address a variety of emotional disorders and psychological problems, including homosexuality, from a conservative Christian perspective.

SPATULA MINISTRIES (FOR PARENTS OF HOMOSEXUALS)
P.O. Box 444, La Habra, CA 90631; (310) 691-7369.
Spatula's aim is to support and restore families who have been affected by homosexuality.

Books—To Understand the Homosexuality Debate

Homosexuality and the Politics of Truth by Jeffrey Satinover (Baker Books, 1996)
Dr. Satinover's book is an excellent analysis of the political debate about homosexuality. Satinover, a physician, examines the nature versus nurture controversy. After investigating the scientific findings of biology, psychology, and sociology, the author challenges the claims of "gay science." He concludes that the public policy debate over homosexual behavior can only be decided on moral, and ultimately religious, grounds.

Homosexuality: Opposing Viewpoints, William Dudley, editor (Greenhaven Press, Inc., 1993)
> An excellent resource for gaining understanding regarding the arguments used both for and against homosexuality, this book is a compilation of essays that feature opposing viewpoints on the following issues: What causes homosexuality? Should society encourage increased acceptance of homosexuality? Can homosexuals change their sexual orientation? Should society legally sanction gay relationships? Includes a directory of organizations concerned with homosexuality, as well as a bibliography of articles and books on the subject.

Books—On the Nature and Treatment of Homosexuality

Homosexuality: A New Christian Ethic by Elizabeth Moberly (James Clarke & Co., 1983, 1993)
> Correlating the insights of psychology and theology, this short but incisive study of the dynamics of homosexual orientation locates the underlying causes in legitimate unmet developmental needs. It challenges long-held beliefs about both the nature of homosexuality and the proper moral, social, and therapeutic responses. This book is written for lay people from an explicitly Christian perspective, informed by psychoanalytical research. The author encourages both therapy and prayer to facilitate the fulfillment of heterosexual development.

Reparative Therapy of Male Homosexuality by Joseph Nicolosi (Jason Aronson Inc., 1991)
> This highly recommended work is an enlightening discussion of male homosexuality from a psychotherapeutic perspective. Incorporating and expanding upon Moberly's work, Nicolosi explains both the psychological dynamics that drive homosexual desire and the therapeutic process that can bring substantial healing. This book is fully compatible with a Christian perspective but not written explicitly from that perspective.

Coming Out of Homosexuality: New Freedom for Men & Women by Bob Davies and Lori Rentzel (InterVarsity, 1993)
> This practical guide for people struggling with same-sex desires is based on proven strategies successfully employed by other Christians. The authors address various aspects of the problem, including the biological, psychological, and relational.

Out of Egypt: Leaving Lesbianism Behind by Jeanette Howard (Monarch, 1991)
> Written by a Christian woman who has come out of a lesbian lifestyle, this honest and practical book deals with such issues as the roots of lesbianism, problems of personal identity, loneliness, nonsexual, same-sex intimacy, and the importance of the spiritual life for recovery.

Books—On the Homosexual Movement

Are "Gay Rights" Right? by Roger Magnuson (Multnomah Press, 1990)

A critical discussion of the national movement for homosexual rights, this book includes a description of the gay community, analysis of the legal implications of "gay rights" ordinances, and a refutation of the arguments most often put forward in defense of legislation protecting homosexuality.

Gays, AIDS, and You by Enrique T. Rueda and Michael Schwartz (The Devin Adair Company, 1987)

A concise, informative discussion of how the homosexual movement is purposely using the tragic AIDS epidemic to promote its own social and political agenda. Stressing the important distinction between homosexual individuals and the pro-homosexual ideology and the lifestyle it advocates, this book focuses on the threat to American society that the movement poses.

The Homosexual Network: Private Lives and Public Policy by Enrique T. Rueda (The Devin Adair Co., 1982, revised 1988)

This book represents one the most exhaustive investigations into the social and political activities and impact of the homosexual movement in the United States. Its fully documented 680 pages deal with such crucial issues as the character of the homosexual subculture, the ideology, organizations, goals, and funding sources of the movement, as well as its relationship to religious and political organizations.

Kinsey, Sex and Fraud by Judith A. Reisman and Edward W. Eichel (Huntington House, 1990)

This book is the result of an intensive and detailed investigation into the methods and motives behind the human sexuality research of Alfred C. Kinsey, which had been the basis for much public discussion and policy decisions on homosexuality. Heavy but profitable reading, it demonstrates that much of the research was methodologically inadequate and unscientific, deliberately deceitful, and driven by a radical social agenda.

Legislating Immorality by George Grant and Mark A. Horne (Moody Press, 1993)

A popular, broad-sweeping analysis of the homosexual political agenda and its inroads into the major cultural institutions in America, including the media, education, politics, medicine, the military, and the church, this book is useful not only for its commentary, but also as a resource. Written from an evangelical perspective, it encourages both firm commitment and compassion in responding to homosexuality.

THE MEDIA

Organizations
ACCURACY IN MEDIA

4455 Connecticut Ave., N.W., Suite 330, Washington, DC 20008; (202) 364-4401.
Billed as "America's media watchdog," AIM works toward the media's adoption of higher standards of reporting and editing and a responsible approach to news.

AMERICAN FAMILY ASSOCIATION
P.O. Drawer 2440, Tupelo, MS 38803; (601) 844-5036.
AFA is a grassroots organization pressing for the restoration of traditional family values.

CENTER FOR MEDIA AND PUBLIC AFFAIRS
2100 L St., N.W., Suite 300, Washington, DC 20037; (202) 223-2942.
CMPA was founded in 1984 by social scientists Robert and Linda Lichter as a nonpartisan organization to hold journalism to its own high standards of fairness and accuracy.

FEDERAL COMMUNICATIONS COMMISSION
Mass Media Bureau, 1919 M. St., N.W., Washington, DC 20554; (202) 418-2600.

MEDIA RESEARCH CENTER
113 South West St., Second Floor, Alexandria, VA 22314; (703) 683-9733.
MRC works to bring political balance to the media through research, education, and public outreach programs.

MORALITY IN MEDIA
475 Riverside Dr., New York, NY 10115; (212) 870-3222.
This organization directs its efforts toward protecting children and adolescents from pornography in the media.

Books

American Evangelicals and the Mass Media edited by Quentin J. Schultze (Zondervan, 1990).

Amusing Ourselves to Death by Neil Postman (Penguin, 1985).

Bridging the Gap: Religion and the News Media by John Dart and Jimmy Allen (The Freedom Forum, 1993).

Book Burning by Cal Thomas (Crossway, 1983).

Hollywood vs. America by Michael Medved (Harper Collins, 1992).

The Media Elite: America's New Powerbrokers by S. Robert Lichter, Linda S. Lichter, and Stanley Rothman (Hastings House, 1986, 1990).

Prodigal Press: The Anti-Christian Bias of American News Media by Marvin Olasky (Crossway, 1988).

Watching America by S. Robert Lichter, Linda S. Lichter, and Stanley Rothman (Prentice Hall Press, 1991).

Periodicals
Forbes MediaCritic is available for $29.95 by calling 1-800-825-0061. *MediaCritic* is a quarterly journal that explores how the media covers the most important topics of the day.

PARENTAL RIGHTS

Organizations
OF THE PEOPLE FOUNDATION
2111 Wilson Boulevard, Suite 700, Arlington, VA 22201; (703) 351-5051.
> Of The People is a national, nonprofit, nonpartisan grassroots organization working to keep public policy on the side of parents by enacting the Parental Rights Amendment to state constitutions and, ultimately, the federal constitution.

Books
Parents' Rights by John W. Whitehead (Crossway, 1985).

PORNOGRAPHY

Organizations
AMERICAN FAMILY ASSOCIATION
P.O. Drawer 2440, Tupelo, MS 38803; (601) 844-5036.
> AFA monitors pornography-related legislation, offers a national porn-addiction referral service, and initiates grassroots efforts to dissuade the entertainment media from presenting indecent programming.

ENOUGH IS ENOUGH!
P.O. Box 888, Fairfax, VA 22030; (703) 278-8343.
> The mission of the Enough Is Enough! campaign is to greatly reduce sexual violence to prevent children, women, men, and families from becoming victims by eliminating child pornography and removing hard-core and illegal pornography from the marketplace. This educational program is designed specifically to mobilize and equip America's women to make a difference in this issue.

MORALITY IN MEDIA
475 Riverside Dr., New York, NY 10115; (212) 870-3222.
> This organization directs its efforts toward protecting children and adolescents from pornography in the media.

NATIONAL COALITION FOR THE PROTECTION OF CHILDREN AND FAMILIES
Compton Road, Suite 9224, Cincinnati, OH 45231; (513) 521-6227.
> The Coalition has local chapters throughout the United States devoted to fighting pornography.

NATIONAL FAMILY LEGAL FOUNDATION
11000 N. Scottsdale Road, Scottsdale, AZ 85254; (602) 922-9731.
>The nonprofit NFLF is dedicated to providing free legal assistance to individuals, legislators, law enforcement officials, and courts in the fight against child pornography, obscenity, broadcast indecency, and sexually-oriented businesses.

Books
Final Report of the Attorney General's Commission on Pornography (Rutledge Hill Press, 1986).

The Mind Polluters by Jerry R. Kirk (Thomas Nelson, 1985).

Pornography: A Human Tragedy, Tom Minnery, editor (Tyndale, 1987).

RELIGIOUS LIBERTY

Organizations
ALLIANCE DEFENSE FUND
11811 N. Tatum Blvd., Suite 3031, Phoenix, AZ 85028; (602) 953-1200.
>ADF's mission is to assist with strategy, training, and providing the funding for those defending religious liberty, the sanctity of human life, and family values in our nation's courts.

AMERICAN CENTER FOR LAW AND JUSTICE
P.O. Box 64429, Virginia Beach, VA 23467; (804) 579-2489.
>The ACLJ is a not-for-profit public interest law firm and educational organization dedicated to the promotion of pro-liberty, pro-life, and pro-family causes. The organization is also developing a national network of attorneys committed to the defense of religious and civil liberties for Americans.

BECKET FUND FOR RELIGIOUS LIBERTY
2000 Pennsylvania Ave., N.W., Suite 3200, Washington, DC 20006; 1-800-BECKET-5.
>The Becket Fund is a nonpartisan, ecumenical, public interest law firm that defends the civil rights of people from all religious traditions.

CATHOLIC LEAGUE FOR RELIGIOUS AND CIVIL RIGHTS
1011 First Ave., New York, NY 10022; (212) 371-3191.
>Founded in 1973, the nation's largest Catholic civil rights organization works to safeguard the religious freedom and free speech rights of Catholics wherever they are threatened. They are a lay Catholic organization, not an official arm of the Catholic church.

CENTER FOR LAW AND RELIGIOUS FREEDOM
4208 Evergreen Lane, Suite 222, Annandale, VA 22003-3264; (703) 642-1070.
>This arm of the Christian Legal Society, a national volunteer network of attorneys and laypersons, works to protect the religious rights of believers. This group has

been instrumental in litigation on important issues regarding clergy malpractice, tax exemption for churches and ministries, and equal access for religious groups in public schools.

INSTITUTE ON RELIGION AND DEMOCRACY
1331 H St., N.W., Suite 900, Washington, DC 20005; (202) 393-3200.
IRD works to advance and strengthen democracy and religious liberty around the world through the church. Founded in 1981 by both Protestants and Catholics, IRD strives to effect a more constructive Christian involvement in social and political issues through education and resources.

LIBERTY COUNSEL
P.O. Box 540774, Orlando, FL 32854; (407) 875-2100.
Liberty Counsel is a nonprofit religious civil liberties and legal defense organization.

RUTHERFORD INSTITUTE
P.O. Box 7482, Charlottesville, VA 22906-7482; (804) 978-3888.
Rutherford is a nonprofit legal and educational organization that defends people whose First Amendment religious liberties have been threatened by state action. The Institute also educates the public on key issues confronting the religious community.

Books

The Culture of Disbelief: How American Law and Politics Trivialize Religious Devotion by Stephen L. Carter (HarperCollins, 1993).
Carter, a professor of law at Yale University, surveys the role of religion in American law, politics, and culture. He defends the right—and the need—for religious practices and convictions to be prominently included in public discourse.

Religious Liberty in the Supreme Court: The Cases that Define the Debate over Church and State, Terry Eastland, editor (Ethics and Public Policy Center, 1993).
This book reviews 25 of the most significant Supreme Court cases regarding the First Amendment's religion clause, ranging from prayer in public schools to tax exemption for property owned by religious organizations. Commentary pertaining to many of the specific cases, as well as insights by three legal scholars regarding related trends by the Court, is included.

Articles of Faith, Articles of Peace: The Religious Liberty Clauses and the American Public Philosophy, Os Guinness and James Davison Hunter, editors (Brookings Institution, 1990).

Faith & Freedom: A Complete Handbook for Defending Your Religious Rights by Mathew D. Staver (Crossway, 1995).

A Fragrance of Oppression: The Church and Its Persecutors by Herbert Schlossberg (Crossway, 1991).

Legal Defense Handbook for Christians in Ministry by Carl F. Lansing (NavPress, 1992).

The Politics of the American Civil Liberties Union by William A. Donohue (Transaction Books, 1985).

The Rights of Religious Persons in Public Education by John W. Whitehead (Crossway, 1991).

Twilight of Liberty: The Legacy of the ACLU by William A. Donohue (Transaction Publishers, 1994).

SEX EDUCATION

Organizations
JOSH MCDOWELL MINISTRY
P.O. Box 1000, Dallas, TX 75221; (214) 907-1000.
> This ministry provides a variety of materials designed to help adults teach teens about sexuality from a Christian perspective.

MEDICAL INSTITUTE FOR SEXUAL HEALTH
P.O. Box 4919, Austin, TX 78765-4919; (800) 892-9484.
> MISH informs people of the worldwide challenges we face from sexually transmitted diseases and provides education, training, and information to assist in the preservation of human health and life.

NATIONAL ASSOCIATION FOR ABSTINENCE EDUCATION
6201 Leesburg Pike, Suite 404, Falls Church, VA 22044; (703) 532-9459.
> NAAE functions as a clearinghouse for abstinence education resources and research. It provides related information to teachers, parents, school boards, and other interested parties.

RESPECT INC.
P.O. Box 349, 231 E. Broadway, Bradley, IL 60915; (815) 932-8389.
> This for-profit organization offers materials relating to sex education from a Christian perspective.

TEEN-AID
723 E. Jackson, Spokane, WA 99207-2647, (509) 482-2868.
> This group strives to reduce the many adverse consequences of sexual activity among teens by encouraging abstinence as a premarital lifestyle.

Books
Sex, Lies and . . . the Truth (Focus on the Family, 1994).
> This educational curriculum is designed to aid public school educators, youth leaders, and others who desire to present information on sexuality to adolescents

from a pro-abstinence perspective. A Focus on the Family video by the same name offers a powerful message about the dangers of sex in the 1990s and brings viewers face to face with the realities of unwanted pregnancies, sexually transmitted diseases, and AIDS.

How and When to Tell Your Kids About Sex by Stanton L. Jones and Brenda B. Jones (NavPress, 1993).

Kinsey, Sex and Fraud by Judith A. Reisman and Edward W. Eichel (Huntington House, 1990).

The Myths of Sex Education by Josh McDowell (Here's Life, 1990).

School-Based Clinics, the Abortion Connection by Richard D. Glasow (National Right to Life, 1988).

School-Based Clinics, and Other Critical Issues in Public Education, Barrett L. Mosbacker, editor (Crossway, 1987).

Sex Education: The Final Plague by Randy Engel (Human Life International, 1989).

SOCIAL WELFARE

Organizations—Poverty
CHRISTIAN COMMUNITY DEVELOPMENT ASSOCIATION
3827 W. Ogden Ave., Chicago, IL 60623; (312) 762-0994.
> CCDA is the premier network of evangelical churches and organizations that are addressing the needs of the poor in rural and urban areas. Ministry services range from addiction counseling to economic and housing development.

Books—Poverty
The Problem of Poverty—Abraham Kuyper, James W. Skillen, editor (Baker Book House and the Center for Public Justice, 1991).
> Dutch statesman, philosopher, clergyman, and journalist Abraham Kuyper (1837-1920) fought for sweeping social and educational reforms a century ago. This text of Kuyper's speeches remains a powerfully relevant message for concerned Christians.

With Justice For All by John Perkins (Regal Books, 1982).
> Perkins offers a passionate plea for racial reconciliation in America and justice to black America. Eschewing the traditional social welfare solutions, Perkins advocates his "three R's" of community development—relocation, reconciliation, and redistribution—as a means toward a spiritual and economic awakening for blacks.

Beyond Hunger: A Biblical Mandate for Social Responsibility by Art Beals (Multnomah, 1985).

Freedom, Justice, and Hope: Toward a Strategy for the Poor and Oppressed by
Marvin Olasky, Herbert Schlossberg, Pierre Berthoud, and Clark H. Pinnock
(Crossway, 1988).

Out of the Poverty Trap by Stuart Butler and Anna Kondratas (Free Press, 1987).

Prosperity and Poverty: The Compassionate Use of Resources in a World of Scarcity
by E. Calvin Beisner (Crossway, 1988).

Organizations—Homelessness
DOOR OF HOPE
669 N. Los Robles, Pasadena, CA 91101; (818) 304-9130.
> Door of Hope is a Christian ministry for homeless families. A residency program
> integrates biblically based classes on the topics of self-esteem, finances, marriage,
> and parenting.

GOLDEN GATE COMMUNITY, INC.
1387 Oak St., San Francisco, CA 94117; (415) 552-1700.
> This organization's Oak Street House program is a comprehensive facility to
> assist and rehabilitate homeless individuals. The program includes practical care
> services, job development opportunities, counseling, Christian discipleship, and
> residential support.

HABITAT FOR HUMANITY
121 Habitat St., Americus, GA 31709; (912) 924-6935.
> This Christian housing ministry, designed to provide suitable shelter for those
> lacking such, has projects here and abroad.

TREVOR'S CAMPAIGN FOR THE HOMELESS
3415 West Chester Pike, Room 203, Newtown Square, PA 19073, 1-800-Trevors.
> Trevor's is a nonprofit humanitarian organization that coordinates street out-
> reach; offers transitional housing and services for the homeless; and conducts
> public education and advocacy work for the homeless across the United States
> and in France.

UPTOWN BAPTIST CHURCH
1011 W. Wilson Ave., Chicago, IL 60640; (312) 784-2922.
> Uptown Baptist has a significant outreach to the local homeless community
> through a variety of programs and can serve as a model for other churches.

Books—Homelessness
The Dispossessed by George Grant (Crossway, 1986).

The Excluded Americans: Homelessness and Housing Policies by William Tucker
(Regnery Gateway, 1990).

Organizations—Urban Ministry
CIRCLE URBAN MINISTRIES
118 N. Central, Chicago, IL 60644; (312) 921-1446.

> From a Christian perspective, Circle Urban Ministries addresses the spiritual, physical, social, and economic issues in the Austin community of Chicago. Numerous programs include pastoral care and visitation, care and resources for families in emergency situations, educational development for children and adults, Christian leadership development for youths, health care services, and legal assistance.

JOHN M. PERKINS FOUNDATION FOR RECONCILIATION AND DEVELOPMENT
1581 Navarro Ave., Pasadena, CA 91103; (818) 791-7439.

> The Foundation is committed to developing leaders from urban areas who, once equipped, can return to their communities to assist others in the social, economic, education, and spiritual aspects of life. Through such development, the foundation aims to combat crime, immorality, and other issues that plague urban areas.

THE URBAN ALTERNATIVE
P.O. Box 4000, Dallas, TX 75208; (214) 943-3868.

> The Urban Alternative, led by Dr. Anthony (Tony) Evans, seeks to bring the gospel to black communities. Various outreaches include a worldwide daily radio ministry, materials on marriage and the family, a counseling ministry, and regional conferences.

VOICE OF CALVARY MINISTRIES
1655 St. Charles St., Jackson, MS 39209; (601) 353-1635.

> Founded by John M. Perkins, Voice of Calvary is a black Christian community development outreach that works through local churches. Specific program areas include a family health center that tends to 12,000 patients annually, a housing development providing homes to low-income families, and family and youth development programs designed to strengthen and better participants both socially and spiritually.

Books—Urban Ministry
The General Next to God: The Story of William Booth and the Salvation Army by Richard Collier (Harper & Row, 1965).

Help is Just Around the Corner by Virgil Gulker (Creation House, 1988).

Seeing the City with the Eyes of God by Floyd McClung (Zondervan, 1991).

Organizations—Welfare Reform
CENTER FOR PUBLIC JUSTICE
P.O. Box 48368, Washington, DC 20002; (410) 263-5909.

> The Center has undertaken the task of examining the moral and conceptual roots of the welfare crisis and offers innovative policy solutions to the poverty problems.

FAMILY RESEARCH COUNCIl
700 13th St., N.W., Suite 500, Washington, DC 20005; (202) 393-2100.

HERITAGE FOUNDATION
214 Massachusetts Ave., N.E., Washington, DC 20002; (202) 546-4400.

Books—Welfare Reform

Welfare in America: Christian Perspectives on a Policy in Crisis, Stanley W. Carlson-Thies and James W. Skillen, editors (Eerdmans, 1996)
> In this work, several Christian scholars address basic questions about human nature, society, responsibility, government, and welfare.

The Tragedy of American Compassion by Marvin Olasky (Crossway, 1992)
> The author, a professor of journalism at the University of Texas, traces the evolution of charity throughout American history. Acknowledging the failure of public assistance programs, Olasky proposes that such government efforts be replaced by private charitable initiatives.

Beyond Entitlement: The Social Obligations of Citizenship by Lawrence Mead (Free Press, 1986).

Losing Ground by Charles Murray (Basic Books, 1984).

The New Politics of Poverty: The Nonworking Poor in America by Lawrence Mead (Basic Books, 1992).

Wealth and Poverty by George Gilder (Basic Books, 1981).

Notes

Chapter 2

1. Richard J. Neuhaus, *The Naked Public Square: Religion and Democracy in America* (Grand Rapids: William B. Eerdmans Publishing Co., 1984,1986).
2. James C. Dobson and Gary Bauer, *Children At Risk: The Battle for the Hearts and Minds of Our Kids* (Waco, Texas: Word, 1988), 19-20.
3. James Davison Hunter, *Culture Wars: The Struggle to Define America* (New York: Basic Books, 1991).
4. Harold J. Berman, *Faith and Order: The Reconciliation of Law and Religion* (Atlanta: Scholars Press, 1993), 214-16.
5. *McCollum v. Board of Education*, 333 U.S. 203 (1948).
6. Stephen L. Carter, *The Culture of Disbelief: How American Law and Politics Trivialize Religious Devotion* (New York: Basic Books, 1993), 122-23.
7. Ibid., 22.
8. A facsimile of this letter can be found in Dobson and Bauer, *Children at Risk*, 26.
9. Joe Klein, "The Out-of-Wedlock Question," *Newsweek* (13 December 1993): 37.
10. As quoted by John W. Whitehead, *The Second American Revolution* (Elgin, Ill.: David C. Cook, 1982), 50.
11. Richard J. Neuhaus, *First Things*, (June/July 1994): 69.
12. Russell Kirk, "Civilization Without Religion?" The Heritage Lecture Series (Washington, D.C.: The Heritage Foundation, 1992), #404.
13. George Washington, "First Inaugural Address, in the City of New York, April 30, 1789," *A Compilation of the Messages and Papers of the Presidents* (New York: Bureau of National Literature, Inc., 1897), I:45.

14. Ibid., "Farewell Address, 1796," I:212-13.
15. John Adams to Zabdiel Adams from Philadelphia on June 21, 1776, contained in *The Works of John Adams, Second President of the United States*, Charles Francis Adams, ed., (Boston: Little, Brown, 1854), IX:401.
16. Ibid., "To the Officers of the First Brigade of the Third Division of the Militia of Massachusetts, October 11, 1798," IX:229.
17. Ibid., "To Dr. Benjamin Rush from Quincy, August 11, 1811," IX:636.
18. This phrase does not appear in the Constitution but rather in the personal correspondence of President Thomas Jefferson to "Nehemiah Dodge, Ephraim Robbins, and Stephen S. Nelson, A Committee of the Danbury Baptist Association, In the State of Connecticut, January 1, 1802," *The Writings of Thomas Jefferson* (Washington, D.C.: The Thomas Jefferson Memorial Association, 1904), XVI:282.
19. Thomas Jefferson, "First Inaugural Address, 1801," *A Documentary History of the United States* (Bloomington: Indiana University Press, 1952), 68-9.
20. Thomas Jefferson, Query XVIII, "The particular customs and manners that may happen to be received in that state," Saul K. Padover, ed., *The Complete Jefferson* (New York: Tudor Publishing, 1943), 677.
21. James Madison, "Memorial and Remonstrance to the General Assembly of the Commonwealth of Virginia, 1785," Robert Rutland, et al., eds., *The Papers of James Madison* (Chicago: University of Chicago, 1973), VIII:299.
22. Alexis de Tocqueville, *Democracy in America* (New York: Vintage, 1945, 1990), I:305-7.
23. As quoted in James Madison, *Notes of Debates in the Federal Convention of 1787* (New York: W.W. Norton, 1787,1987), 209-210.
24. "President Sides with Religious Right on Tithing Case," The Morning Edition (Washington, D.C.: National Public Radio, September 24, 1994), Transcript #1444-12, page 4.
25. Garry Wills, *Under God: Religion and American Politics* (New York: Simon & Schuster, 1990), 97.
26. Mary Baird Bryan refers to the 16th Amendment, federal income tax; 17th Amendment, popular election of U.S. Senators; 18th Amendment, Prohibition; and the 19th Amendment, women's suffrage as among the policies successfully advocated by William Jennings Bryan. Cf. Bryan and Bryan, William Jennings and Mary Baird, *The Memoirs of William Jennings Bryan* (New York: Haskell House Publishers, Ltd., 1971), 462-471.
27. Martin Luther King Jr., "I Have a Dream" speech, Washington, D.C., June 15, 1963. King was citing Isaiah 40:4-5.
28. The Thirty Years War, 1618-38, and the English Civil War, 1642-48, were the last of the great religious wars. The Reformed Protestant thinking on the relationship of church and state during that era is demonstrated by the

Westminster Confession of Faith, 1647, which affirms the magistrate's "power of the sword . . . that all blasphemies and heresies be suppressed, all corruptions and abuses in worship and discipline prevented or reformed. . . . " Cf. Phillip Schaaf, ed., *The Creeds of Christendom* (Grand Rapids: Baker Books, 1931,1985), II:652-53.

29. Carl F. H. Henry, "Response," *No Longer Exiles: The Religious New Right in American Politics*, Michael Cromartie, ed. (Washington, D.C.: Ethics and Public Policy Center, 1993), 76-77.

30. As quoted in Maroon Borden, *Jews, Turks, and Infidels* (Chapel Hill, N.C.: Univ. of North Carolina, 1984), 64.

31. Data was obtained in an interview with Margaret Mary Dalton, principal, Charles J. Riley Public School Number 9, Paterson School District, Paterson, New Jersey, on January 13, 1994.

32. Jean-Jacques Rousseau, *The Social Contract* (New York: Free Press, 1969).

33. As cited by Will J. Herberg, *Protestant-Catholic-Jew* (Garden City, N.Y.: Anchor, 1955,1960), 84.

34. Mark Silk, *Spiritual Politics: Religion and America Since World War II* (New York: Touchstone, 1989), 87-107.

35. Os Guinness, *The American Hour: A Time of Reckoning and the Once and Future Role of Faith* (New York: Free Press, 1993), 222-238.

36. The New York State Board of Regent's Prayer was a voluntary, brief, non-descript, nondenominational prayer contested in the famous *Engel v. Vitale* (1962) supreme court case. The prayer is as follows: "Almighty God, we acknowledge our dependence upon Thee, and we beg Thy blessings upon us, our parents, our teachers and our country." In a pluralistic nation, the problem that this voluntary prayer accentuates for those who choose to participate is: To which God am I praying? Allah? Jehovah? The Trinity? Pontifex Maximus?

37. Terry Eastland, "Protestant Christianity Is America's Religion," *Religion in America*, Julie S. Bach and Thomas Modl, eds. (San Diego: Greenhaven, 1989), 37. Italics added for emphasis.

38. Wolfhart Pannenberg, "Christianity and the West: Ambiguous Past, Uncertain Future," *First Things* 48 (December 1994): 19-20.

39. Cf. Matthew 13:24-30, 36-43.

40. In *Torcaso v. Watkins*, 367 U.S. 488 (1961), Justice Hugo L. Black, writing for the majority, lists "Secular Humanism" in a footnote as being among religions in the United States "which do not teach what would be considered a belief in the existence of God."

41. *Abington School District v. Schempp*, 374 U.S. 203 (1963).

42. In *Guidry v. Calcasieu Parish School Board*, a district court upheld a school principal's decision to eliminate the valedictorian from the graduation

program when she refused to comply with the censorship requirement. This case was later affirmed on jurisdictional grounds in *Guidry v. Broussard*, 897 F.2d 181 (5th Cir., 1990).

43. In *Settle v. Dickson County School Board*, WL 261590 (6th Cir., 1995), the court upheld a teacher's decision to do just this, even though other subjects approved by the teacher included "Spiritualism," "Reincarnation," and "Magic Throughout History."

44. Focus on the Family and several other organizations have publicly supported the concept of a religious equality amendment to the Constitution. An amendment of this kind, which would articulate a principle of government neutrality, is now a necessary corrective to supreme court jurisprudence that has more recently interpreted the First Amendment's religious freedom clauses to be freedom *from* religion. Various versions of a religious equality amendment have circulated. Professor Michael W. McConnell of the University of Chicago School of Law has advanced legal arguments on its behalf.

45. Universal Declaration of Human Rights, Article 26.3.

46. International Covenant on Economic, Social, and Cultural Rights, Article 13.3.

47. The Constitution of the Republic of South Africa 200 of 1993, Section 32(c).

Chapter 3

1. See chapter 1 of this book: William Bennett, "Revolt Against God: America's Spiritual Despair," 10.

2. Christopher Dawson, *The Historic Reality of Christian Culture* (San Francisco: Harper & Row, 1960), 20-21.

3. Allan Bloom, *The Closing of the American Mind* (New York: Simon & Schuster, 1987), 25.

4. Gottlob Frege, "The Thought: A Logical Inquiry," reprinted in *Philosophical Logic*, Peter Strawson, ed. (New York: Oxford University Press, 1987), 29.

5. William James, *Principles of Psychology*, vol. I (New York: Cambridge University Press, 1983), 24.

6. George Barna, *Virtual America* (Ventura, Calif.: Regal Books, 1994), 82, 283.

7. Ibid., 85, 230.

8. George Skelton, "Most Americans Think Abortion Is Immoral," *Los Angeles Times*, 19 March 1989.

9. Kenneth Clark, *Civilisation* (San Francisco: Harper & Row, 1969), 3.

10. Aristotle, *Works of Aristotle Vol. 9: Nicomachean Ethics*, W.D. Ross, ed. (New York: Random House, 1940), Book I, 1094-1181.

11. David Hume, *An Enquiry Concerning Human Understanding*, Selby-Brigge, ed. (Oxford: Clarendon Press, 1894), Section 4, Part 1, p. 139.

12. David Hume, *A Treatise of Human Nature*, Selby-Brigge, ed. (Oxford: Clarendon Press, 1898), 252.
13. Hume, *Enquiry*, 163.
14. Immanuel Kant, *Critique of Pure Reason*, N. Kemp Smith, trans. (New York: St. Martin's Press, 1965 [1929]), B xxxix, 34.
15. Protagoras, as quoted in E. Hussey, *The Pre-Socratics* (New York: Scribners, 1973), 109.
16. Hilary Putnam, "Philosophers and Human Understanding," *Philosophical Papers*, vol. III (Cambridge: Cambridge University Press, 1983), 204.
17. Joe Klein, "The Out-of-Wedlock Question," *Newsweek* (13 December 1993): 37.
18. Ibid.
19. Aristotle, *Works of Aristotle Vol. 9*, Book I, 1095b, 14-22.
20. Charles Colson, *Against the Night* (Ann Arbor, Mich.: Servant Publications, 1989), 44.
21. Hilary Putnam, *The Many Faces of Realism* (La Salle, Ill.: Open Court Publishing Co., 1987), 79.
22. Hilary Putnam, *Reason, Truth and History* (New York: Cambridge University Press, 1985), 133.
23. C.S. Lewis, *Christian Reflection* (Grand Rapids: Wm B. Eerdmans, 1973), 73.
24. Don Whatley, "Make Way for Character Education: It Counts," *Daily Report Card*, 17 October 1994.
25. Irving Singer, *Meaning in Life: The Creation of Values* (New York: Free Press, 1991).
26. John-Paul Sartre, *Existentialism and Human Emotions* (New York: Citadel Press, 1957), 49.
27. "A White House Promise," *National Review* (7 April 1989): 15.
28. Shirley MacLaine, *Out on a Limb* (New York: Bantam Books, 1986).
29. Bloom, *The Closing of the American Mind*.
30. Judith Wallerstein, *Second Chances: Men, Women and Children a Decade After Divorce* (New York: Ticknor & Friends, 1990). Also see Glenn Stanton, "Twice as Strong: The Undeniable Advantage of Raising Children in a Traditional Two-Parent Family," a social research paper available from Focus on the Family, Colorado Springs, CO 80995.

Chapter 4
1. Matt. 22:39.
2. James 2:8.
3. John R.W. Stott, *Decisive Issues Facing Christians Today* (Old Tappan, N.J.: Revell, 1990), 19.
4. *Lausanne Occasional Papers: No. 21 Grand Rapids Report: Evangelism and Social Responsibility: An Evangelical Commitment* (Wheaton, Ill.: Lausanne

Committee for World Evangelization/World Evangelical Fellowship, 1982), 23.

5. Ibid., 21-24.
6. R. Pierce Beaver's introduction to Samuel Escobar and John Driver, *Christian Missions and Social Justice* (Scottdale: Herald, 1978), 7-9.
7. Op. Cit. [Note 4], 43-44.
8. The reader should note that the abolition movements in England and America were deeply Christian.
9. C.S. Lewis, *The Weight of Glory* (Grand Rapids: William B. Eerdmans Publishing Company, 1949,1965,1974), 14-15.
10. Gen. 12:3; 1 Pet. 3:9.
11. C.E.B. Cranfield, "The Christian's Political Responsibility According to the New Testament," *Scottish Journal of Theology* 15 (1962): 176-92.
12. Francis A. Schaeffer, *A Christian Manifesto* (Westchester: Crossway, 1981), 67.
13. For further reading on these questions, see Appendix A, "Reclaiming the Culture: An Annotated Bibliography."
14. Op. Cit. [Note 3], 12.

Chapter 5
1. Pronounced KI-ras.
2. James Davison Hunter, "What Americans Really Think About Abortion," *First Things* (July 1992), quoted in William J. Bennett, *The Index of Leading Cultural Indicators* (New York: Touchstone, 1994), 70.
3. Os Guinness, *Winning Back the Soul of American Business* (Washington, D.C.: Hour Glass, 1990), 32.
4. According to the National Opinion Research Center, the following are reasons for which large numbers of Americans would condone abortion: strong chance of serious defect (82 percent); wanting no more children (48 percent); cannot afford more children (50 percent); not being married (48 percent); if woman wants an abortion for any reason (46 percent). Cited in *General Social Survey Trends, 1972-1994*.
5. Cf. Acts 13:43, 14:19, 18:4, 19:26, 21:14, 26:26; 2 Cor. 5:11, 10:5.
6. R.C. Sproul, *Lifeviews* (Old Tappan, N.J.: Revell, 1986), 20.
7. 1 Cor. 3:6.
8. Donald P. Shoemaker, "Social Concern for a Sinful Culture" (Grace Community Church, 138 8th Street, Seal Beach, CA).
9. Quoted in Mark Hartwig, "How You Can Be More Credible," *Citizen* (15 March 1993): 5.
10. Ibid.
11. Quoted in Mark Hartwig, "Check Your Facts Before You Act," *Citizen* (17 May 1993): 6.

12. Ibid., 5.

13. Ibid. Italics added for emphasis.

14. This is as true of Christians as it is of others. It was to His followers that Jesus said, "I have much more to say to you, more than you can now bear" (John 16:12).

15. Quoted in Michael Ebert, "How Washington Defeated Death," *Citizen* (17 February 1992): 2.

16. Hartwig, "Check Your Facts Before You Act," 5.

17. James Nuechterlein, "Life at the Intellectual Barricades," *First Things* (October 1994): 12.

18. Matt. 7:12; Luke 6:31.

19. Mark Patinkin, "I've Wronged the Religious Right," *Rocky Mountain News,* 20 November 1992.

20. Quoted in *Rutherford* magazine (February 1993).

21. Phil. 2:3-4.

22. Donald S. Lutz, "The Relative Influence of European Writers on Late Eighteenth Century American Political Thought," *American Political Science Review* (1984), 189-97; cited in John Eidsmoe, *Christianity and the Constitution* (Grand Rapids: Baker Books, 1987), 52.

23. C.S. Lewis, "Before We Can Communicate," *God in the Dock* (Grand Rapids: William B. Eerdmans, 1970), 257.

24. I also like to point out that the truths that are in the Bible do not become any truer when we identify their location, such as saying, "In Romans 1:18 . . ."

25. Ebert, "How Washington Defeated Death," 2.

Chapter 6

1. For further discussion on this point, I refer the reader to chapter 4, "A Biblical Case for Social and Political Involvement."

2. Ps. 22:28; Gen. 18 and 19; Gen. 41; John 15:5.

3. Rom. 7 and 8.

4. For further reading, I direct the reader to *Victory over the Darkness* and *The Bondage Breaker* by Neil Anderson and *Spiritual Warfare* by Tim Warner.

5. Cf. Job 1 where the Sabean and Chaldean raiders are prompted by Satan and Daniel 10 where a demon is described as the "prince of the Persian kingdom" with powers to influence national events.

6. Luke 9:54-55.

7. As cited in Philip Yancey, *Disappointment with God* (Grand Rapids: Zondervan, 1988), 92.

8. J. Edwin Orr, *The Flaming Tongue* (Chicago: Moody, 1973), 17-18, 8, 17.

9. 1 Tim. 2:1-3.

10. *The Book of Common Prayer*, John W. Suter, custodian (New York: The Church Pension Fund, 1945), 18.

11. *The Book of Common Prayer*, Charles M. Guilbert, custodian (The Church Hymnal Corporation/Seabury Press, 1977), 242, 207, 209, 260.

Chapter 7

1. Os Guinness, *Winning Back the Soul of American Business* (Washington, D.C.: Hourglass, 1990), 4.

2. The factual details of this account are taken from Garth Lean, *God's Politician* (Colorado Springs: Helmers and Howard, 1987) and Charles W. Colson, *Kingdoms in Conflict* (New York and Grand Rapids: Morrow and Zondervan, 1987), 95-108.

3. Op cit., 4-5.

4. Ezek. 14:14.

5. Dan. 6:10; 9:23; 2:49; 6:5; 5:17.

6. In John 17:15, Christ prays that His followers will remain in the world in order to fulfill His ministry. In Romans 12:1-2, we are urged not become corrupted by the world in which we live.

7. For further study on this subject, I direct the reader to chapter 4, "A Biblical Case for Social and Political Involvement."

8. Garth Lean, *God's Politician* (Colorado Springs: Helmers and Howard, 1987), 64.

9. Dan B. Allender and Tremper Longman III, *Bold Love* (Colorado Springs: NavPress, 1992), 63.

10. 1 Cor. 15:19.

11. J.I. Packer, "How to Recognize a Christian Citizen," *Christianity Today Institute*, 4.

12. Jurgen Moltmann, *Theology of Hope* (New York: Harper & Row, 1967), 337.

Chapter 8

1. I am referring to Professors Nathan Hatch, George Marsden, and Alvin Plantinga.

2. Francis A. Schaeffer, *The Great Evangelical Disaster* (Wheaton, Ill.: Crossway Books, 1984), 90-91.

3. Francis A. Schaeffer, *The Complete Works of Francis Schaeffer: A Christian Worldview*, vol. IV, book iii (Wheaton, Ill.: Crossway, 1982), 190.

4. As cited by John Hendrik deVries, "Biographical Note: Abraham Kuyper, 1837-1920," in the introductory pages to Abraham Kuyper, *Lectures on Calvinism* (Grand Rapids: Eerdmans, 1931,1987), iii.

5. William Shakespeare, *The Tempest*, II, i.

6. Franky Schaeffer, *Bad News For Modern Man: An Agenda for Christian Activism* (Wheaton, Ill.: Crossway, 1984), 108.

7. James C. Dobson and Gary L. Bauer, *Children At Risk: Winning the Battle for the Hearts and Minds of Your Children* (Waco, Texas: Word, 1990), 19.
8. Louis Berkhof, *Systematic Theology* (Grand Rapids: Eerdmans, 1939,1984), 440.
9. Ibid., 441-443.
10. *Citizen* magazine (20 November 1995): 3.

Chapter 9
1. "Woman Helps Topless Dancers Out of Clubs, Into New Lives," *Citizen* (December 1994): 14.
2. Esther 4:14.
3. "Church Members Permeate State Capitol with Prayer," *Citizen* (July 1994): 14.
4. "Resident-Home Walls Can't Contain Stroke Victim's Influence," *Citizen* (December 1994): 15.
5. "'Joe Citizen' Stops Card Casino Referendum," *Citizen* (April 1994): 15.
6. "Home-school Family Helps Repeal Special Rights for Gays,"*Citizen* (January 1994): 14.
7. "Fifth-grader's Anti-graffiti Campaign Cleans Up School,"*Citizen* (January 1994): 15.
8. "Church Elder Turns Gays' Resentment into Rapport," *Citizen* (January 1994): 15. Readers may call (215) 947-4416 for more information.
9. Nolan Head. Letter to John Eldredge, December 9, 1994.
10. "Contractor Stands Against Abortion: Company Loses, But Conscience Wins," *Citizen* (March 1994): 14-15.
11. "Fourth-graders Rise Up Against MTV's Anti-heroes," *Citizen* (May 1994): 14.
12. "Pastors Cross Denominational Lines, Shut Down Erotic Dancing," *Citizen* (May 1994): 15. For a complimentary information package, readers may write to the American Lutheran Church at P.O. Box 199, Long Prairie, MN 56347.
13. Elizabeth McClinton, "Cable Channel Cleans Up Obscene Programming," *Citizen* (December 1993): 14.
14. "Grandfather Makes the Grade: School Board Adopts Values," *Citizen* (October 1994): 15.

Chapter 10
1. Luke 19:41-44
2. Matt. 28:19-20
3. C.S. Lewis, *God in the Dock: Essays on Theology and Ethics* (Grand Rapids: Eerdmans, 1970), 281.

Notes

4. Ibid., 280.
5. H. Richard Niebuhr, *Christ and Culture* (New York: Harper Tourchbooks, 1951), 191.
6. I am indebted to my colleague Greg R. Jesson for this aphorism.
7. E.M. Bounds, *The Complete Works of E.M. Bounds on Prayer* (Grand Rapids: Baker Book House, 1990), 317.
8. James W. Skillen, *Christians Organizing for Political Service* (Washington, D.C.: Association for Public Justice, 1980), 29-30.
9. Andrew Murray, *Andrew Murray: The Best From All His Works* (Nashville: Thomas Nelson, 1988), 259.
10. Albert E. Day, *An Autobiography of Prayer* (New York: Harper and Brothers, 1952), 146.
11. Compare also Prov. 1:5; 11:14; 13:10; 19:20,21; 20:18; 27:9.
12. Stephen R. Covey, *The Seven Habits of Highly Effective People: Restoring the Character Ethic* (New York: Simon & Schuster, 1989), 262-263.
13. These concepts are discussed at length in a book by Leonard D. Goodstein, et al., *Applied Strategic Planning: A Comprehensive Guide* (San Diego: Pfeiffer & Company, 1992). Though developed for business planning, this book contains excellent insights for Christian organizational endeavors.

Appendix A
1. 1 Pet. 3:15.
2. Irving Kristol, "Taking Religious Conservatives Seriously," *Disciples and Democracy: Religious Conservatives and the Future of American Politics*, Michael Cromartie, ed. (Grand Rapids: Ethics and Public Policy Center/Eerdmans, 1994), vii.
3. James C. Dobson, Focus on the Family's monthly newsletter, October 1994.

About the Contributors

William J. Bennett is a Distinguished Fellow in Cultural Policy Studies at The Heritage Foundation, co-director of Empower America, and a senior editor of *National Review* magazine. He received his B.A. from Williams College, J.D. from Harvard University, and Ph.D from the University of Texas.

Lawrence F. Burtoft is a social research analyst for Focus on the Family. He received his B.A. from Biola University, M.Div. from Talbot Theological Seminary, and Ph.D. in social ethics from the University of Southern California.

Charles W. Colson is the 1993 recipient of the prestigious Templeton Prize for Progress in Religion. He is a highly regarded author, speaker, and columnist, and is founder and chairman of Prison Fellowship Ministries.

Alan R. Crippen II is Senior Fellow for Family and Social Policy Studies at Focus on the Family's Institute for Family Studies. He received his B.S. from Philadelphia College of Bible and M.A.R. from Westminster Theological Seminary.

John Eldredge is public policy seminars and research director for Focus on the Family. He received his B.A. from California Polytechnic University and M.A. from Colorado Christian University.

Diane Hesselberg is editor of Focus on the Family's weekly Family Issues Alert fax news service. She received her B.S. from Regis University.

Greg R. Jesson is Senior Fellow for Philosophical and Cultural Studies at Focus on the Family's Institute for Family Studies. He received his B.A. from the University of California at Los Angeles, M.A. from the University of Southern California, and is currently pursuing doctoral studies at the University of Iowa.